MURDERED MIDAS

ALSO BY CHARLOTTE GRAY

Mrs. King: The Life & Times of Isabel Mackenzie King

Sisters in the Wilderness:
The Lives of Susanna Moodie and Catharine Parr Traill

Flint and Feather:
The Life and Times of E. Pauline Johnson, Tekahionwake

Canada: A Portrait in Letters

The Museum Called Canada

Reluctant Genius: The Passionate Life and Inventive Mind
of Alexander Graham Bell

Nellie McClung: Extraordinary Canadians Series

Gold Diggers: Striking It Rich in the Klondike

The Massey Murder: A Maid, Her Master,
and the Trial That Shocked a Country

The Promise of Canada:
150 Years—People and Ideas That Have Shaped Our Country

CHARLOTTE GRAY

MURDERED MIDAS

A MILLIONAIRE, HIS GOLD MINE, AND A STRANGE DEATH ON AN ISLAND PARADISE

HarperCollins*PublishersLtd*

Published by HarperCollins Publishers Ltd

First edition

HarperCollins Publishers Ltd
Bay Adelaide Centre, East Tower
22 Adelaide Street West, 41st Floor
Toronto, Ontario, Canada
M5H 4E3

www.harpercollins.ca

Library and Archives Canada Cataloguing in Publication
information is available upon request.

Maps on pages xviii–xxi by Mary Rostad.
Endpaper image, *Toronto Daily Star* (Page 3, Feb 11, 1938),
courtesy Toronto Public Library.

Photograph on p. 1: Tough-Oakes Mine, MUSEUM OF NORTHERN HISTORY.
Photograph on p. 77: British Colonial Hotel, Nassau, ALAMY. Photograph on
p. 165: Supreme Court Building, Nassau, THE BAHAMAS NATIONAL ARCHIVES.

ISBN 978-1-4434-4934-2

Printed and bound in the United States
LSC/H 9 8 7 6 5 4 3 2 1

For Jacqueline May Anderson

CONTENTS

PART THREE: LOSING IT

TIMELINE

1874   Harry Oakes is born in Sangerville, Maine

1890s Oakes attends Foxcroft Academy, and then Bowdoin College, in Maine

1897   News of a huge gold strike in northern Canada reaches the Eastern Seaboard; Oakes joins the Klondike gold rush

1902   Construction of the Temiskaming and Northern Ontario Railway (T&NO) begins, opening up Northern Ontario

1903   Huge veins of silver are discovered at T&NO Mile 103, triggering the Cobalt silver rush

1908   Cobalt produces 9 percent of the world's silver

1909   Massive gold strike at Porcupine Lake jump-starts a new gold rush

1911   Oakes arrives in Swastika, Ontario

1912   Oakes, the Tough brothers, and Bill Wright stake claims around Kirkland Lake

1914   Oakes fails to sell stock in Lake Shore Mines Ltd.

1916   Oakes strikes the richest vein of gold ore ever seen in Canada and finds American investors

1918   Lake Shore Mines pays its first dividend

1923   Oakes marries Eunice McIntyre

1924   Nancy Oakes is born

1924   Oakes buys the Schoellkopf mansion in Niagara Falls, remodels it, and renames it Oak Hall

1927   Sydney Oakes is born

CAST OF CHARACTERS

SIR HARRY OAKES, owner of Lake Shore Mines and multimillionaire
EUNICE MYRTLE, Lady Oakes, née McIntyre
NANCY OAKES, Sir Harry's eldest child and third wife of Alfred de
   Marigny
SYDNEY OAKES, heir to the Oakes baronetcy
SHIRLEY LEWIS OAKES
WILLIAM PITT OAKES
HARRY PHILLIP OAKES

COUNT MARIE ALFRED FOUQUEREAUX DE MARIGNY, husband of
   Nancy Oakes
RUTH FAHNESTOCK, de Marigny's second wife
GEORGES DE VISDELOU-GUIMBEAU, de Marigny's cousin and best friend

MAINE

WILLIAM AND EDITH OAKES, Harry's parents
LOUIS OAKES, Harry's elder brother
GERTRUDE, JESSIE, AND MYRTICE OAKES, Harry's sisters
JOHN CLAIR MINOT, Harry's classmate at Bowdoin College
GEORGE BABSON, husband of Jessie Oakes
DR. EUGENE WHITTREDGE, Dover-Foxcroft dentist

KIRKLAND LAKE

WILLIAM (BILL) WRIGHT, British butcher turned prospector
JIMMY DOIG, owner of the Swastika general store
TOM, GEORGE, BOB, AND JACK TOUGH, railway workers turned
   prospectors

Roza Brown, early resident of Kirkland Lake and friend of Harry Oakes

Ernie Martin, Harry Oakes's first employee

Charlie Chow, hotel owner

James McRae, Canadian prospector and editor of the *Northern Miner*

Arnold Hoffman, American prospector and author

Albert Wende, manager of the Wright-Hargreaves mine

David Freeman-Mitford, Baron Redesdale, British landowner and prospector

Joseph Burr Tyrrell, geologist, dinosaur bone discoverer, and mining investor

FLORIDA

Walter Foskett, lawyer

LONDON

Sir Joseph Duveen, British art dealer

Lord Luke of Pavenham, the "Bovril King" and fundraiser for London hospitals

Sir Joseph Ball, former MI5 officer and Conservative Party operator

George, Duke of Kent, younger brother of Edward VIII and Nazi sympathizer

NASSAU

Harold Christie, founder of H. G. Christie Real Estate, Nassau

Frank Christie, Harold's brother

Axel Wenner-Gren, Swedish industrialist, multimillionaire, and Nazi sympathizer

Rosita Forbes, British travel writer

Duke of Windsor, governor of the Bahamas (1940–45), and the Duchess of Windsor

Leslie Heape, colonial secretary of the Bahamas (1940–43) and acting governor during the governor's absence

Sir William Murphy, governor of the Bahamas (1945–50)

SIR HARRY'S DINNER GUESTS

CHARLES HUBBARD, retired Woolworth executive

MRS. DULCIBEL "EFFIE" HENNEAGE, wife of a British Army Officer

DE MARIGNY'S DINNER GUESTS

ALFRED CERETTA, American engineer

DOROTHY CLARKE, wife of a Royal Air Force officer

JEAN AINSLIE, wife of a Royal Air Force officer

BETTY ROBERTS, girlfriend of Georges de Visdelou-Guimbeau

BAHAMAS POLICE AND PROMINENT RESIDENTS

COLONEL R. A. ERSKINE-LINDOP, commissioner of the Bahamas Police Force

MAJOR HERBERT PEMBERTON, deputy commissioner of the Bahamas Police Force

LIEUTENANT JOHN DOUGLAS, Bahamas Police Force

CAPTAIN EDWARD SEARS, Bahamas Police Force

NEWELL KELLY, Oakes's business manager

MADELINE GALE KELLY, American singer, wife of Newell Kelly

DR. HUGH QUACKENBUSH, local physician

DR. LAWRENCE FITZMAURICE, acting chief medical officer of the Bahamas

DR. ULRICH ERNST OBERWARTH, medical officer at Nassau jail

ÉTIENNE DUPUCH, owner and editor of *Nassau Daily Tribune*

EUGENE DUPUCH, *Nassau Daily Tribune* reporter and Étienne's son

AMERICAN POLICE AND EXPERTS

CAPTAIN EDWARD MELCHEN, chief of the homicide bureau, Miami Police Department

CAPTAIN JAMES BARKER, Supervisor of the Laboratories of the Miami Police Department

FRANK CONWAY, retired fingerprint expert, New York Police Department

CAPTAIN MAURICE O'NEIL, supervisor of the New Orleans Police Department's Bureau of Identification

COURT OFFICIALS

SIR OSCAR BEDFORD DALY, Chief Justice of the Bahamas

THE HONOURABLE ERIC HALLINAN, Attorney General

THE HONOURABLE ALFRED ADDERLY, junior lawyer for the prosecution

THE HONOURABLE GODFREY HIGGS, lawyer for the defence

ERNEST CALLENDER, junior lawyer for the defence

JAMES SANDS, foreman of the jury

WITNESSES AND REPORTERS

RAYMOND C. SCHINDLER, private detective

ERLE STANLEY GARDNER, reporter for the Hearst newspaper chain and creator of Perry Mason

RUTH REYNOLDS, reporter for the *New York Sunday News*

PROFESSOR LEONARDE KEELER, inventor of a lie-detector apparatus

MURDERED MIDAS

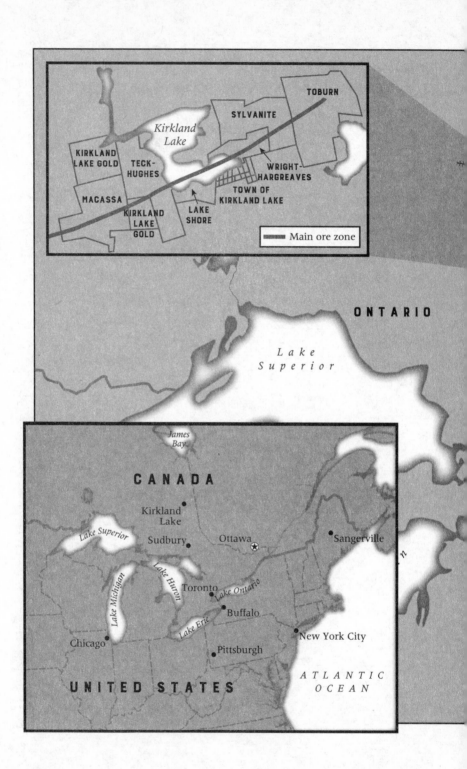

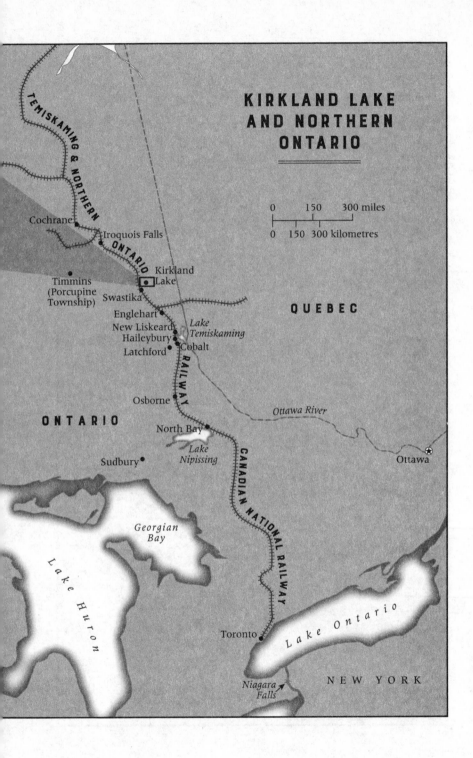

KIRKLAND LAKE
AND NORTHERN
ONTARIO

0   150   300 miles

0   150 300 kilometres

TEMISKAMING & NORTHERN

Cochrane

Iroquois Falls

ONTARIO

Kirkland
Lake

Timmins
(Porcupine
Township)

Swastika

Englehart

New Liskeard

Haileybury

Latchford

Cobalt

Lake
Temiskaming

QUEBEC

RAILWAY

Osborne

ONTARIO

North Bay

Sudbury

Lake
Nipissing

Ottawa River

Ottawa

CANADIAN NATIONAL RAILWAY

Georgian
Bay

Lake Huron

Toronto

Lake Ontario

NEW YORK

Niagara
Falls

THE BAHAMAS

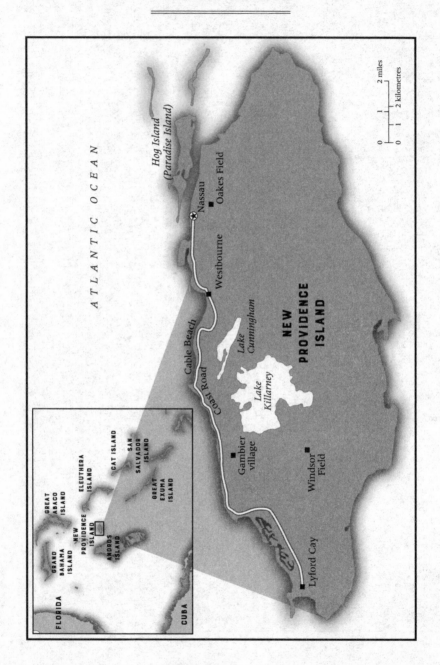

THE MURDER SCENE AT WESTBOURNE

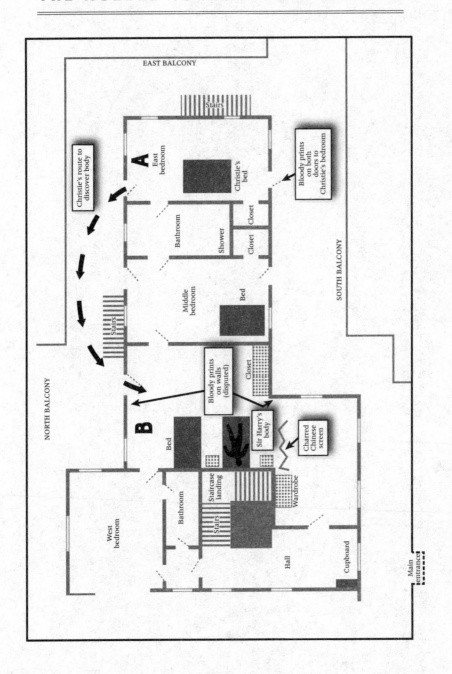

EAST BALCONY

Stairs

Christie's route to discover body

A

East bedroom

Christie's bed

Bloody prints on both doors to Christie's bedroom

Bathroom

Shower

Closet

Closet

SOUTH BALCONY

Middle bedroom

Bed

Stairs

NORTH BALCONY

Bloody prints on walls (disputed)

Closet

B

Bed

Sir Harry's body

Charred Chinese screen

Staircase landing

Wardrobe

West bedroom

Bathroom

Stairs

Hall

Cupboard

Main entrance

INTRODUCTION

A Corpse Is Open to All Comers

The battered and burned body sprawled across the bed's blood-soaked covers, face up, with bare feet hanging over the edge. The victim's skull bore four puncture marks above his left ear, and his face was smeared with blood. There were bloodstains on the wall, and rusty drops and pools of dried blood on the carpet. On the night table next to the bed, a set of false teeth sat in a glass of water.

Someone had deliberately set a fire, and the odour of scorched fabric and charred flesh lingered in the air of the second-floor bedroom. The mosquito net had been incinerated; the sheets and covers were burned; patches of the carpet were singed; and both a nearby Chinese screen and the door to the hallway bore scorch marks. In the next-door bathroom there were black cinders on the floor and burnt material in the wash basin. A pillow had been ripped open, and a fan that whirred quietly had blown feathers around. Some floated in the hot, sticky air, while others clung to the charred corpse or settled lazily next to the false teeth and foot powder on the bedside table.

The police report described the grisly murder scene on the Bahamian island of New Providence, but each detail raised questions: What was the weapon that had made the four strange, angular puncture marks? Why did it appear as though blood from the wounds had flowed *uphill* towards the nose? Had the body been turned to lie face up? Were the bloodstains on the wall handprints? Did the blood on the floor mean there had been a fight? When the murderer tried to burn the body, why hadn't the bedding gone up in flames or the fire engulfed the rest of the room? How many murderers were there? Had the pillow been deliberately ripped?

However, only one question really mattered: Who had done this? Who had killed Sir Harry Oakes, the owner of a Canadian gold mine, a man said to be worth over $200 million (an unusually large fortune back then, and equal to more than $3 billion in today's terms)? (All dollar figures in the text are Canadian, unless otherwise specified.) Who had bludgeoned to death the megamillionaire, who was frequently described in the press as "the richest man in the British Empire" or tagged as "Midas," after the mythical Greek monarch who had the gift of turning everything he touched to gold? Who would want to murder the largest landholder and investor in the Bahamas and friend of the Duke of Windsor, the governor of the Bahamas? As the sea breeze from nearby Cable Beach dispersed the last traces of the mysterious fire in Westbourne, Sir Harry's bougainvillea-covered mansion, the news of his death surged across the English-speaking world to New York City, then across the Atlantic to London, the imperial centre, and north to the remote Canadian mining town of Kirkland Lake, in the Ontario bush. It would quickly become celebrated as "the crime of the century."

====

THE MURDER OF Sir Harry Oakes was committed over seven decades ago in a colonial backwater, yet it continues to exert a dark appeal. Fascination persists because the one question that really mattered has never been answered. No murderer was brought to justice.

But it is not only the lack of a neat resolution to this whodunit that grabs attention; there are additional layers of mystery. A member of the British royal family, the former King Edward VIII, was involved, and he took far too close an interest in how the murder was investigated. Then there are the recurrent mutterings about illegal financial transactions, Mafia involvement, spy activities. Murder is always shocking, but this crime was committed at a time of raw nerves and global tension; while Sir Harry's life was cut short in a paradise of palm trees, turquoise seas, and white-sand beaches, thousands of much younger men were fighting and dying for their countries in Europe and the Far East. An added ingredient to the story is the glitter of Sir Harry's gold. Nothing brings out greed and suspicion faster than the image of a stack of gold bars; where did the mine owner's fortune end up?

Since the news of the multimillionaire's death first broke, suspicions about what might have happened have bloomed. The mythology of the murder has taken flight, thanks to several true-crime books, episodes in novels by writers including Timothy Findley and William Boyd, and movies with titles such as *Passion in Paradise* (1983, starring Marlon Brando), *Eureka* (1984, starring Gene Hackman), *Passion and Paradise* (1989, starring Rod Steiger), and *Murder in Paradise* (2010, with Gillian Anderson).

So, after all these treatments—several shamelessly sensationalist, as accounts of brutal murders tend to be—is there any more to say about Harry Oakes and his untimely end?

I think there is. In contrast to the tsunami of ink and celluloid spent on his death, little has been written about his *life*.

The murder victim is usually dismissed as an unpleasant man whose death caused few regrets. Few spoke up for Harry. His extraordinary achievement in striking gold, retaining control of his gold mine, and helping to establish Toronto as a centre for the mining industry in the 1920s has been forgotten. The sinister friendships with pro-Nazi appeasers that he made in London during the 1930s, which probably secured his baronetcy and may have been a factor in his death, have been quietly obscured; the only connection with this crowd that is remembered today is his relationship with the Duke of Windsor. The person who should have been the leading suspect in his death was never properly investigated. Oakes's financial dealings have remained invisible.

And there is a further aspect of the Harry Oakes story that deserves notice. Coverage of the crime soon shifted in tone; a matter of public interest slid into being of purely prurient interest. The articles, books, and movies that have explored the Oakes murder have built on each other, blatantly incorporating speculation as fact and personal bias as history. False facts litter this particular narrative, and those assertions have demonized Oakes while deflecting attention from the most obvious murder suspect, the man who stood to gain the most from Oakes's death.

As a biographer, I know how easy it is to shape reputations posthumously. The tools are subtle adjustments, sly cuts, colourful embellishments, exaggeration. In the words of Jean-Paul Sartre, "A corpse is open to all comers." And Sir Harry Oakes is the kind of man for whom few people shed a tear these days—a wealthy old white man who could treat people abominably. But his flaws were rooted in his early struggles to realize his ambitions, and in his tenacious pursuit of a dream. Hardened by years of isolation and resentment, the former prospector was singularly unprepared for the sophisticated circles into which his immense wealth propelled him. Some people admired him as a hero and a benefactor; others haughtily dismissed him as an uncouth bully. Only the latter image has survived in the popular imagination.

So, yes, I think there is more to say about Harry Oakes, who during his lifetime was both admired and reviled but after his death was recalled only for his murder—a gruesome death that was increasingly interpreted as his just deserts. There is more to say about the identity of the man who was probably responsible for the murder, and how he evaded scrutiny. And there is more to say about the way that writers can skew the story, reframe events, and manipulate history to suit their own purposes.

But let's start at the beginning . . .

PART ONE

MAKING IT

CHAPTER 1

Roaming the Globe for Gold

He never stopped. Every morning he started at dawn, and he stopped when it was too dark to see. He did this seven days a week. Fifty-two weeks a year. Leap year he worked an extra day. The memory we all had of Harry was of a little guy . . . broke, his bare ass sticking out of his pants because he couldn't afford to buy any more, always working, always alone.

A CANADIAN PROSPECTOR, 1947

Had Harry Oakes once again arrived too late for a big strike? In Toronto in the spring of 1911, the thirty-six-year-old stared at the geological charts and topographical maps in Ontario's Department of Mines, noting the extensive grid of prospectors' claims superimposed on the region north of North Bay, bang in the centre of the immense expanse of Canada. On paper, Northern Ontario looked as though government surveyors had already outlined its features and its potential. By now, the provincial bureaucrats suggested, the land had been "tamed."

Oakes traced with his stubby, stained finger the settlements strewn across the grim monotony of forest, rock, water, and muskeg swamp. The charts recorded only mining camps; the cartographers had ignored the numerous Indigenous communities, although their presence showed up in the Ojibwa or Cree names of several features, such as Lake Temagami. Most of the network of links connecting mining camps consisted of rough, winding trails, but there were also newly laid railway tracks, punctuated at regular intervals by stations.

The muscular little Yankee ignored the chatter of the engineers around him. He muttered to himself the names of the town sites that were roughly sketched around those stations: Osborne, Latchford, Cobalt, New Liskeard, Englehart, Cochrane . . .

The Temiskaming and Northern Ontario Railway, begun ten years earlier, drove the new mining boom in this region. As it slashed its way due north, it had opened up the sullen landscape of northeastern Ontario, west of the Ottawa River and Lake Temiskaming. But it appeared to Oakes that all the land around gold and silver strikes had been staked out by eager prospectors before his arrival. The government geologists told the newcomer that the best claims might already have gone, and that there had been few new mineral strikes. Recent claims were little more than "moose pasture," as mining old-timers liked to say.

Perhaps the Northern Ontario mining boom was slowing down. Wasn't that predictable, given the pattern of previous high-rolling mining booms? The 1848 California gold rush had tapered off by 1855. British Columbia's Cariboo gold rush in the 1860s had lasted only three years. The Klondike gold rush of the 1890s was over before the century ended. Had Harry Oakes missed his chance again? Would he have to turn around and seek his fortune elsewhere—in South Africa, perhaps, where new veins were still being discovered?

Harry Oakes's eyes remained fixed on the charts. As a youngster, he had reached the Klondike goldfields months after the excitement had peaked. Since then, he had been a Johnny-come-lately at gold rushes all over the globe, arriving after local prospectors had already staked the best ground. He had never been in the right place at the right time (luck remains the key to most prospectors' success), so fortune had eluded him.

But he had the bug. Wiry and determined, he was not easily discouraged. For Oakes, as for most of the thousands of prospectors who shared his quest, searching the wilderness for the elusive glint of precious ores was much more than a gamble on Lady Luck or an escape from the drudgery of urban life. It was an obsession. And Canada's vast northern landscape glittered with potential wealth.

Oakes was a foot soldier in the army of drifters, fortune hunters, and prospectors roaming the globe in the period before the First World War. It was a time of change but also a time of jarring disruptions, in a pattern that would repeat itself in the early twenty-first century. Technological breakthroughs were upending ways of life that had been settled for centuries. First the telegraph, then the telephone and mass-market newspapers had revolutionized communications. Steamships, railways, and most recently automobiles had speeded up transportation systems and shrunk distances. Mechanization had vastly increased industrial production. Medicine was transformed by science; the nature of germs had been identified, and then Aspirin and X-ray machines had been developed. Between 1880 and 1900, cities in the United States grew at a dramatic rate, by about 15 million people. Much of this flow of people consisted of immigrants from beyond American shores, but there was also a steady migration from rural North America. The Carnegies, Rockefellers, and Van Hornes who drove the industrial revolution amassed immense fortunes, while ordinary Americans and Canadians found themselves uprooted, impoverished, and dispersed.

The sense of dislocation accelerated when economies took a downswing in the early 1890s. So it is no wonder that, in the middle of all the upheaval, young men who were either unemployed, scratching out a living on tired old family farms, or stuck in badly paid office or factory jobs they hated dreamed of escape and embraced get-rich-quick schemes. Walt Whitman had serenaded such an escape in his "Song of the Open Road" (*Afoot and light-hearted I take to the open road / Healthy, free, the world before me . . .*). Newspapers such as London's *Daily Mail*, Nebraska's *Omaha World-Herald*, and Halifax's *Morning Herald* breathlessly chronicled the instant wealth discovered by prospectors in distant lands. Novelists such as Bret Harte and Jack London romanticized life in mining camps. Life on the frontier looked immeasurably exciting compared to a cramped existence in a filthy, overcrowded city.

Years later, when some of those fortune hunters sat down to write their memoirs, many were suffused with nostalgia for the physical challenges they had overcome, the friendships they'd forged with like-minded adventurers, and the frenzy of successful strikes. In an exuberant account of his adventures entitled *Call Me Tomorrow*, a former prospector named James McRae who later wrote for mining newspapers recalled the "stampede and excitement" that followed a silver strike, and the sense of moving in a thrilling "world of fables and of dreams. . . . Enthusiasm seemed to know no bounds. Untrammelled optimism reigned everywhere." Arnold Hoffman, an American prospector who disappeared into the Canadian bush in 1922 and re-emerged a wealthy man, would later write with passion about "the richness of our life, the deep satisfaction of complete self-reliance and the glowing health which only the north can give. We quailed at nothing, for there were no creaking joints to favor, or family ties which gave us reason to pause. Weather meant nothing to us;

rain and snow were part of the bush, just as were flies, windfall and the long portages."

Harry Oakes nursed his dreams alongside everybody else, and in later years would recall with satisfaction the way he had realized those dreams through sheer, muscle-cramping, solo effort. But in 1911, he spoke little, smiled rarely, and never romanticized his quest. Those who met him remarked on his "intense, humorless quality . . . as though he has a mission in life which must be performed, a destiny that is almost a burden." Nothing could distract him, and he scorned prospectors who wasted precious time by swigging rotgut whisky and trading tales in dirt-floored bars. At this stage in life, he did not touch alcohol, he rarely smoked because he was slightly asthmatic, and he stuck to his own company. By his mid-thirties, he was reclusive and driven. Perhaps he felt that time was running out, that his body could not take much more of such a harsh life. So far, he had nothing to show for the thirteen years he had spent chasing his dream.

THE TANGLED BUSH, unnamed lakes and impenetrable forests of the Northern Ontario landscape were uninviting to most city dwellers, but to a prospector, every bare rock face was worth investigation; every moss-covered boulder might be the motherlode. And Oakes was no rookie rockhound; the square tip of his steel rock hammer was battered with use. From his years in Australian and American mining camps, he knew that porphyry, a reddish, highly crystallized volcanic rock, was associated with gold deposits. Porphyry is magma that worked its way into the folds of older granite as the Earth's crust cooled: quartz and feldspar are frequently found in such formations. Back then, it was frequently tagged "red granite," because it was as tough to break up as the dense rock surrounding it. In Toronto that spring,

Oakes had grilled geologists about rock formations north of North Bay. He paid particular attention to a handful of claims on which porphyry was plentiful near a small patch of water named Kirkland Lake, located 10 kilometres east of the rail tracks. The nondescript lake had been named after Winnie Kirkland, a secretary in the Department of Mines, although Winnie herself hadn't been within 500 kilometres of it.

Years later, in 1931, Harry Oakes told the *Northern Miner* that, although the country around Kirkland Lake had already been claimed, "most of the prospectors seemed to be afraid of what they called the 'red granite,' but I recognized their red granite as being real porphyry. . . . I could never understand those engineers who walked in, turned up their noses and walked out again." He prided himself on being methodical in his approach to prospecting. "I plan my work, then I work my plan," he liked to say. He was well acquainted with the Canadian rules governing mineral exploration claims. If he reckoned a plot of mud and scrub that had not been claimed deserved more attention, he knew that he should immediately stake out a square plot of about 16 hectares.

In theory, the protocol for doing this was simple. A prospector first had to mark one corner of the plot with the Number One post, then take four hundred strides (roughly a metre each) southward and mark the Number Two post, either by blazing a tree or banging into the ground a second picket. From there, he needed to walk 400 metres west to mark Number Three post, and finally northward for the same distance to mark Number Four post. Once back at Number One post, he would write or carve his name, licence number, and the date and time staked. Then he would have to record the claim at the local mining recorder's office within thirty-one days and collect metal tags to affix to the four corner posts.

In practice, claims were rarely so neat. Prospectors fought their way through undergrowth and thickets of wild raspberry bushes, waded through swamps, and ducked overhanging branches as they paced out their claims. When your face was furred with mosquitoes and your boots were squelching through mud, it could be hard to keep walking in a straight line. But Harry Oakes would grit his teeth, lower his head, and shoulder his way through the tangle of bushes.

There was an additional rule to which Oakes paid particular attention. The Department of Mines required claimants to spend at least twenty days a year on each claim, doing what was loosely described as "assessment work." If a claimant didn't do such work, he forfeited his claim and the ground was then available for someone else to stake.

Carefully examining those departmental maps in 1911, Oakes quietly noted claims around Kirkland Lake that were due to revert to the Crown the following January because the original prospector had not done the assessment work required by law. Then he paid five dollars for an Ontario prospector's licence.

IN TORONTO THAT DAY, the stocky American must have appeared to the officials at the Department of Mines as just one more dreamer with a rock pick, intent on getting rich quick. But Harry Oakes was a much more complicated character than that, in ways that set him apart from other fortune hunters converging on Northern Ontario.

First, he wasn't interested in striking pay dirt on a claim only to turn round as fast as he could and sell the land to investors. He wanted to retain control from first strike to full production, ensuring that he ended up owning his own mine. And it couldn't be just *any* mineral that he was going to dig out of the ground. While still a teenager, he had dreamed of getting rich from his own private gold mine. Since then, the dream had become an obsession.

Second, Oakes had deliberately chosen this way of life. He was not escaping poverty or drudgery. He was an educated man from a prosperous family; he might have been a professional—a teacher like his mother, a lawyer like his father, or a doctor, perhaps. When he decided to take off into the wild and look for gold, his family back in the New England state of Maine supported him with both encouragement and money.

There are many picturesque areas in Maine, but Oakes's birthplace, Piscataquis County, is definitely not on the list. Far from the state's dramatic seashore or the peaks of the Appalachian Mountains, it is characterized by humid summers, frigid winters, and above-average rainfall. Once dominated by the wool trade, many of its shabby settlements of wooden buildings, battered by recessions, had already passed their peak by the mid-nineteenth century.

Harry Oakes was born in the little Piscataquis County town of Sangerville, population 1,200, on December 23, 1874. Sangerville already had one claim to fame—as the birthplace of Hiram Maxim, who began life there as an apprentice coach-builder before he realized there was no future for him in that dreary community. He went on to train as a mechanical engineer, after which he founded an arms company and eventually became wealthy on the sales of the Maxim machine gun. Like Maxim, Oakes came from a comfortable family that had lived in Sangerville for several generations. His father, William Pitt Oakes, was one of four brothers who had all trained as lawyers, but William now worked as a land surveyor and occasionally taught school. Young Harry's mother, Edith Nancy Lewis, was the daughter of a tradesman; she also taught school and would become a school supervisor.

Harry was the middle child of five and the second of two boys. His older siblings were Louis and Gertrude; after his own birth came two sisters, Jessie and Myrtice. There were evidently close ties between family members; throughout his life, Harry Oakes would remain in touch with his siblings, and they would support him. The Oakes boys inherited their father's distinctive features: a square, jutting jaw, long nose, deep-set and intense eyes. The family lived in a two-storey clapboard house with a shady porch and a large stable. Their neighbours prided themselves on their New England rectitude, which included good work habits and support for the temperance movement. Edith shared both these characteristics. William paid lip service to them, but had a reputation for slipping off the wagon.

William Oakes was determined to keep his sons in the professional class. When Harry was fourteen, his father moved them 10 kilometres east through the thick New England woods to Dover-Foxcroft, the main town in Piscataquis County. The move enabled William to send his children to Foxcroft Academy, the best high school in the neighbourhood. Louis, the elder son, had already decided that he wanted to work outdoors, like his father. After he graduated from Foxcroft, he went off to the University of Maine to study forestry.

At this stage, Harry had no clear ambition. So his father enrolled him in Bowdoin College, in Brunswick, Maine. Bowdoin is a small liberal arts school that has always catered to the sons of the state's establishment. Its graduates include statesmen, legislators, and many of Maine's doctors, lawyers, and judges—and, by the time Oakes arrived there, two of the country's best-loved writers: Nathaniel Hawthorne and Henry Wadsworth Longfellow. One of the nineteenth century's most powerful anti-slavery novels, *Uncle Tom's Cabin*, had been composed in the school library by Harriet Beecher Stowe while her husband was teaching at Bowdoin.

Harry Oakes left little mark on Bowdoin. According to a report in the school archives, he was "a quiet unassuming boy of average scholastic ability. In athletics he did not make any of the varsity teams, but he was a member of his class gymnasium team in his freshman and sophomore years. . . . Although he did not have outstanding personal qualities, he was well-liked by his classmates for his quiet way and friendly disposition." He joined the Zeta Psi fraternity, and he took all the Bowdoin courses on geology and mineralogy. His 1896 graduation photo shows a serious young man with a furrowed brow, unruly dark hair, and a stern expression as he gazes into the distance, lips tightly shut. One account of his early life states that he was invited to give the oration at a class dinner, but he was so tongue-tied he was not asked again.

However, behind the reserve was a steely ambition. Oakes boasted that he was going to make a million dollars. One classmate, John Clair Minot, would later tell Geoffrey Bocca, a British magazine journalist who became Oakes's first biographer, about a conversation he had with Oakes in the school quadrangle. Minot asked him *how* he was going to make his million. Oakes replied that he had no intention of making money "out of my fellow men, no matter how honestly I may be able to do it. The thought repels me."

According to Bocca, Minot scoffed: "'This is absurd,' he told Oakes. 'There's no other way. Money doesn't come down out of the sky or up out of the earth.' As soon as he said that, he realized that he had made nonsense of his own logic. Oakes' deep-set eyes were fixed on him. 'Are you certain of that?' he asked ironically. 'Isn't the earth the ultimate source of all riches?'"

Minot half-believed Oakes. Others were more skeptical. George Babson, another classmate who would become a prominent local businessman in Foxcroft-Dover and would marry Myrtice Oakes, mocked Oakes's claim that he would make a million dollars. In later years, prominent Maine business leaders would enjoy recalling for Bocca that Babson had said to Oakes, "That is pretty clever of you to have it worked out so easily. Have you figured out what you will do with it when you die?" Oakes apparently replied, "I don't care about death. I shall die violently, with my boots on, I hope." With an angry glance at Babson, he then turned on his heel and walked away. Babson had never had much time for the brother of his fiancée, Jessie Oakes, so he shrugged. "Harry Oakes is not going to make a fortune. Mark my words, he won't make a cent as long as he lives."

Those who recalled such anecdotes enjoyed the smack of hubris.

WHERE DID HARRY OAKES go after Bowdoin College? It appears that he spent the next couple of years studying medicine at the University of Syracuse, while working part time for the Carter Ink Company. But he didn't stick with these activities. Instead, he went on dreaming about an instant fortune, and he started paying attention to what was happening on the other side of the continent, in the remote Canadian territory of Yukon.

In 1896, on a narrow brook called Rabbit Creek, an American prospector and his Indigenous brother-in-law had stumbled on a seam of raw gold lying between flaky slabs of schist rock. The yellow layer was so thick it looked like cheese in a sandwich. News of this strike deep inside Yukon took months to travel from the distant, frozen North down the Pacific coast. Once it reached the ports of Vancouver, Seattle, and San Francisco, the Klondike gold rush was on. A wild stampede of gold diggers streamed west for thousands of kilometres, north across the St. Elias Mountains, and into the Arctic cold that gripped the territory for eight months of the year.

Oakes could read all about this crazy stampede in any American newspaper. He learned that Rabbit Creek was soon renamed Bonanza Creek, and how the Klondike valley echoed with the thuds of claim stakes being hammered into frozen soil. The closest mining camp to the goldfields was on a mudflat squeezed between the wide, silty Yukon River and its tributary Klondike River. The mudflat had once been a traditional fishing ground for the Hän people, but they had been rudely shoved aside as the camp mushroomed into Dawson City, an exuberant and squalid boom town. Within two years of that first gold strike, Dawson had become the largest Canadian city west of Winnipeg, outpacing both Vancouver and Victoria. Over 30,000 people crowded its boarding houses, casinos, and brothels. The crush of wooden shacks, grimy tents, and lean-tos teemed with scruffy young men, confident they were *this close* to a big strike. Harry Oakes hungered to join them.

Harry's family did not balk at his ambition. In 1897, his mother gave her twenty-three-year-old son a big chunk of her savings so he could afford to make the journey and acquire all the equipment he would need to survive his first subarctic winter. A prospector's outfit included tent, blankets, candles, matches, sewing kit, a file for sharpening axes, fly oil, notebooks, pencils, compasses, geological picks, axes with leather covers for the heads, whetstones, and pots that cunningly telescoped into one another. At the start of the gold rush, there were no stores in Yukon, so a prospector heading north had to stock up on provisions too: tea, flour, dried prunes, beans, peas, rice, and a large slab of bacon. Louis Oakes, now well established in the lumber business, promised his younger brother $75 a month until he made his strike. Harry's eldest sister, Gertrude, who had a job as a secretary in Washington, D.C., promised to send him everything she could spare. And off went Harry, hell bent on making a mint.

To all intents and purposes, Harry Oakes disappeared for the next thirteen years. There are wisps of information in the written record. In 1925, while stuck on a train with a bunch of North American mining executives ("buzzards of Bay Street," in his opinion), Oakes boasted, "I know gold mines. I've been in the Philippines, Australia and the Yukon, Alaska and the American West . . ." In 1949, Lady Oakes sent Bowdoin College a "Biographical Record of Harry Oakes" that mentions the Philippines, the Alaskan mining town of Nome, Honolulu, China, Japan, the Samoan Islands, Australia, New Zealand, Mexico, South Africa, and Nevada. But this globetrotting record is more striking for its gaps than for its haphazard itinerary. The only characteristic common to most of these places is the eruption of gold rushes.

Gaps in a subject's life are black holes—immensely frustrating to a careful biographer. I know the strategies that writers can adopt: we can skate past them or attempt to bridge them with carefully harvested anecdotes, the subject's self-mythologizing, or our own imaginations. I found a colourful (and probably fanciful) account of the Oakes trajectory during these years in the biography written by Geoffrey Bocca, who construed Oakes's early life as a strange mix of boyish *Robinson Crusoe* adventure and sinister *Heart of Darkness* fable. Bocca drew many details from conversations with Dr. Eugene Whittredge, who had been a contemporary of Oakes's at Foxcroft and went on to be the dentist in Dover-Foxcroft.

According to this account, Harry Oakes quickly grasped that he would not make his fortune in the Klondike—and not simply because the entire region had already been staked. More to the point, although he had studied geology, he had no prospecting skills. He didn't know what he was doing. He needed to learn how to find alluvial gold—the loose flakes and nuggets that were washed down Yukon creeks. So he carefully watched grizzled prospectors panning the creeks, sinking shafts, building flumes and sluice boxes. Once he knew how to pan for gold, he shouldered his pack again and headed west, into Alaska. Working with a Swedish partner, he did find small amounts of gold in a riverbed. Although the seam was soon exhausted, Oakes was now smitten with gold fever.

In the fall of 1899, the young prospector heard of a fresh gold strike on the beaches of Nome, a godforsaken little town on the windswept coast of the Bering Strait. He joined the stampede, and then, with a Danish partner, bought a boat to explore some more beaches. Biographer Bocca let his imagination rip as he described events.

Neither of them [Oakes and his Danish partner] were seamen and soon the boat was wildly out of control. The world turned for the dizzy prospectors from crests as high as mountains to coffin-like troughs. With plaintive desperation they dabbed inexpert oars into the foam, seeing black rocks loom up ahead. Somehow the boat hit shingle and the two men fell exhausted on the freezing ground. Tugged into awakening by the discomfort of his soaking clothes, Harry Oakes climbed to his hands and knees and shook his head. The mists cleared and he found his eyes on a level with a pair of magnificent polished top boots. Not wishing the mirage to disappear before he could fix it firmly in his mind, he forced his eyes to rise slowly. Above the top boots were a pair of baggy trousers brilliantly scarlet. Still higher Harry saw a vivid white military tunic, then a fiercely moustached face, and a wild fur hat that could signify only one thing—a Cossack!

In this hyperbolic account, the tall Dane and the little American were soon surrounded by Cossack soldiers who prodded them with rifles. "By now it had dawned on Harry what had happened," Bocca wrote. "His boat had been blown on to the coast of Siberia and he was a prisoner of the Czar." It had been only three decades since the Russian Empire sold Alaska to the United States for $7.2 million.

Luckily, the Cossack officer decided that the sodden and filthy castaways were of no use to him. With a dismissive gesture, he indicated they could return to Alaska as soon as the storm had abated. The Cossack story was an irresistible part of the Harry Oakes legend.

Bocca went on to describe how Oakes abandoned the icy beaches of Alaska and headed off to the other end of the world. He made his way to Seattle, then signed on as a ship's purser bound first for the Philippines and then Australia. He tried his luck in Western Australia, in the Kalgoorlie goldfields, without success. By now he was tough, single-minded and increasingly antisocial. Rubbing shoulders with men much coarser than himself had scoured off all his Bowdoin polish, and the years of disappointment had worn him down. With women, he was either pathologically shy or just plain rude. Geoffrey Bocca spoke to an old prospector in Sydney who knew the young American during these years. He learned that, in Kalgoorlie, Oakes got a girl pregnant and had to leave the district in a hurry. The incident apparently made his behaviour with women even more surly.

Lady Oakes believed that her husband spent a year farming in New Zealand but was soon drawn back to the prospecting life. Returning to the United States, he spent the years 1906 to 1911 on the Nevada side of Death Valley—the lowest, driest, and hottest area in North America. An eerie landscape of salt pans and deserts, with huge rocks and menacing canyons, Death Valley is one of the least inviting places on the continent. But that didn't stop Harry, who trudged through cacti and mesquite, searching for rocky outcrops. Oakes himself loved to talk about the time he crawled into a cave to sleep and woke the next morning to find that he had spent the night in a nest of rattlesnakes. Like many self-made men, Oakes enjoyed portraying himself as a rugged survivor who, by luck and judgment, overcame obstacles that would have killed other, softer individuals.

Stories like these enhanced the Oakes mythology in Dover-Foxcroft, but Bocca suggests that Harry Oakes's former classmates, most of whom were living humdrum lives, ridiculed his fierce determination to strike gold. They circulated amongst themselves the postcards that occasionally arrived from him, with messages such as "Still pursuing that elusive fortune. Health good. Regards to the fellows," or "Luck hasn't broken yet but I'll be with you someday." As the years went by, Harry Oakes became a target of derision for friends back home—but never to his family. When he ran out of money, he could always rely on his mother and his siblings Louis and Gertrude to send him whatever funds they could spare.

But there's no doubt that years of failure took their toll on Harry Oakes. He had never stayed anywhere long enough to make friends, and the long periods of solitude that the life of a prospector entailed had left him an antisocial loner. "He was a hard man, hard," a fellow prospector told Arnold Hoffman, the American who wrote about his own years in the bush in his memoir *Free Gold: The Story of Canadian Mining.* "Too bloody serious all the time. Never once did I see him enjoy a belly laugh, and a man like that ain't right. No balance."

CHAPTER 2

Anatomy of a Gold Rush

In the next century . . . it is not improbable that the mineral wealth of Canada will equal or even exceed that of the United States. . . . As yet there are between one and three million square miles of country in Canada practically unprospected, and the mineral wealth that lies hidden in this vast area will be an important factor in the progress of this northern continent.

JOSEPH B. TYRRELL, JANUARY I, 1901

W hat was the life that Harry Oakes had flung himself into? What hunger drove him to endure the cruel winters and sticky summers of North America's bleak landscape, as he swallowed repeated failures and dashed hopes?

Men like Harry Oakes had been tramping through forests, across swamps, and through tundra for centuries, in search of resources—rocks, furs, logs, oil. Europeans recognized that this vast land mass was a treasure chest from the moment they first landed on its shores. The raw wealth of the northern half of North America would help fuel first Britain's Industrial Revolution, and then the growth of the Canadian economy.

Demand for the various treasures changed over the centuries. Precious rocks were the first glittering lure. As early as 1576, the Yorkshire seaman Martin Frobisher had set off to find the Northwest Passage, and instead discovered some glittering pebbles on a windswept Arctic beach. He proclaimed that he had discovered gold, and shipped 1,350 tons of the rocks back to Queen Elizabeth I's London. Alas, the mineral was identified as worthless iron pyrites.

The wrong rocks, but the right idea. Indigenous peoples had always enjoyed this land's abundance and known about "special" stones. A hundred years later, an Algonquin guide showed a vein of silver to the Chevalier de Troyes, leader of a French military expedition to what is Lake Temiskaming in today's Ontario. Troyes sent a few lumps of ore back to Quebec City, where nobody paid any attention to them. It would be another 225 years before prospectors like Harry Oakes headed into the same region.

In the seventeenth and eighteenth centuries, lust for glittering minerals was overshadowed by a new European appetite: luxurious, thick pelts that could be fashioned into hats, collars, and cloaks. Fur traders from the Hudson's Bay Company rarely gave the earth beneath their feet a second look as they penetrated farther and farther into the northern half of the continent. But the nineteenth century saw renewed interest in what lay below the tangled forests of the northern wilderness. Britain's Industrial Revolution generated a ravenous demand for steam power and metals, and its colonies were scoured for coal deposits and mineral ores. This is why the Geological Survey of Canada was founded, twenty-five years before British North America morphed into the Dominion of Canada. The collection of Canadian mineral-bearing rocks that the Survey exhibited in Great Britain in 1851, at London's famous Crystal Palace Exhibition, caused a sensation. The treasure chest was about to be plundered.

Towards the end of the century, railways began to snake their way across the new dominion, revealing even more hidden wealth. During excavation for the Canadian Pacific Railway railbed, engineers stumbled over seams of valuable minerals—particularly in the more remote areas of Ontario. In the northwest of the province, above Lake Huron, CPR labourers blasted their way into extensive nickel-copper concentrations in the Sudbury basin. Word spread fast. Soon, hundreds of stubble-chinned prospectors boarded the CPR's transcontinental trains, where they mingled with thousands of settlers who would turn Canada's prairies into the breadbasket of the Empire.

Mine promoters and politicians bragged that Ontario's mines would be the engine that drove Canada's prosperity. They were prescient; by the mid-twentieth century, minerals and petrochemicals would dominate trade, and natural resources have been a mainstay of the economy ever since. From the early days, interest came from some surprising quarters. Amongst the first to sniff around in Ontario's bush was American inventor Thomas Edison, who had heard about the rich nickel and cobalt deposits discovered near Sudbury. He arrived in 1901, eager to see whether they might be useful in the manufacture of his electrical equipment. They weren't, so he fled the mosquitoes and blackflies and returned to New Jersey. But Sudbury's population swelled as production of copper and nickel increased. In 1902 the International Nickel Company, which was later renamed Inco and would become one of the largest mining complexes in the world, was created in New York. (In 2009, it was renamed Vale Canada, after a takeover by the Brazilian mining company now known as Vale SA.)

The prospectors who talked up the limitless potential of Northern Ontario were operating on a wing and a prayer. Although the provincial government had established a Bureau of Mines in the 1890s to explore the region's mineral potential, the hobnailed-boot brigade did not know exactly where to look under the surface layers of moss and decaying vegetation. Exploitation of this uncharted region required transport and communications—and, as yet, there were barely moose trails.

The Canadian government paid no attention to demands for a railway that headed north towards Hudson's Bay. Ottawa was interested only in railways that ran east to west, knitting together the new dominion from the Atlantic Ocean to the Pacific. However, the Ontario government was much more sympathetic, recognizing that a northbound railway was in the provincial interest.

Farms and villages were already beginning to appear in this wilderness, and a few hardy souls had identified an area with agricultural potential—the so-called Clay Belt, comprising more than 12 million acres of potential farmland on the same latitude as the prairies. A railway would funnel immigrants into the region, which the Ontario immigration office quickly tagged New Ontario. (The word *north*, with its connotations of cold and distance, was shunned.)

Provincial politicians were also keen to exploit the abundant forest resources and mineral discoveries. They resented the fact that the Sudbury mining camp was owned by British and American companies that continued to treat the country as a colony and ship Sudbury's ores out of Canada for refining. And they hoped that a new mineral strike might persuade Toronto big shots to invest in refineries within Ontario, which would create employment and revenue within provincial borders and ensure that some of the profit from Ontario's mines stayed there, rather than being funnelled into British and American financial centres. Up until now, the cautious Methodists who ran Toronto's banks had pursed their lips at the idea of dodgy investments in the uncharted bush of their own backyard. They preferred to direct funds into less risky projects, such as street railway companies in Canadian, Caribbean, and South American cities.

But some Ontario government engineers dreamed bigger. Perhaps Toronto might finally mount a serious challenge to its rival, Montreal? Montreal remained the country's financial capital; it was the major port for central Canada, and home to the dominion's banks and insurance companies. Founded more than a century before the provincial capital of Ontario, Montreal was a much larger, wealthier city than Toronto, with a more affluent merchant class and a much grander self-image. It boasted an art gallery, boulevards lined with splendid stone mansions, and the most glamorous balls north of Boston. Ontario boosters dreamed of undercutting Montreal's swaggering monopoly on seagoing trade by constructing a railway all the way to James Bay, establishing a port at its northern terminus. This railway could be the stimulus needed to move Toronto beyond the penny-pinching civic ambitions of its *nouveau riche* owners of department stores, furniture workshops, and farm-implement factories.

In 1902, Ontario's government decided to take the plunge, announcing that it would finance the Temiskaming and Northern Ontario Railway, or T&NO, a standard-gauge railway that would run the 150 kilometres from North Bay to the raw young settlement of New Liskeard. The sweaty and expensive labour of laying steel tracks (made in Sheffield, England) across unyielding Precambrian rocks and around lakes began almost immediately. Forests of spruce, black and yellow birch, cedar, hemlock, balsam, and maple had to be felled; rivers had to be bridged, and swamps drained. There was talk of extending the rails as far as James Bay, but that was too big a gamble for politicians. (When it did happen, in 1932, it never produced a major port.)

The arrival of steel rails was bad news for the Ojibwa communities in the Temagami region, which had never been covered by a land treaty. Since Confederation, the Ontario government had resisted granting any land rights to the Ojibwa because it didn't want to lose access to the valuable timber. Indigenous people watched, with dismay, the inexorable advance of logging gangs chopping and sawing their way through red and white pine forests. Chief Ignace Tonené, a revered elder of the Temagami band, had warned in 1879 that "the whitemen were coming closer and closer every year and the deer and furs were becoming scarcer and scarcer." In a few years, he warned, "Indians could not live by hunting alone." But worse was to come, once the railway construction workers started looking more closely at the rocks.

It wasn't long before the dull mineral gleam of this region— the gleam that would pull prospectors like Harry Oakes north— emerged.

Fred LaRose, a blacksmith who had set up his forge on the shores of a piece of water called Long Lake, 130 kilometres north of North Bay, was one of the first lucky strikers. LaRose flung his hammer at either a fox or a rabbit, but the hammer missed its four-footed target and instead chipped off a piece of rock to reveal a rich vein of what the blacksmith thought was copper. LaRose promptly filed a claim with the Department of Crown Lands.

In fact, the metal was silver, and two T&NO lumbermen had already identified it. J. H. McKinley and Ernest Darragh had been scouting for timber that could be cut for railway ties. As they walked along the lakeshore, they detected the gleam of metal flakes in both pebbles and rock outcrops. The white metal was so soft that they could bend it with their teeth. They immediately staked a claim, and by 1904 the McKinley-Darragh mine was up and running. It was quickly joined by several more enterprises.

At first, miners did not need costly equipment, because the silver lay close to the surface; a man who owned only a pick and shovel might become a millionaire overnight. However, as surface veins were exhausted, heavier equipment was required to dig deeper.

Soon, the T&NO railway cars were filled with flannel-shirted prospectors and smooth-talking promoters. Chief Tonené acquired a prospector's licence, learned the rules, and began staking some claims. One claim was particularly promising, but it was promptly jumped by a newcomer who wrote on one of the claim stakes, "Damn the Indian who moves this post." The Department of Indian Affairs in Ottawa failed to secure redress for Chief Tonené. This was a white man's stampede. The Ojibwa were elbowed aside.

Long Lake, where silver was first discovered, was soon renamed. The provincial geologist nailed a board to a post near the new railway stop and painted on it, "Cobalt Station, T.&N.O. Ry." The site of the silver mines acquired its name from the element that was also found in rocks that littered the vicinity, and which produced a rose-coloured bloom on exposed rock surfaces.

The silver seams proved even richer than hoped; one shipment of ore was described in the papers as consisting of "slabs of native metal stripped off the walls of the vein, like boards from a barn." Canvas sacks of silver bullion were often piled up like sandbags and left unguarded in wagons and along Cobalt's dusty, crooked roads. The government declared the Timiskaming area a "mining division" and appointed a mining recorder to live close to Cobalt, in the more salubrious town of Haileybury, to issue miners' licences and deal with claims.

These were intoxicating times for men who had spent years tapping rocks. By 1905, sixteen mines were operating, and Cobalt, stuck in the middle of tangled swamps, was a raucous boom town, spawned by hope and poverty. A disorderly jumble of mine buildings, tents, and log cabins surrounded the little stone

T&NO railway station. They were jammed together on land to which their owners had no legal title, and where there was no sanitation or water supply. Soon, the population topped eight thousand, with fortune seekers continuing to arrive at the rate of a hundred a month. Eventually, there would be over a hundred mines; it wasn't long before this squalid little town became the third-largest producer of silver in the world.

Some mines were well managed and productive, with a steady flow of ore reaching the surface. One of the best was owned by Noah and Henry Timmins, sons of a general store owner in Mattawa, a sleepy stop on the Canadian Pacific Railway in the Ottawa Valley. They knew nothing about mining, but they were risk takers. When they heard through the grapevine about the Cobalt silver strike, they and a friend bought out blacksmith Fred LaRose. Now the three men owned the richest silver mine in the district, which within the next two decades would produce an astonishing 25 million ounces of silver. By then, the three canny operators had sold their claim and become millionaires, and they were looking around for their next big play.

Other mines were little more than pipe dreams. Unlike Harry Oakes, most prospectors had stumbled on lucrative claims by luck, and they had no interest in developing their claims themselves. It was easier to sell them to promoters, and then move on to the next potential strike. Meanwhile, the promoters lined their pockets by selling shares in what they promised were surefire mineral strikes, which were nothing of the kind because they were either undeveloped or yielded no metal. In Cobalt's heyday, it was childishly easy for a crooked promoter to float a company and fleece the suckers. Shady lawyers stored sheaves of corporate applications in their desk drawers; the promoter simply filled in the blanks and paid the incorporation fee. Then he would print out some fancy stock certificates, circulate an enthusiastic prospectus, pay for advertisements in any paper that would take them, and start selling.

The whole area was suffused with euphoria and desperation. In Cobalt, private boarding houses rented out bedrooms on a shift basis. Under provincial law, no liquor could be sold within five miles of a mining camp. This allowed Haileybury, just outside that limit, to flourish. It soon boasted a "Millionaires' Row" of mine owners' mansions and turreted hotels. These establishments displayed pretentious names like the Matabanick, Vendôme, Maple Leaf, and Attorney, and featured long, polished bars and a choice of every whisky known to man. Instant millionaires sported dinner jackets each evening, while their wives and girlfriends glittered with diamonds. Both Haileybury's plutocrats and the roustabouts in Cobalt's illegal drinking establishments, known as "blind pigs," raised their glasses and roared the town anthem:

For we'll sing a little song of Cobalt,
If you don't live there it's your fault.
Oh you Cobalt, where the big gin rickies flow,
Where all the silver comes from,
You'll live a life and then some.
Oh you Cobalt, you're the best old town I know.

Cobalt residents were not the only people laughing all the way to the bank. Back then, Toronto had only a handful of brokerage houses, but the brokers bubbled with excitement as the luscious prospect of quick profits opened up. The Toronto mining exchange started to take off. In 1905, the Bank of Commerce sent a manager north to pitch a tent and declare its Cobalt branch open for business. This was no Klondike gold rush, where the mines were separated by thousands of kilometres and a gruelling three-month hike from any financial centre. The Cobalt silver mines could be reached in comfort. The T&NO's regular Cobalt Special offered its passengers a first-class dining car, comfortable sleeping compartments, club car, and library car. Financiers, engineers, and sightseers boarded the train in Toronto in the evening and, after a stopover in North Bay, disembarked in Cobalt after breakfast.

In the unpretentious lakeside town of Orillia, Ontario, the Canadian humourist Stephen Leacock watched the trains steam north, and described them in *Sunshine Sketches of a Little Town*: "On a winter evening about eight o'clock you will see the long row of the Pullmans and diners of the night express going north to the mining country, the windows flashing with brilliant light, and within them a vista of cut glass and snow-white table linen, smiling negroes and millionaires with napkins at their chins whirling past in the driving snowstorm."

The Ontario silver frenzy made headlines throughout North America. On the Cobalt Special, members of Toronto's business elite clinked glasses with deep-pocketed investors from the industrial cities of the northern US—Buffalo, Chicago, Detroit, Pittsburgh. Stock exchanges pulsated with excitement about every new mine incorporation. In 1906, New York City police had to break up mobs of people on Wall Street who were frantically trying to buy silver mining shares.

Between 1904 and 1920, Cobalt mines supplied almost 90 percent of Canada's silver production; at its peak, in 1911, silver production hit an all-time high of 31.5 million ounces. Equally important, the hardrock mining skills and capital acquired here were crucial to subsequent mineral discoveries in Northern Ontario. The Cobalt silver rush laid the foundations for the Canadian mining industry and the rise of Toronto as Canada's financial centre.

===

WHERE WAS HARRY OAKES during all this excitement? On the other side of the continent, in Nevada's scorching Death Valley. And in the unlikely event that news of the Cobalt rush had reached his ears, he would probably have ignored it. He cared only about yellow metal. What was so exciting about silver, valued in 1911 at 53.34 cents an ounce, when gold was worth $18.92 an ounce—nearly forty times as much?

However, the Cobalt silver rush was only the beginning. The T&NO Railway forged north, its mounting construction costs ($30,000 a mile) now justified by the wealth it was revealing. The immigrants who performed the hard physical labour—laying ties and tracks, hauling rocks from dynamite blasts, digging gravel and slag for the ballast or railbed—were paid a dollar a day. But with mines paying $1.50 for underground workers, these Finns, Swedes, Italians, Poles, and Bulgarians began to abandon the railway in favour of rock picks.

In 1909, there was a massive gold strike, and the Ontario stampede went into overdrive. The stampeders into the Canadian north would far outnumber those who had joined the great gold rush in California in the year 1849. And gold production from this region would outstrip production from the rushes in both California and the Klondike.

The 1909 strike was triggered when the railway reached Mile 228, north of North Bay, giving prospectors access to a region where the presence of gold around a fair-sized lake had been suspected since the 1890s. The lake was shaped like a porcupine, so it had long been known as Porcupine Lake. A Chicago promoter sent eight men, including a tough little guy called Harry Preston, up to Porcupine Lake, with equipment and food to last for several months. While scrambling through thick underbrush, Preston slipped down a slight incline and dug in his heels to prevent a fall. His boot stripped the moss from a vein that showed yellow flecks. Preston traced the vein to a large mound that, once the moss was scraped away, proved to be a dome "all covered with gold." The large vein was promptly tagged the "golden staircase," as the surface gold was like candle drippings, hanging down the hillside.

Preston was not the only man to make a lucky strike. A couple of independent prospectors, Benny Hollinger and Alec Gillies, were scraping away in the same area, hammering in claim posts and tapping at the rocks with their picks. Years later, Gillies would recall how Benny suddenly let out a roar and threw his hat at him. "At first I thought he was crazy, but when I came over to where he was it was hard not to find the reason." The gold was so rich that it looked as though it had been poured on the ground. This was just the beginning of a vein about 6 feet wide, with a visible length of 60 feet. It was the kind of strike that every prospector, from grizzled veteran to guileless rookie, hardly dared to dream about.

The two men feverishly staked six claims each, fearing that other prospectors were close by. On the way back south on the T&NO, they met a Scottish iron moulder named Sandy McIntyre and told him what they had seen. McIntyre, known as a hard drinker but a superb bushman, puffed on his pipe and scratched his dark beard as he listened carefully to the men's excited account. Then he quickly headed north and staked claims adjacent to theirs. These men had now staked what would become the three biggest-producing gold mines in the Porcupine region: Dome, Hollinger, and McIntyre.

Within weeks, prospectors converged on the new strike, with promoters, prostitutes, pimps, and moonshine producers hot on their heels. The coaches of the T&NO Railway were cluttered with packsacks and dunnage, and the fug of warm bodies and raw spirits grew stifling. The clatter of the wheels along steel rails

beat time for endless tuneless renderings of the newly composed
Porcupine anthem (as corny as its Cobalt counterpart):

I've got rings on my fingers,
Bells on my toes,
Claims up in Porcupine,
Crumbs in my clothes.
So strap on your snowshoes
And hit the trail with me
To P-O-R-C-U-P-I-N-E, that's me.

News of the Porcupine gold strike rippled across North
America, and this time, when Harry Oakes heard about it, he
paid attention. Would he finally achieve his private gold mine on
the Canadian Shield? He decided to abandon Death Valley and
head north.

By now, he had staked and panned and shovelled and tun-
nelled; his hands were scarred with old cuts, his nails were
broken, his back ached, and his skin was mottled by the sun. He
knew that there was plenty of porphyry on the Canadian Shield,
so the presence of gold was likely. But he had a major problem:
he was broke. His experiences in Yukon and Alaska in the 1890s
had taught him that he needed a canoe, toboggan, tent, utensils,
food, and far warmer clothing than he had required in Australia,
Arizona, or California. Before he could join the Ontario gold
rush, he had to go back once again to his long-suffering friends
and relatives to beg for funds.

Meanwhile, miners continued to pour into the Porcupine
Lake area. James McRae, the eager young prospector who would
later edit the *Northern Miner* (the bible for the Northern Ontario
mining industry), recalled rattling north on T&NO rails. "The
atmosphere thrilled me. Bottles of whisky were being passed from

hand to hand in the coach." Soon, the town of South Porcupine, now tagged the Golden City, boasted rough-timbered buildings, wooden planks as sidewalks over the dirt roads—and, like all mining camps, dozens of seedy bars and "cathouses" with names like the White Rat. The mackinaw-clad miners would stumble home under night skies where, on winter nights, stars twinkled like diamonds while timber wolves howled. It was almost enough to make a man forget that this was a sweaty, dirty, dangerous life.

One particular danger in every resource town surrounded by forest, then and now, was fire. Just as a wildfire would devastate Alberta's Fort McMurray in May 2016, flames engulfed South Porcupine in July 1911, destroying the pit heads of the mines and filling the air with an acrid whirlwind of sparks and ashes. At the West Dome Lake Mine, fifteen people who had hidden deep in the mine shaft died of asphyxiation as the fire sucked out all the oxygen. In a panic, residents grabbed blankets and food supplies and ran towards the lake. Men and women drowned as they tried to get as far as possible from the searing heat by clinging to canoes that capsized.

During this deadly inferno, there was a miracle birth. In an unpublished memoir, Mrs. Eva DeRosa recalled the story of a heavily pregnant woman who went into labour as she waded into the lake. The local doctor found himself managing an underwater delivery while waist-deep in water.

> There were eight men who held the blanket, and the doctor worked, and eight other men held the blanket on top of her. And they kept throwing water on the blankets, so it wouldn't be too hot. And when it got too hot for the men they'd change and some others went in. And that's the way the doctor delivered the baby. . . . The mother was fine, so was the daughter.

The safe birth was the only good news. More than seventy lives were lost in South Porcupine that day. On the same day, a similar firestorm destroyed the town of Cochrane, a railway town north of Porcupine Lake, leaving three thousand people homeless. Fires destroyed plenty of other communities, too, including Cobalt and Haileybury. But in the days following each of these tragedies, refugees limped back to the townsites and began rebuilding.

Talk of forest fires and mine cave-ins never scared Harry Oakes; they were just occupational hazards that left underground ore deposits unaffected. In fact, the torrential rain that followed the Porcupine fire exposed more quartz veins powdered with gold, and most of the prospectors had rebuilt their cabins within a couple of months. Boom towns were exactly the kind of communities that Harry Oakes felt at home in—blue-collar, resilient, and home to gritty loners like himself, focused on the only thing that mattered: the glint of precious metals. He didn't care that often the only meat available was moose, or that scurvy was a risk every winter because of the shortage of fresh vegetables. Only weeks after the conflagrations, Oakes was sitting on the hard wooden seats of the T&NO, staring out at a monotonous green landscape occasionally interrupted by mounds of sawdust burning purposelessly next to sawmills, or lonely clearings still studded with blackened tree stumps and roots.

CHAPTER 3

Harry's Claim

Mining towns are homely. Mining towns are rough. They nurture their own and their own love them. Not like the town laborer do mining dwellers become dull, nor like the grower of things narrow-minded. Theirs is the inheritance of a dash of romance, theirs is the nomad life. . . . Theirs is a true frontier breed.

NORTHERN MINER, MARCH 6, 1930

W hether Harry Oakes landed in Kirkland Lake by design or dumb luck is not clear. The Oakes legend, which flourished after his success, includes the story that the T&NO conductor booted him off the train at the tiny settlement of Swastika because he was flat broke and had no ticket. (The station was probably named after a piece of jewellery shaped like a swastika—then a symbol of good luck—worn by the daughter of one of the town's founders. When the Nazis subsequently adopted the symbol, someone suggested that the settlement's name be changed to Winston. The local physician and drugstore owner, Doc Edis, had matchbox covers printed with the slogan "Hitler be damned. This is our sign since 1922." The name stuck.)

Oakes resented the story that he had been thrown off the train. Although he readily admitted that he had barely two cents, he insisted that luck had nothing to do with his fortune. He had studied the claims in this area at the Bureau of Mines in Toronto, and probably in the mining recorder's office in Matheson, and he had identified the rock formations in the Kirkland Lake region as having potential. The surfeit of porphyry there had suggested to him a break, or fault, through which molten minerals from the Earth's core—including gold—might have penetrated the surrounding granites. He also dropped into the office of the Swastika Mining Company, on one of the earliest gold claims in the region, and looked carefully at their ore samples. They confirmed his instincts.

Oakes was a cagey man who kept his cards close to his chest. He was particularly interested in a handful of soon-to-be-abandoned claims near Kirkland Lake, 9 kilometres east of Swastika along a rough forest track, but he didn't want anybody to notice that he was accumulating claims there. He persuaded a local prospector, Melville McDougall, to stake some Kirkland Lake land, and then quietly arranged for the claim to be transferred to him. Meanwhile, he continued to explore around the lake, working thigh-deep in muskeg and bogs, and sleeping in either his tent or one of three lean-to shelters he had fashioned out of sacks and sticks.

Some prospectors, camping alone in the backwoods, relished glimpses of forest wildlife—a beaver repairing his dam; a black bear standing belly-deep in a brook, flicking fish out of the water; a red fox crouching low as an unwary rabbit approached; a moose dipping her massive head deep into murky waters in search of water-lily roots. James McRae wrote nostalgically of such sights, including "a porcupine hunched in the crotch of a tree, and maybe waiting there for night and the opportunity to chew my boots, tumpline or straps, for their salty accumulations of sweat." McRae loved to boast of the way that he had "lived and experienced the full gamut of the music the wilderness plays."

Harry Oakes had no patience for wilderness music. "I was up every morning before daybreak and on the go all day," he recalled years later. "At night I would make for the nearest of the little camps, cook myself a bite of supper and fall asleep, dead tired. I worked hard, harder than a lot of those grubstake, syndicated prospectors think they have to work today. I am a great believer in a prospector working for himself and I think a district gets opened up faster if it has men working on their own."

Oakes was not the only person digging through the bush around Kirkland Lake. Amongst other prospectors in the area was a mild-mannered chain-smoker, a former butcher named William H. Wright who loved horses and had fought with the British cavalry in the South African wars. A small, quiet man with a handlebar moustache, Wright had arrived in Canada from England five years earlier. First he worked on a farm, handling the six- and eight-horse teams that pulled the lumbering steam threshing machines, and then he moved to Cobalt and supported himself by painting houses. After he had saved $40—enough to stake himself for a few weeks in the bush—he and his brother-in-law Ed Hargreaves, another butcher, travelled north and started digging around on the eastern shore of the lake. Wright noticed gold flecks in the rock, so he staked three claims—the maximum allowed under the Mining Act—plus two more in Hargreaves's name. By then, the two men had run out of money.

This was the first time anybody had seen—rather than suspected—gold close to Kirkland Lake. The metal is usually so finely disseminated through the rock that it is not visible to the naked eye, and the rocks have to be processed by assayers to determine its presence. Porcupine's "dripped candle wax" gold deposits were highly unusual. So Wright's staking aroused only desultory interest because the evidence of gold was so scanty. Hargreaves would sell his claims within the next few weeks.

But Harry Oakes knew about those claims, and the gold flecks. And he continued to survey the lake's shoreline and wait for the ground he wanted. All his instincts told him that this was gold-bearing ground. Although he hadn't seen any gold flecks, he was certain that the rock formations, sediments, and lavas indicated he was close to a vein. He had developed a theory (on what grounds, he never explained) that all gold veins in the north country ran under lakes, so he concentrated on the land under the lake and to the west of Wright's discovery. As always, he was dogged. "I plan my work, then I work my plans." And he kept his eye on some claims beyond the five Wright-Hargreaves claims: the prospectors who had staked them several years earlier had not done the development work on them required by law, so they were about to revert to the Crown. But he was bedevilled by his usual problem: empty pockets. At one stage, he was down to his last four dollars.

In later years, when Oakes was polishing anecdotes about his tough times in the north, the story of the four dollars was one of his favourites. Apparently, one day he discovered that rabbits had been in his tent while he was out prospecting, and had found the sweat-stained notebook in which he had hidden his last two $2 bills. They had chewed the notebook to shreds. In desperation, Oakes crept on his hands and knees over every inch of the clearing in which his tent was pitched. He claimed that he found one of the bills, rolled into a tight little wad that had proved too tough for a rabbit to swallow.

But in late 1911 Oakes cursed his poverty. Wrapping his scarf across his face for protection against the numbing cold, he trudged back to Swastika and wrote desperate letters to his mother, brother, and sister, begging them to trust his instincts. Then he dropped into a general store run by a man called Jimmy Doig to equip himself for a few months in the bush. Doig usually extended credit, so Oakes didn't even bother to ask as he picked up a pair of overalls and bundled them into his backpack. But Doig brusquely told Oakes to put them back on the shelf. Oakes stared at him and (according to biographer Bocca) snapped, "Put them on my account. My brother is sending me money from Maine."

Doig replied, "Sorry, Harry. If you can't pay, put them back."

Oakes flushed scarlet, yanked the overalls out of his pack, and flung them on the counter. "You'll be sorry for that, Doig," he said. Oakes never forgot his grudges, and this particular grudge would cost Doig dearly.

In 1911, Swastika was doing well because it had two working mines—the Swastika Mine and the Lucky Cross Mine. Besides Doig's store, a hardware store, the railway station, a post office, bunkhouses, and homes, it boasted the Swastika Hotel, with a bar that was usually thick with tobacco smoke and crowded with lumbermen, railway workers, and miners. One bitterly cold evening in January 1912, either in Doig's store or in the hotel, Harry Oakes bumped into four large young men: the Tough brothers, T&NO contractors who had all been bitten by the prospecting bug. The four brawny brothers—Tom, George, Bob, and Jack—towered over Oakes, but the latter had a powerful presence that commanded respect. Oakes told the brothers that he knew of claims that were about to lapse, and said he would share the information if they would help him stake the claims and then develop them. Tom Tough asked when the claims would be open. Oakes pulled out his watch, then replied, "In about four hours."

The Tough brothers took the bait, and agreed that Tom and

George should set off immediately with Oakes, despite four inches of new snow and a marrow-chilling temperature said to be -52°F. According to one author, "Some said Harry Oakes was wearing five pairs of pants; others said he never owned that many pairs of pants in his life until he struck it rich." The moon was so bright and the sky so clear that Oakes did not need to use his lamp. The three men trudged on snowshoes through snowdrifts and across frozen swamps; it was long after midnight before Oakes looked around, caught sight of the old claim stakes, and then announced they should start staking.

It took two men to drive each claim stake into the rock and frozen ground: one held the stake, rotating it downwards as the second wielded a heavy mallet. Altogether, Harry Oakes and the two Toughs staked five claims: three for themselves, two more for the other two Toughs. They may have staked a further six, although the record is unclear. At one point, according to an interview that George Tough gave to *Gold* magazine in 1934, Oakes went out onto nearby Gull Lake and the ice gave way. Fortunately, the water was not too deep, and the Tough brothers heard him yell for help. They hauled the sodden, shivering prospector out of the ice and mud. "Then we cut down an old pine and built a fire," George Tough recalled. "He stripped off all his clothes and we had a good laugh over it." Oakes danced around the flames in his long underwear, trying to keep warm, while his outer clothes were strung over the fire. "You'd think we were displaying samples for a clothing factory." After hammering in the claim stakes, they were exhausted. As dawn broke, they huddled around a fire on which they had brewed some tea.

A panting, bundled-up figure suddenly came crashing through the undergrowth. The Tough brothers recognized Bill Wright and welcomed him warmly as they explained he was too late. Oakes had never met the Englishman; now the two prospectors shook hands before Wright hurried off to stake new claims next to the Tough-Oakes claims.

The icy trudge through the night paid off. Jack and Bob Tough joined their brothers, and along with Oakes started digging through the icy ground, panting with the effort of breaking up dirt that was frozen as hard as the granite below it. Within three days, they found more rock that glittered with gold flecks.

Meanwhile, Oakes had also teamed up with Bill Wright in an unlikely alliance; together, the college-educated American and the British butcher staked more claims along Kirkland Lake. Wright agreed to lend Oakes the cash he needed to pay his share of the recording fee for all the different claims in which he had an interest. This meant that, in addition to the claims he had staked on his own, Oakes was part owner of two more potential gold mines: the Tough-Oakes claims and the claims he and Wright intended to develop farther along the lakeshore.

However, Harry Oakes still needed money. Unlike the San Francisco or Klondike gold rushes, where rubber-booted prospectors needed only a pan with which to sift through the alluvial gravel of riverbeds to find nuggets, Ontario's gold was locked deep underground in hard rock. A man who wanted to develop his own gold mine would need labour, machinery, engineers, steel, timber, electricity, cyanide, arsenic, and dynamite.

DR. EUGENE WHITTREDGE, the Dover-Foxcroft dentist, was shocked by the appearance of his old school friend in 1912. When Whittredge described the encounter to Geoffrey Bocca in 1958, he was still shaking his head at Oakes's deterioration. Whittredge had last seen Oakes around fourteen years before this encounter, when the latter was a strapping young adventurer in a smart suit and trim haircut. But here was the same Harry, only thirty-eight years old but looking like an aging tramp in his threadbare over-coat and mouldy bowler hat. Whittredge could see that years of gold digging had not been kind.

Harry Oakes was oblivious to the poor impression he made that late-January afternoon. He had undertaken the long, com-plicated journey from the north to his little hometown in Maine to persuade family and friends to lend him some money, and he had ducked into Whittredge's dental office seeking shelter from a steady downpour outside. He immediately started his pitch. More than four decades later, Eugene Whittredge described the scene to Bocca, who enlivened it by reconstructing the dialogue. According to Bocca, Oakes told the dentist, "If you will lend me a thousand dollars I shall make you a rich man."

"Where do you think I can find a thousand dollars?" Whittredge protested. "I am a country dentist."

Oakes didn't falter. "Raise it. You will have as much as you put into it back almost at once. . . . By the end of 1913 I will pay you that much back in dividends alone."

Once again, Whittredge protested that such a sum was out of reach, and even if he had it, he wouldn't invest in a gold mine: "The *Wall Street Journal* will tell you that it is the most specula-tive stock a man can own."

Oakes came straight back at him. "I can sell you shares for a few cents today that ten years from now will be worth thirty dollars, forty dollars, a hundred dollars."

Whittredge told his visitor that there was no point in pursu-ing the issue because he did not have that kind of money. "It's no use," he insisted, but he asked Oakes why he needed the money.

Oakes fixed his gaze on the dentist, according to his biog-rapher, and told him he had found "the biggest gold mine in Canada," or maybe "the biggest gold mine in the world. All I need is some capital, and not much of it at that, so that I can exploit it. . . . I can recognise a gold mine when I see one, and I can recognise a bonanza. This is a bonanza and I don't intend to sell it to a lot of fancy-pants bastards from Toronto. I am going to keep it and suck it dry."

Oakes was keen to tell his story, even though he would get no money out of his old friend. He and Whittredge spent the next five hours in the dental office, one speechless with amazement while the other barely drew breath as he recounted his global search for gold. Night fell, but Whittredge was too mesmerized by his visitor to rise and switch on the light. Then Oakes rose abruptly, nodded to Whittredge, jammed his sodden hat on his head, and headed off into the rain in the direction of his mother's house.

It took Whittredge a few minutes to recover from the encounter—his old friend had been so forceful, so passionate. The quiet, unassuming boy he had known at Bowdoin had become a man obsessed with a hunger for gold. Whittredge still didn't know whether Oakes knew what he was talking about, or whether the years of hardship had bred delusions. He did not regret his decision not to offer to stake him.

But Harry Oakes's mother had faith. She, or perhaps her elder son Louis, must have found some funds for Harry, because in the spring of 1912 he was back in Kirkland Lake with enough cash to hire a young English immigrant named Ernie Martin, paying him a few dollars a day.

CHAPTER 4

Flashy Fellows and Big Spenders

In scores of . . . promotions, stock was marketed for a nickel or a dime and even rose to a quarter or more, before the insiders silently folded their tents and stole away as the bottom dropped out of the market, leaving the shareholders with nothing but finely engraved certificates useful only as wallpaper.

DR. CHRISTOPHER ARMSTRONG, 1997

O nce Harry Oakes was back in Canada, he and Martin set to work on the claims along the shore of Kirkland Lake, chipping away at quartz outcrops. Oakes was encouraged by the presence of tellurides in the rock—telltale greenish grains that he had also seen in the Australian gold camps. The tellurides seemed to confirm his theory about gold seams running under the lake, because a vein of quartz at the water's edge was speckled with gold.

However, the gold, which would subsequently become the productive "Number One vein" in Harry Oakes's mine, looked like fairy dust rather than layers of creamy, rich minerals. That is why Oakes had a problem convincing visiting engineers that the surface show indicated a much richer vein deeper down. To his irritation, the only mines attracting the heavy capital investment required for hardrock mining were those clustered around Porcupine Lake, 127 kilometres farther north.

What made visiting engineers skeptical about the Kirkland Lake claims was not simply the lack of clear evidence of a rich vein. They also knew that mining stocks were riddled with fraud. Too many guileless punters, eager to take a flyer on a penny stock, lost most of their money in "bucket shops," where operators simply "bucketed" their clients' orders rather than actually acquiring shares in mining enterprises. Anecdotes about unscrupulous share pushers were commonplace because investors had almost no legal protection, so dubious salesmen operated with brazen impunity.

Bucket shops for mining stocks existed in all the major North American financial centres that had stock exchanges, from San Francisco to Chicago, New York City to Philadelphia. Toronto's stock exchange was still in its early days at the start of the twentieth century, but everybody in the mining sector knew where to go to pick up tips, snag prospectors, and lure investors: the King Edward Hotel on King Street, the city's first luxury hotel. Desk clerks at the "King Eddie" welcomed dishevelled prospectors to its opulent lobby while bellboys struggled under the weight of battered suitcases packed with rock samples.

Hector Charlesworth, the future editor of *Saturday Night* magazine, the Toronto social and literary weekly, would recall that in 1910, "one could not go into the King Edward Hotel at Toronto without seeing scores of crooks at work trying to separate victims from their money, flashy fellows and big spenders. This was true also of every large hotel in Canada and in every village . . . [where] 'strong arm' salesmen were at work endeavouring to bamboozle ignorant men and woman out of their savings."

Beyond Canadian borders, the young dominion gathered an

unsavoury reputation for mining swindles. London investors, already burned by Canadian railway stocks that had gone sour, kept their distance. In Toronto, *Saturday Night* started a new column, "Gold and Dross," to expose shady dealings. Such warnings were justified: between 1904 and 1933, fewer than one in fifty of the mining companies incorporated in Ontario reached production.

Meanwhile, Harry Oakes could barely raise a cent to finance his mine.

Undeterred, he and his partners sweated on. By the time the snow had finally melted, Wright and the Tough brothers were also working rich quartz veins in their claims—veins that convinced them they would soon strike pay dirt. The Toughs had access to more funds than Oakes, so the Tough-Oakes mine could hire more men to hack out the rocks with picks and bag the ore (the rock from which gold might be extracted). Wright and the Tough brothers proceeded in a helter-skelter fashion, driven by the sheer exhilaration of prospecting and the hope of being able to quickly sell shares in their claims to willing promoters. Harry Oakes was more methodical as he and Ernie Martin started digging the Number One shaft on his claim. It was back-breaking work that involved drilling a round hole, putting a stick of dynamite down it, blasting it out, and then mucking it out with a windlass arrangement and a wooden bucket. Drill, blast, load. One man would stay in the shaft, filling a barrel with ore, while the other climbed to the surface, hauled up each heavy barrel-load, emptied it, and waited for the next one. If Oakes could secure some sophisticated equipment and more employees, he would be able to build a more efficient winching system as the shaft deepened. But where could he find the funds?

At Tough-Oakes, the Tough brothers managed to fill fifty-two bags of hand-picked high-grade ore that year—over a hundred tons. After the 1912–13 winter freeze-up, they conveyed it to Swastika on the wagon trail and loaded it onto a southbound T&NO train for transport to a smelter in New Jersey. The ore yielded $46,221, a remarkable $457 per ton. Harry Oakes got a share of the profit, after all the expenses and debts were paid.

Seven gold mines would eventually be consolidated along the lakeshore, but development was slow: Tough-Oakes would not pour its first gold brick until 1915. This was paltry compared to what was going on in Porcupine, where that same year, the gold mines delivered more than $2 million to shareholders and pushed Ontario into the lead for gold production in Canada.

Nevertheless, as Kirkland Lake grew, a typical northern cast of prospectors, loners, and eccentrics drifted into the settlement. Earlier arrivals, happy to meet others who shared their faith in the region, welcomed each wave of hungry, tired, but hard-working miners, and shared their meals with them. One of the first to arrive was Charlie Chow, a Chinese cook who opened a boarding house and popular lunch counter. Chow let Oakes pay for dinner with shares, at the rate of thirty cents each, instead of cash.

Women were in short supply in mining camps. "The odds were good," as one woman had remarked during the Klondike gold rush, "but the goods were odd." One of the oddest characters in Kirkland Lake was a woman named Roza Brown, who had met Oakes when he first stepped off the train in Swastika. Brown is one of those characters who are irresistible to writers like Geoffrey Bocca, Pierre Berton, and me—an eccentric about whom plenty of stories accrued, and who typifies the unpredictable nature of communities far from big-city conventions. Once met, never forgotten, Roza claimed an intimate knowledge not only of the northern wilderness but of the nature of gold itself. She was much given to mystical pronouncements about the mineral everybody was looking for. "Gold has a mind of its own," she would tell anybody she could buttonhole. "Gold is a woman. All the gold in the world is waiting for just one thing, for the right man to find it." In her hip-high rubber boots and smelly beaver coat, with a pack of mangy dogs in tow, she cut an eye-catching figure in a community of hefty miners.

Roza Brown had worked as a baker in Cobalt before moving on to Swastika, and then to Kirkland Lake. She paced around the cramped little settlement, between the raw tree stumps, open trenches, and shafts, and worked out where the main streets would be. Would they run parallel to the lakeshore, or would they lead down to it? Brown guessed (correctly) the former, and quietly bought up lots along the muddy trail and at its inter-sections. She hired a man to build her a bakeshop and laundry, and then to cobble together a boarding house and properties she could rent out, usually to bootleggers and prostitutes.

Brown prospered as her tight-fisted, hard-nosed habits paid off. She began trading in claim shares, and managed to accumu-late enough capital to grubstake the rare prospector that she decided to trust. She also staked a couple of claims herself, then sold them at a considerable profit. This allowed her to indulge her affection for the British royal family. She kept track of all the royal birthdays and celebrations, and regularly cabled her con-gratulations to Buckingham Palace.

Roza Brown developed an affinity for Harry Oakes. Perhaps she liked him because he was as ornery and pugnacious as she was. They certainly shared a determination never to be taken advantage of. Oakes never forgave the engineers who urged him to sell out, who told him that his claims were worthless and that a simple prospector lacked the financial and technical skills to develop a mine from first strike to first corporate dividend. Throughout his life, he resented the financiers in Buffalo and

Toronto who smiled politely when he called on them but declined to invest. Roza Brown's belief in Harry was firm.

By now, the Tough-Oakes claims (which the Tough brothers did all the work on) were producing a steady stream of high-yielding ore. Harry Oakes decided to sell his interest in the property, since he didn't like sharing ownership. Then he could invest everything in the claims he had staked exclusively in his name along the south shore. He commissioned a Cobalt investor named Clem Foster, a friend of the Toughs, to sell some of his stock in the Tough-Oakes property. Foster made a deal in England—one that included a secret commission for himself on the side. Oakes heard about this and was enraged; he reckoned Foster was trying to cheat him. He launched a bitter lawsuit, Foster countersued, and then the Toughs sued Oakes. All of these actions concerned gold that many engineers insisted didn't exist. The litigation tied up development for months; Oakes's recalcitrance ensured that he had no access to any easy cash. "Stubborn" was the way Oakes's partners described him. His critics used stronger language. When Oakes finally won the case in 1941 and collected $40,000 from Foster, he sent cheap reprints of the judgment to three or four hundred mining friends. He would talk about the swindle for the rest of his life.

"He overdid the work, and it made him one-sided," recalled a Cobalt engineer who met him during these years. "He wasn't like most of the boys here, ready for a joke, handy with a bottle. . . . Harry had a genius for making unnecessary enemies."

SOMEHOW, WITH HIS share of the Tough-Oakes profits, money sent to him by his family, and perhaps a bit of help from Roza Brown, by 1913 Harry Oakes had managed to buy the steam boilers and compressors he needed to burrow deeper. He was finally able to afford a headframe, a tower constructed directly over the shaft and housing a rickety wire cage that could transport men and rocks between surface and seam. The elevator cage was raised and lowered by means of a greased metal cable wound around a drum that was connected to a wheel. Because the shaft was relatively deep, the wooden tower was supported by angled braces, which gave the whole structure an awkward, lopsided look. Headframes were already icons of the north, just as grain elevators had become prairie landmarks.

Oakes employed six men to help him keep working on his Number One vein, recovering just enough ore to keep going. He was convinced that his theory the veins of gold ran under the lake was correct, and that his drill bit was within centimetres of a thick layer of gold within the hard porphyry rock. Although it still eluded him, he was more optimistic about his future than he had been in years.

Around this time James McRae, a decade younger than Oakes but already a veteran of the Cobalt and Porcupine stampedes, visited him in a shack by the lake. Oakes was clad in heavy, wrinkled woollen pants, tucked into high-legged boots; he wore no top shirt, although it was a chilly day. Instead, his stained suspenders were stretched over a filthy fleece-lined undershirt, and he stank of sweat. McRae introduced himself to the grubby, unkempt figure who was working like a dog and asked him if he had found any "colour," as the miners called gold. Oakes was happy to show his visitor the quartz vein glinting with gold.

McRae found Oakes to be more good-humoured and hospitable than he had expected, given the latter's reputation as a loner. "Although I was a complete stranger to him, he placed two tin plates and two tin cups upon his homemade table and insisted that I share with him a helping of mulligan stew and a hot cup of freshly-brewed coffee." Oakes spoke of his canniness in recognizing Kirkland Lake's possibilities when he had checked the geology charts. Besides, he insisted, "The name of Swastika sounded good to me. It sounded like good luck. That's what gave me my hunch."

Oakes's confidence in his hunch would never waver, but there were setbacks. Three hundred feet down, the rock was yielding steadily less gold. According to mining historian Philip Smith, "The local sages all nodded with satisfaction and muttered, 'Just another flash in Harry's pan.'" Nobody around him shared his crazy idea about the vein running under the lake, but Oakes kept digging. In 1914 he formed Lake Shore Mines Ltd. and tried to sell stock. The company had a nominal capital of two million shares with a par value of one dollar each. But this unknown American prospector had no traction in Toronto. The Toronto *Globe* refused to carry his advertisements, and the mining exchange pegged Lake Shore at fifteen cents per share. Visiting mining engineers continued to raise their eyebrows at Oakes's claims; they doubted the area's potential. By 1916, only 300,000 shares had been sold, at prices ranging from fifteen to thirty cents.

These were lean years for Lake Shore employees, with food scarce and stock often offered in place of wages. War had broken out in Europe, which meant a shortage of labour and little cash available for risky mining projects. Unlike his friend Bill Wright, Harry Oakes felt no obligation to go to war—he was an American; why should he defend the British Empire? His grim determination was as solid as the Canadian Shield itself. He managed to scrape together enough money to hire a diamond-drilling crew, and he ordered them to drill horizontally from the bottom of his Number One vein shaft, northward under the lake.

Still no luck. The drill encountered a vein, but it proved to be poor. The crew manager, who had taken part of his salary in shares, promptly sold them for ten cents each. But Oakes kept at it. In one final throw of the dice, he told the drillers to blast out a crosscut shaft that would dig deep under the lakebed. This time, the drill hit high-grade ore in what became Number Two vein. Twelve metres wide, it would yield some of the richest ore ever seen in Canada.

Four years after Oakes staked his original claim on the edge of Kirkland Lake, he had his gold mine. He strutted and crowed like a bantam rooster, gleeful that his hunch had paid off. The manager's ten-cent Lake Shore shares would trade for as much as $64 each by the mid-1920s. Oakes even dared to divert some of his own energy from the mine into an upgrade of his living conditions, from tarpaulin shelters. He hired two men to cut the logs for a modest cabin. Two days later, he flew into a rage when he discovered they had cut only thirty poles. He fired them both and took on the job himself; in a single day, he is said to have trimmed and felled seventy trees, ready for the proposed building. Two friends helped him put up the walls, and in no time at all he had a square, one-and-a-half-storey log building with a wraparound porch, surrounded by white birch. After his death, an old-timer recalled the story, adding, "Harry Oakes was a bear for getting things done."

Not that Oakes was putting on airs—his shirts were as sweaty as ever and his manner as truculent. But at the age of forty-two, for perhaps the first time in his life, he was happy and triumphant. His hunch about where he would find gold had paid off, and he had proved the naysayers wrong.

But Harry Oakes continued to be frustrated at every stage. He still needed a lot of money, to allow him to drill even deeper through the dense layers of rock and build a mill so that he would no longer have to ship his ore south for refining into bullion. He tried to persuade the Timmins brothers, and others who had done well in Cobalt, to put some money into Lake Shore, but there were still no bites. In 1916, he made a public offering of 150,000 Lake Shore shares at forty cents each to raise the money for a 100-ton mill. But the prewar exhilaration about fortunes being made in New Ontario had given way to gloom and caution about the immense loss of young lives in the trenches of France. Lake Shore stock attracted few buyers.

If Oakes's failure to raise funds wasn't bad enough, Kirkland Lake itself seemed trapped in a fog of gloom. Although gold had been found in several claims, the settlement remained small and dispiriting. Unlike Cobalt or Porcupine, this was no exuberant boom town. Thick bush crowded the meagre human habitations, and the only prosperous-looking spot was Tough-Oakes, where they had electric power and light. In other mining towns, the community lived on the edge of the mineral field, and though the streets were muddy there were wooden sidewalks and a semblance of order. The centre of town was usually the shingle-roofed train station. But Kirkland Lake had no centre and, as yet, no train station; visitors still left the railway at Swastika and then caught a ride with Walter Little's horse-drawn freight wagon over the rutted 8-kilometre track to Kirkland Lake. There, they discovered buildings clustered higgledy-piggledy around the five mines now at different stages of development: Tough-Oakes, Lake Shore, Teck-Hughes, Kirkland Lake, and Wright-Hargreaves.

A muddy path (known officially as Government Road and unofficially as the Mile of Gold) wound its way around shaft openings and headframes, and the once-sparkling lake was disfigured and polluted by the toxic tailings from the mines. Roza Brown's boarding house and cabins were usually full, and two brothers, Hyman and Max Kaplan, had set up a new store that sold everything a prospector might need—dry goods, meat, coal oil, cheese, nails, cabbages, beer, boots. The Kaplans' store often looked like an old Hudson's Bay fur-trading post because it was a gathering place for the local Ojibwa who belonged to the Beaver House Lake band. When they came into town to buy supplies, they liked to sit on the store's stoop, smoking and chatting, as they watched the passing traffic. But there was no bank (a bank officer came up each week from Haileybury to transact business and distribute wages), and Kirkland Lake could be cut off for days at a time in winter. After one March storm in 1917, a metre of snow blocked the road to the T&NO station in Swastika, and Walter Little used thirteen teams of horses pulling a wooden plough, plus eighteen men with shovels, to clear the 8-kilometre distance. Kirkland Lake was in limbo, with everybody waiting for serious money to come into town so production could ramp up.

For all his flintiness, Oakes was prepared to make a deal when he needed one, and he could see that he needed one now. After the 1916 public offering of Lake Shore Mines cratered, he stomped over to the Wright-Hargreaves mine to talk to its manager, Albert Wende. Wende was a broad-shouldered, affable American hardrock miner with deep-pocketed contacts in Buffalo. He had purchased a three-eighths interest in Wright-Hargreaves for only $3,000 and was now running the mine while Bill Wright, who had volunteered for service in the British army when war broke out, was away fighting in Europe. Oakes told Wende that if the latter could help him sell Lake Shore stock in Buffalo, Wende would receive a commission of 60,000 shares from Oakes's personal holdings.

Wende knew that a rising tide lifts all boats; he was anxious to see Lake Shore go into production, because that would strengthen the case for investing in its neighbour, Wright-Hargreaves. He invited several wealthy business associates from Buffalo to visit the Lake Shore mine. Two Buffalo financiers, Canadian-born Conrad Wettlaufer and realtor Edward L. Koons, hired a special train to take twenty-two Canadian and American potential investors from Toronto to Swastika, and filled it with champagne and fine food.

The American investors settled comfortably into the club car's plush seats, and as the train made its way north, they chatted affably as they stared through the train windows at the rapidly thickening bush and dwindling number of settlements. The railcar attendant made sure their glasses were full and their Havana cigars lit. By the time they were chugging through the swampy wilderness north of North Bay, many of the champagne bottles were empty and the decibel level had risen. Harry Oakes sat amongst them, incapable of such conviviality and uncomfortable in a lounge suit he had bought off the rack in Toronto.

I can speculate on Oakes's discomfort as he accompanied his trainload of investors north, thanks to the American prospector Arnold Hoffman, author of *Free Gold*. Hoffman found himself sitting opposite Oakes on such a train, and the younger man detected a "definite note of contempt in [Oakes's] glance as he [surveyed] the men about him." Hoffman assumed that Oakes shared his own impatience with their companions' ignorance of Canada, "this land of timbered silence . . . [and] the shifting colours of northern lights." More likely, Oakes glowered because he couldn't stand men who, in his view, made their money on the backs of hard workers like himself who risked everything.

Hoffman was fascinated by Oakes: "He is a small man, but the square face and jutting chin give a sense of largeness and power. . . . His voice, that of an assertive self-made man, breathes defiance and conviction." He could see that the owner of Lake Shore Mines Ltd. deeply resented the power of cigar-chomping plutocrats to make or break his dreams. Hoffman noted that

Oakes was inclined to launch into rants about anybody who derided his ideas. "His close-set eyes burn with a fierce light as he recounts his wanderings. He has been misunderstood and ridiculed everywhere, and as he speaks of his detractors his hands twitch nervously as though he would destroy anyone with the temerity to oppose him. He is impressive in his strength but obviously riddled with fixations, a mixture of the rare and the common, bright hues matched against the dullest grey." As the jovial hubbub in the bar car grew noisier, Oakes abruptly rose and went elsewhere.

Hoffman did not record the reaction of the well-fed plutocrats to the dingy mining camp at Kirkland Lake. Doubtless they were quickly shepherded past Roza Brown's boarding house, the blind pigs, and the seediest parts of the community. Despite the town's squalor and Oakes's manners, Wende's manoeuvre with the Buffalo investors paid off handsomely. Once Wettlaufer and friends had seen the Lake Shore layout and samples, and examined the ore taken from the most productive veins, they agreed to help finance the mill. Oakes sold them half a million shares at 32½ cents each—one-quarter of all Lake Shore Mines stock—and the agreement was signed on a sheet of brown wrapping paper. The deal yielded $162,000 for Oakes, his first serious cash with which to develop his mine. The Buffalo investors were rewarded when Lake Shore paid its first dividend in 1918; over the next twenty years, they would receive dividends totalling more than $32 million.

CHAPTER 5

Kirkland Lake Comes of Age

GOLD OUTPUT TO JUMP 50%: CANADA'S NEW BOOM SHAPING UP
Evidence piles up convincingly that Canada is entering upon a gold mining boom. . . . Gold mining is today the most flourishing branch of Canadian industrial life. It was never so lush in profits. The Public, so obsessed with the worries of other phases of Industrial life, appears to have paid little attention to what the gold mines are doing, and the remarkable change that is taking place.

NORTHERN MINER, MAY 29, 1930

Finally, Lake Shore could let rip! Harry Oakes ordered mechanical rock crushers from the States and hired local carpenters to construct a mill, tool house, and (eventually) a two-storey mine office and a bunkhouse. The mill went into operation in March 1918. Before the year was out, Lake Shore had produced gold valued at $416,414 and the company had paid its first dividends—$100,000 worth. That was a huge sum in an era when a Ford Runabout cost $500, and the annual salary of a male teacher hovered around $1,000 a year.

There were still problems. Oakes faced a technical challenge with his operation. The deep vertical Lake Shore shaft was adjacent to the lake, but his employees were now digging the Number Two shaft horizontally, under the lake, and work was constantly interrupted because water kept seeping into it. Quicksand posed a danger to the miners and made it difficult for the engineers to see the surface of the rock.

Another issue was a shrinking labour pool because so many miners had gone to war. One edition of the *Northern Miner* reported shutdowns in seven shafts in the area because of a shortage of men, money, or machinery. Oakes struggled on, and production slowly increased. Finally, on November 11, 1918, a chorus of mine whistles in Kirkland Lake—and the burning of the Kaiser in effigy in Swastika—signalled the armistice and the end of the grim European conflict. Soon, returning soldiers appeared at mine offices, looking for work, and Kirkland Lake's employee shortage evaporated.

Harry Oakes, now forty-four, had realized his childhood dream. More than two decades after setting off in search of gold, and seven years after his arrival in Northern Ontario, he was on the way to being a very rich man. He owned nearly 50 percent of the shares in Lake Shore, and ownership of the rest was so diffused that no one could challenge his supremacy. He was making several other people wealthy, too, including his own family, with whom he was still in close touch. (His mother could not believe her first dividend cheque was real, and waited a long time before she dared to cash it.) Several Kirkland Lake merchants, such as restaurant owner Charlie Chow, who had accepted shares instead of cash, found themselves rich beyond their wildest fantasies. Oakes gave his first employee, Ernie Martin, shares worth more than $100,000. Lake Shore shares spiralled upwards in value: the 60,000 shares that Oakes gave Al Wende for luring the Buffalo investors to his mine would be worth $3.75 million within a decade.

Oakes's partners and friends were not the only beneficiaries. As news of the Lake Shore bonanza filtered south, stockbrokers in Toronto, Montreal, Buffalo, and New York took a much closer look at Ontario's mines in general, and Oakes's in particular. Trading on North American stock markets soared through the 1920s, with sharp rises in volumes on all the well-established exchanges. There were even more dramatic increases in dealings in speculative mining shares on Toronto's Standard Stock and Mining Exchange, where every speculator dreamed that he had discovered "the next Lake Shore" and might emulate Harry Oakes's success. The gush of gold production in Kirkland Lake and the Porcupine region prompted new investors to plunge into the market, often using borrowed money to buy stock.

Oakes watched the town of Kirkland Lake, and his own company, benefit from all this excitement, but he continued to resent the way that smooth-talking investors were making so much money off the sweat equity of miners like himself. In 1928, a newspaper feature about Kirkland Lake quoted him saying with satisfaction, "Quite a large interest in the camp is still held by the original prospectors, whose interest [is] in the profit from the ore rather than the money to be taken from the other fellow's pocket via the stock market."

Stock traders shrugged off such unrealistic sentiments; they were busy offering silent prayers of thanks to prospectors like Oakes for building the industry. Equally grateful was the provincial government, now making money from land rentals, the ten-dollar mining licence fee, and the 3 percent royalty on production. Between 1920 and 1940, the Ontario mining industry prospered as never before; its value increased fivefold and it far outstripped manufacturing as the backbone of the provincial economy. The annual value of gold alone mined in Ontario in these years jumped from $11,679,483 to $125,574,988—and a big chunk of that came from a single mine: Lake Shore.

Lake Shore's neighbouring mines were also thriving. Bill Wright had returned from the war to find the Wright-Hargreaves mine shipping almost as much gold as Lake Shore. Wright had hung on to a one-quarter interest in the mine and also held 250,000 Lake Shore shares, and now he became vice-president and a director of both Lake Shore and Wright-Hargreaves. These were the two most productive mines in Kirkland Lake, but others did well too. For years, town residents would rhyme off, like beads on a rosary, the names of the seven mines that were eventually developed: Lake Shore, Wright-Hargreaves, Teck-Hughes, Kirkland Lake Gold, Macassa, Sylvanite, and Toburn (renamed from Tough-Oakes). The Porcupine-area mines had a greater output than the Kirkland Lake mines, but Porcupine gold was lower grade.

And the town of Kirkland Lake finally began to grow up. By 1919, it had 1,170 residents. The newly elected council of the Municipal Corporation of the Township of Teck rented a small wooden building for $30 a month to serve as an office and a lock-up, and splashed out on wages for a police officer, supplies for an emergency office, and a pump and horse-drawn water pumper to fight fires. The Imperial Bank (precursor of today's CIBC) built a bricks-and-mortar branch office on Government Road. Charlie Chow opened a new hotel, where he enjoyed telling gullible guests that he was really Charlie Chan, the famous movie detective. A bowling alley and a pool hall sprang up next to Charlie's hotel, and the Kaplan brothers built a gimcrack movie house called the Lyric that doubled as a synagogue on Saturdays and a Baptist church on Sundays.

Al Wende was canny enough to see that all the men arriving

to work in the mines would need roofs over their heads. He commissioned a survey to divide up available land into housing plots, then became the sales agent. Soon there was a gas station, a drugstore, and a hall in which church services were held. There were also rock dumps by each mine that were popular haunts for men off shift, who would poke through the refuse, looking for gold to set into their watch chains.

Nobody could pretend that Kirkland Lake was pretty, but it was now full of life and promise.

All this growth was built on one of the toughest, noisiest, dirtiest resource industries known up until then. In Kirkland Lake, hardrock mining continued twenty-four hours a day, seven days a week. A miner tramped off to work in a flannel shirt, overalls, a cloth cap, and stout leather lace-up boots. Conditions were primitive—there were no safety standards, and mine owners did not supply hard hats, gloves, ear plugs, or protective clothing. If men were working in a particularly damp shaft, they might be given rubber pants and jackets. Many of the shafts were now 1,000 to 2,000 feet deep; eventually the deepest Lake Shore shaft would sink over 8,000 feet. Underground workers began their days by cramming themselves into cages under the headframe, so that they could be lowered to the rock face. Once underground, they had to manoeuvre heavy machinery along the tunnels.

Magne E. Stortroen, a Norwegian miner who arrived in Kirkland Lake in 1925, never forgot the effort required to lift the drills. "I believe the smallest machines weighed 145 pounds and the heavier ones 180 pounds," he wrote in his memoirs years later. "When the drills started, all work orders between driller and helper had to be done in sign language. Just try to imagine the noise of a bulldozer in a small kitchen, and after working for an hour or two with the rubber suits on, we were soaking wet from sweating." The echoing roar of the drills left him temporarily deaf each day.

Lake Shore was particularly notorious, according to a young Ontario man named Alan Collier who arrived in Kirkland Lake looking for work in the 1930s. Oakes's mine was "too darn dangerous for the likes of me," he wrote to his fiancée.

> At that mine a human life has the value of a piece of machinery; it is OK if it gets out the ore but if it is lost it is too bad but can be replaced. . . . They jealously guard their title of "The World's Greatest Gold Producer." I suppose you must have seen in the papers the last few days of the three men being killed, and then three others injured next day. They were both the result of the "rush without precaution" policy. They are such a powerful outfit that they can get away with flagrant breaches of the Mining Act.

In the first years, there were no toilets in the subterranean depths, just buckets. In the damp, stuffy tunnels, the smell could be revolting. (But one man happily hung on, for years, to the contract to collect and empty the "honey buckets"; it was later discovered that he had used them to smuggle gold out of the mine's depths.) Dust and noise were occupational hazards, and accidents involving careless use of dynamite, fuses, and blasting caps were frequent. The only defences during rockfalls were luck and prayer.

Why did men put up with these brutal conditions? Because jobs were scarce and the wages steady. Underground workers like Stortroen earned $4.24 per eight-hour shift, and surface employees $3.50. During these years, a worker in a meat-packing plant—another dirty, dangerous workplace—earned around $4.00 for an eight-hour shift. A man who was lucky enough to have a clerical job in Toronto could not expect much more—and he did not get the opportunity to pick up a gold nugget from the tailings pile.

Living conditions for the miners were rudimentary. Most lived in mine bunkhouses where incessant applications of roach powder failed to keep bedbugs and cockroaches at bay. At least the fare for these hard workers was reliable, as they needed to consume at least five thousand calories a day to sustain their efforts. Breakfast included porridge, bacon and eggs, toast, cold meat, and pies; on the table were tea, coffee, jams, and prunes. There were endless supplies of meat pies, stews, cakes, and suet puddings. Fresh produce was rare, and social facilities within these dormitories nonexistent.

Soon after war's end, the Western Federation of Miners, a labour union with a successful strike record in British Columbia and Britain, arrived with the intention of organizing the mines' workforces. It had little traction. Conditions might be terrible, but there were too many men desperate for employment to ignite enough resentment for a strike.

Harry Oakes, the newly minted multimillionaire, started to enjoy his wealth in the midst of all the tailing ponds, pit heads, and chimneys. He built himself a fancy twenty-room mansion, known as the Chateau, adjacent to the Lake Shore headframe; from its shaded porch, he could survey all his mine buildings and the rapidly shrinking lake. He landscaped some of the despoiled area around his shafts with birch and pine because, like his father and brother, he enjoyed the science of forestry. (When some provincial forestry men arrived to cut a fire ring, he met them at the property line and threatened to sink an axe into the first man to touch one of his trees.) Next, as a reminder of his genteel origins, he added a nine-hole golf course near the tailing ponds.

He persuaded his older sister, Gertrude, to abandon the comforts of life in Washington and her modest clerical job there, and join him in the bush. Gertrude, an unassuming woman who had never married and had invested all her spare cash in her brother's adventures, obviously adored Harry. Now she agreed to become a director of Lake Shore; in the early years, she also worked as her brother's secretary-treasurer and personal assistant. She surprised everybody by blossoming in her new role: she embraced Northern Ontario and helped soften the Oakes image in town. She built herself a large log lodge called Red Pines, on Kenogami Lake west of Kirkland Lake, and became a keen skier and hunter.

There was even a hint that the grumpy prospector had begun to warm to some of his investors—especially those who bothered to make the journey to the annual meetings of Lake Shore Mines, held at the Chateau. In the files at the Museum of Northern History is a copy of a gracious letter written by Oakes to Wettlaufer, the Buffalo financier. Wettlaufer had offered him a brace of pheasant so he could start breeding them; Oakes wrote that the birds would be unlikely to survive the winter, but "next spring I hope to fix the place up so that we can . . . have enough feed around the Chateau to keep pheasants and partridges." He added that he hoped Wettlaufer might bring his wife north with him when he came to the next directors' meeting; "It might be interesting for Mrs. Wettlaufer."

Most days, Kirkland Lake residents could watch their resident millionaire stomping around town in his muddy boots and sweaty shirt, whistling tunelessly. Oakes's awkwardness with women didn't improve. A newly arrived teacher who danced with him at a social one warm summer night felt overawed to be with the town benefactor. She spoke admiringly of the community's rapid growth. Oakes snapped, "Slowest camp I ever saw." The conversation ended there.

Oakes was generous to the growing community—but only on his terms. He helped the Kaplan brothers establish a second movie theatre, the Strand. One of the first movies shown was Charlie

Chaplin's *The Gold Rush*; Roza Brown camped out all night so that she could be the first customer through the door. He donated building lots for the construction of a United church, followed by an Anglican church, and then a hospital. He felt some responsibility for his workforce; he built a greenhouse so they could have fresh vegetables, and one winter, it produced seven tons of tomatoes. He presented toboggans to schoolchildren in Swastika, skates to Kirkland Lake kids, and "Books of Knowledge" to students in both towns. He charged below-market rent to a new public school constructed on his land, paid for its tennis courts, and regularly turned out to watch soccer matches on the school grounds because the Lake Shore team usually beat the teams from the other mines. His most significant donation to the community was a handsome indoor hockey arena, where many future NHL players first took to the ice.

But Harry Oakes's philanthropy was not prompted by any larger vision for the town he had helped create. His gifts cost him little of the gold that was now gushing into his pockets from Lake Shore Mines. Farther north, Noah Timmins had done far more for the employees of his mine—Hollinger. After the disastrous 1911 Porcupine fire, he had planned a townsite, subdivided the land for public auction, named it the Township of Timmins, and ensured that a substantial percentage of mining profits was diverted into its municipal coffers. Timmins rapidly became a thriving regional centre with solid public buildings and services. Noah Timmins had even equipped a hospital and brought in the Sisters of Providence from Montreal to staff it.

Such commitment to the community was beyond Oakes. And for all the benevolence that improved conditions for his employees, he rarely showed compassion for individuals. One day, a badly dressed and obviously hungry man approached him on Kirkland Lake's main street and asked him for a dime for a coffee.

Oakes brushed him off: "On your way, you lousy bum. Go to the
Lake Shore gate if you want a job." Stories spread about Harry
Oakes's temper and his need to show who was boss. There was
gossip about the day he had fired seven men because his skis had
not been put in the right place. No wonder that grievances began
to accumulate around the man who was once just another penni-
less prospector and was now often reputed to be the richest man
in Canada.

IT IS OBVIOUS that there were two sides to Harry Oakes. Critics
and supplicants never got beyond his mean, angry shell, but he
always appreciated men who shared his dreams or respected his
accomplishments. Bill Wright continued to be a good friend and
business partner. James McRae, the enthusiastic young man who
had met Oakes camping in the bush, had met a friendly reception
after he expressed his admiration. Another acquaintance with
whom Oakes enjoyed swapping stories was the famous geologist
Joseph Burr Tyrrell, who in his youth had travelled extensively in
the North on behalf of the Geological Survey of Canada.

Tyrrell had discovered dinosaur fossils in Alberta and coal
beds in Alberta and British Columbia, and had then spent seven
years in the Klondike. Hotheaded and arrogant, Tyrrell rivalled
Oakes in his ability to offend people, but he also shared with
Oakes the physical endurance and curiosity that prospecting
required. Tyrrell's career was filled with ups and downs (far
more downs than ups, as his exasperated wife, Dollie, and his
bank manager would remind him). Although now in his sixties,
he had the strength and stamina of a man half his age, and an
unwavering enthusiasm for being in the centre of mining action.
It was this loud confidence that had persuaded the Anglo-French
Exploration Company of London, England, to appoint him as

its Canadian agent. Anglo-French had large, lucrative mines in South Africa, and was interested in expanding its activities into another British dominion.

Joe Tyrrell's tall, commanding figure had first appeared in Kirkland Lake before any of the big strikes had been made. Like McRae, he ran into Harry Oakes when the latter and Ernie Martin were toiling away with a hand windlass, digging the first shaft on Lake Shore property. Oakes and Tyrrell discovered that they were both Klondike veterans, although they had never crossed paths there, so Oakes invited Tyrrell to stay for the usual miner's dinner of bacon and beans. Tyrrell didn't think much of Lake Shore's prospects, and he told his clients to keep out of this "Kirkland Lake fiasco." But he liked his new acquaintance, with whom he traded prospecting stories.

Throughout the First World War, Tyrrell made lengthy annual visits to his bosses in London—visits that he did not enjoy. On April 18, 1916, he wrote to his wife: "This stay of mine in London is getting very tiresome, for after all I am interested in Canada and the people here are interested in England and are not interested in the least in Canada. A Canadian is a new kind of monkey or Indian who is the best fighter in the world, but of course is not fit to associate with *English gentlemen.*" He couldn't wait to get back to the Canadian bush, and particularly to see what was happening in Kirkland Lake.

A couple of years later, Tyrrell took the train from his Toronto home north to Swastika and, clad in a tailored tweed jacket and buttoned-up vest, hiked along the much-improved wagon trail to Kirkland Lake. Meeting up with his old friend Oakes, he stroked his bushy walrus moustache and guffawed upon hearing that Oakes had secured investment from Buffalo and was now making money hand over fist. How those two old tightwads enjoyed the way that Oakes had confounded his critics! Next, Tyrrell persuaded Anglo-French to buy 50,000 shares in Oakes's mine, then turned around and persuaded Oakes to put him on the Lake Shore board.

By 1924 the town was a typically polyglot settlement: one in ten residents spoke French, and there were seventeen different nationalities represented amongst its population of 2,400. One district was known as "Finntown" because it was heavily Finnish, and another called "Pigtown" because the residents kept pigs. There were families with small children, although single men vastly outnumbered married ones and most residents were below the age of forty. Like any self-respecting mining town, it would even have its own song:

Well, whaddaya know? We're from Kirkland Lake.
We're the boys and we're the girls who'll always give and
    take!
It's an old town, a gold town, we're in it with a stake.
We come from near, we come from far to good ol'
    Kirkland Lake!
Now, we think a lot of Cobalt
And Porcupine is great!
But here's to the hub of the whole white North,
Here's to Kirkland Lake!

Did Harry Oakes know the song? Undoubtedly, since it was roared at every sporting event.

But for all its amenities, Kirkland Lake remained a blue-collar community dominated by shrill whistles signalling shift changes at the mines, the roar of rock crushers, and the acrid smell of toxic mine tailings. The most popular leisure pursuits were drinking and gambling, and brothels with names like the Gem Café and Banana Farm proliferated.

And Harry Oakes was increasingly bored. He had a mine manager, R. C. Coffey, to oversee day-to-day operations, but few friends in town. Joe Tyrrell was always eager to return to his handsome home on Toronto's Walmer Road. Even Gertrude Oakes preferred to divide her time between her cabin, Red Pines, and the family home in Maine.

Oakes's closest ally and fellow multimillionaire, Bill Wright, had left town, and reappeared only for Lake Shore board meetings. Wright's fabulous newfound wealth from his own mine, Wright-Hargreaves, and from Lake Shore had allowed him to return to his first love: horses. In the early 1920s he had moved to the town of Barrie, north of Toronto, where he bought an old brick mansion called Statenborough. He purchased the renowned Brookdale racing stables and poured thousands of dollars into breeding stock. (One of his colts, Archworth, would win the King's Plate at Woodbine Park in 1939, in front of King George VI.) But Wright made little use of his fortune otherwise. He lived simply with his sister, and did everything he could to avoid seeing people who might ask him for help or railroad him into speculative investments. His financial affairs slowly slid into chaos, but he didn't care. Distrusting stock promoters, he preferred the company of men with whom he had fought in the trenches or prospected in the North. He always kept his backpack, gold pan, showshoes, and rock pick ready, in case he ever wanted to join another gold rush. He once remarked to Harry Oakes, "Don't you worry sometimes that this is a dream, that it never really happened, that you will wake up some day and find yourself squatting over a plate of cold beans? . . . I do."

Oakes laughed. "I don't."

There were a few unexpected arrivals amongst the newcomers to Northern Ontario, all drawn by the glittering promise of instant fortunes. Amongst them was the English aristocrat David

Freeman-Mitford, Baron Redesdale, who turned up dressed like a Hollywood version of a miner—polished brown leather boots, immaculate white linen shirt. He puttered around a 40-acre claim between Kirkland Lake and Swastika, pickaxe in hand, with no success. Oakes had no patience with such dilettantes, who had not served back-breaking apprenticeships of clawing through frozen dirt.

At this stage, Oakes was not much of a drinker, and his asthma stopped him from smoking. He was now nearly fifty, but after a lifetime in the bush, his face was as scarred and wrinkled as that of a man two decades older. He chewed and muttered to himself; he had forgotten how to use a knife and fork at a dinner table; he often turned his back on anybody who tried to engage him in conversation. He stuck to his prospector's outfit of lumberjack shirt, britches, and boots, even when he was in a city. He owned the second-richest gold mine in the Western Hemisphere (the richest in 1920 was the Homestake Mine in South Dakota, the basis of the Hearst fortune), yet, despite being as wealthy as Croesus, he had no one and nothing to spend his fortune on. He was lonely, bored, and now that he had found his gold mine, he lacked a purpose in life—but he was also incapable of sufficient self-scrutiny to address the problem. He brooded on all the injustices, real and imagined, that he had suffered.

Sometimes, Harry Oakes allowed his bitterness to fuel campaigns of vengeance against anybody who had laughed at him or thwarted him. It didn't matter whether his target was modest or grand. He recalled how the Swastika storekeeper Jimmy Doig had made him look like a fool when he tried to buy some overalls on credit a decade earlier, so he issued orders that no Lake Shore employee would be allowed to patronize Doig's store. Doig soon had to leave town, a ruined man. (Oakes displayed a glimmer of compassion a few years later, when he heard Jimmy was on his last legs. "Serves the bastard right," he said to his secretary. "Send him a check for ten thousand dollars.")

Oakes's mercurial personality meant that he could be unpredictable even towards those who knew him well. Geoffrey Bocca heard an anecdote from a respected geologist, Shirley Cragg, who called Oakes to say hello when the latter was in Toronto, staying at the King Edward Hotel. Cragg, a wealthy man, had often seen Oakes in Kirkland Lake and held shares in Lake Shore Mines. When Oakes answered the phone, Cragg introduced himself and said, "I heard you were in town, so I thought I would telephone and say—" Before he had even finished his sentence, Oakes slammed down the phone. Cragg was furious, and vowed never to speak to Lake Shore's owner again. He saw Oakes a few days later in the street and walked straight past him, cutting him dead. But Oakes hailed him, put his arm round him, and said, "You called me the other day. It was so good to hear your voice. I really appreciated it." Cragg was completely thrown by this contradictory behaviour, and must have wondered if Harry Oakes had started drinking. He had not—yet.

For thirty years, Harry Oakes's whole life had been about finding and developing his own gold mine. Now that his fortune was established, he lost all interest in the mining industry, aside from the occasional investment. But this meant he had little outlet for the enormous drive and tough physical labour he had put into the creation of Lake Shore. Nor did he have any of the financial knowledge or investment skills that might have helped him manage his millions. Like Bill Wright, he found the world of stock exchanges entirely foreign and was never comfortable around financiers, whom he regarded as parasites. It would take a very special financial adviser to breach his defences against entrusting his fortune to somebody else's decisions.

The savvy prospector who knew the difference between porphyry and granite, and who once worked eighteen-hour days digging and drilling, spent less and less time in Kirkland Lake. However, the urge to remodel the ground beneath his feet never left him.

TODAY, KIRKLAND LAKE is a community that has seen better days, an isolated resource town where the resources are exhausted. Of the seven headframes that once dominated its skyline, only one remains: the disused headframe of the Toburn gold mine, which has become a tourist attraction. In the Tim Hortons coffee shop, opposite a small Canadian Tire outlet, old men whisk imaginary flies off their faces as they slowly chew apple crullers. Even the hockey rink that nurtured so many world-famous hockey players has been pulled down. The population, which peaked at 26,000 in 1938, had dwindled to less than 8,000 by 2016. The T&NO railway, now named the Ontario Northland Railway, runs rarely and no longer carries passengers: the spur line that ran to Kirkland Lake in its productive years has long since closed.

Harry Oakes's Chateau, now the Museum of Northern History, is the most impressive mansion in town, and its exterior is unchanged. The attractive green-roofed building, with low eaves and well-maintained gardens, sits on a small rise overlooking those stretches of the lake that weren't touched by mine tailings. Inside, there is little left of Harry Oakes's years there, other than an old rolltop desk that he used when he was in the house. The gift shop has a few books about Oakes, but most of the shelf space is devoted to local crafts.

But when I visited, I noticed in the second-floor room devoted to mining a plastic-covered page detailing an incident that occurred during a Lake Shore Mines board meeting in the early 1930s. Oakes, who was in the chair, had looked out of the window and seen his mine carpenters at work in a driving rainstorm, constructing an access boardwalk across the mine's sludge pond from the Lake Shore bunkhouse to Government Road. The carpenters were wet and exhausted, but they laboured on. "This seemed to get to Oakes and perhaps reminded him of the many occasions he had toiled in the rain and cold while prospecting in the north," read the information page. "Before anyone left the room, he ordered every man present to follow him to the slime fields to help the carpenters. There was no time to get raingear or boots, just follow him and be pleased to be working with the carpenters in the rain in the presence of Harry Oakes." Board members like Joe Tyrrell and Bill Wright might have thrown themselves into the experience, which would have reminded them of their early adventures in the wilderness. For any representatives of Toronto and Buffalo investors, it must have been a shock.

The museum's archivist dug out two files of Oakes papers for me—mainly programs from testimonial dinners and newspaper clippings about his death. In one file, I found an uncatalogued clutch of handwritten notes and awkwardly typed pages. They were reminiscences, collected by local historian Carolyn O'Neil in the 1970s from old-timers who recalled the Harry Oakes who spent his youth obsessed by the hunt for gold. As I read through them, I could almost smell the smoke of the campfires around which they had all sat, and feel the weariness in their limbs after days of hard manual work.

These men knew Oakes when he was one of them—tough, unsophisticated, a bear for work who refused to be discouraged by failure. George Cooper, a member of the Kirkland Lake Fire Department who had worked at Lake Shore in the early days, described him as "one of the finest fellows that ever sat by the side of the highway. He'd give a fellow anything he wanted to get his prospect going." Walter Little's son Art said Oakes was "opinionated and barked a lot, but usually was really quite nice." Another old-timer, Walter Lingenfelter, told O'Neil that "Harry Oakes' problem was that everyone expected him to loan them money regardless of the reason. If he didn't give it to them, he was automatically disliked. . . . Mr. Oakes was a fair man. We need more Harry Oakes to find the mines."

No one who knew the younger Oakes pretended he was an easy man, but they recognized his extraordinary achievements, and the camaraderie he and other weather-beaten prospectors shared. "Oh, he had his share of weakness, but after all, who hasn't?" a Cobalt engineer called Barney would tell Arnold Hoffman after Oakes's death. "Just because he was an uncompromising kind of gent is no reason why those of us who knew him well shouldn't remember his constructive qualities." However, few of the writers who investigated his subsequent journey through life went to Northern Ontario, or caught that side of him.

PART TWO

SPENDING
IT

CHAPTER 6

Taxed into Exile

Like most communities, Niagara Falls suffered considerably during the Great Depression. Nonetheless, the effects of this catastrophic economic downturn were tempered by the . . . efforts of Sir Harry Oakes, well-known for his philanthropy and generosity in providing many opportunities for locals to work on relief projects.

IMAGES OF A CENTURY:

THE CITY OF NIAGARA FALLS, CANADA, 1904–2004

n 1923, the multimillionaire decided to visit South Africa to check out the mining technology employed in the famous Witwatersrand gold mines there. He travelled on a small freighter via Sydney, Australia, where a blue-eyed Australian woman embarked. Although his dark suspicions of gold diggers made him bristle at anybody who tried to befriend him, his defences were breached by Eunice McIntyre, who was half his age and towered over him. The twenty-four-year-old daughter of a government official, Eunice worked part time in a Sydney bank and was travelling to England via South Africa.

It had been a long time since Harry Oakes had met a young woman who reminded him of the educated and decorous girls he knew growing up in Maine. The women he met in mining towns were not all eccentrics and hookers, but most were tough survivors with little patience for chivalry. According to Brian Martin, nephew of Oakes employee Ernie Martin, Eunice "had an innocence and decency the world-weary Oakes found irresistible. She was a good conversationalist on many topics, while Oakes, with his staccato delivery, struggled with a repertoire limited to mining. Smitten, Oakes knew he had found gold of another kind."

As the boat steamed away from Sydney, Oakes found himself seeking out Miss McIntyre's company. At Cape Town, Eunice learned that her father had died unexpectedly; Oakes immediately offered to accompany her on her voyage home. Within weeks, Eunice had become Mrs. Harry Oakes, after a wedding on June 30, 1923, at the large brick Anglican Church of St. Mark's in Darling Point, near Sydney.

The two could not have been more different: the stocky forty-eight-year-old Yankee millionaire, with his abrasive manner and weather-beaten face, and the statuesque Australian beauty who was always happy to go along with her husband's plans. Somehow, the ingenuous Eunice Oakes managed to turn a blind eye to her husband's shortcomings and to soften the harsh edges within their private relationship.

When the newlyweds arrived in Canada, Oakes took his new wife straight north. From the moment that Eunice Oakes stepped out of the train at the Swastika station, she was loved within the community. The local children collected money to buy her a bouquet as a welcoming gesture. She was so wide-eyed, so easily swayed to tears, and, unlike her husband, so generous. When she suggested to the local firemen that they might extinguish a fire "by throwing snowballs at it," they laughed indulgently. She was also completely loyal to her husband, and overawed by his achievement in finding gold, establishing Lake Shore Mines, doggedly retaining control, and accumulating a fortune. His roughneck manners didn't seem to bother her.

Soon, one of the Chateau's upstairs rooms had been converted to a nursery for the Oakeses' first child, Nancy, who was born in 1924 and rapidly became her father's little darling. Eunice poured her energy into creating imaginative surroundings for her first born: the plasterwork of Nancy's room featured animals, birds, characters from nursery rhymes and fairy stories, plus inventions such as hot-air balloons, trains, and airplanes. Oakes employed an English couple, Mr. and Mrs. Duke, as his chauffeur and cook. Mrs. Duke never warmed to her boss; he was "too brusque and demanding." But she loved the Oakes children, to whom she would read stories and for whom she organized parties with local children.

Now that Harry Oakes had started a family, he decided that he needed a more splendid home, in a larger town than Kirkland Lake. He told one of his senior employees what he was looking for. They were walking down Toronto's Bay Street when Oakes noticed a poster showing Neuschwanstein, the kitschy mountainside castle of mad king Ludwig II of Bavaria. (Neuschwanstein later became the model for Disneyland's Sleeping Beauty Castle.) "Something like that," Oakes told his manager. "That is what I want." He didn't find anything quite as bizarre as Neuschwanstein, but in 1924 he bought a magnificent property in the lively tourist town of Niagara Falls.

Why Niagara Falls? Local historian Sherman Zavitz suggests the simplest of all reasons: Oakes saw an advertisement for an estate that fit his dreams, in a world-renowned location. The stone mansion was perched half a mile above the falls on Clark

Hill. It faced east towards the falls' mists and rainbows, and it overlooked the Dufferin Islands in the Niagara River on the south side. Walter Schoellkopf, a member of a prominent family from Niagara Falls, New York, was the previous owner; he had helped develop the hydroelectric plant on the American side of the falls. The house was not exactly Neuschwanstein, but it was certainly the most impressive home on the Canadian side of one of the Earth's greatest wonders. Its dining room featured English oak panelling that had originally lined Cardinal Wolsey's room at Hampton Court, and the estate included 22 acres of land and several outbuildings. Moreover, it was close to Buffalo, with its clutch of Lake Shore investors.

Oakes purchased the property for half a million dollars (about $16 million today), and over the next four years he spent almost the same amount enlarging and transforming the Schoellkopf mansion into a thirty-seven-room Tudor-style baronial edifice. Perhaps he had nurtured grandiose fantasies about his future home during the rough years living in tents and caves as a penniless miner: he certainly didn't stint now. The mansion was enlarged to include a three-car garage, a great hall with a minstrel's gallery, seventeen bathrooms, air conditioning, water-softening units, an elevator, and an indoor marble swimming pool. Oakes renamed the house Oak Hall and commissioned a stonemason to carve the motto "Oak Standeth Ever," resting on a bed of oak leaves, on the stone portico at the front of the house. When the family moved into their splendid new home in 1928, they opened the leaded windows and listened to the sound of water gushing over the most powerful waterfall in North America.

Harry returned regularly to Kirkland Lake to oversee developments at his mine and conduct board meetings in the Chateau. He also visited old friends, including Hyman Kaplan, the Polish Jew whose cinemas he had helped finance. "Whenever he is coming here to Kirkland Lake he is first seeing me. Bet your life!" Kaplan would tell the former prospector Hoffman. "He is sitting many times on the same chair you are and I always have a bottle of schnapps for him." But over the years, Kaplan began to detect a growing ennui in the billionaire. "Why he's not happy? Because he ain't working. . . . He stops working and begins to loaf and then starts his troubles, and what troubles!"

Despite his growing malaise, I suspect that the Niagara Falls years constituted the happiest period of Harry Oakes's life. He was still in the first flush of marriage. The Oakeses' three sons were born while he lived there: Sydney in 1927 (while the Oakeses were still living in Oak Hall's gatehouse), William Pitt in 1930, and Harry Phillip in 1932, along with a second daughter, Shirley Lewis, who arrived in 1929. Moreover, the city is the only place where even today he is remembered with unalloyed gratitude.

Oakes spent these years playing golf, attending boxing matches, and putting a few of his millions into real estate. Altogether, he bought and sold nineteen parcels of land in Niagara Falls. His acquisitions were often for his own benefit; he spent over half a million dollars on a factory belonging to Canadian Ohio Brass, because it was situated across the road from Oak Hall and its two large chimneys belched smoke across his estate. The factory, which manufactured high-voltage insulators, was forced to relocate to the city's north end. At one point, Oakes owned over 488 acres of land around Oak Hall.

The 1920s were good years to invest in Niagara Falls real estate. The city grew rapidly, and as car ownership spread, tourism took off and gas stations, car dealerships, hotels, and campgrounds proliferated. The second-most popular destination in the city was its liquor store: Prohibition was lifted in Ontario in 1926, while across the river, the state of New York remained "dry." But it was still a more conventional, subdued place than it is today: Movieland, Ripley's Believe It or Not!, the Skywheel, and other garish delights all came later. Most of the breadwinners amongst its 15,000 residents clocked in for nine-to-five jobs at such local enterprises as the Spirella corset factory and the Bell Telephone exchange, and on Saturday nights the gentry enjoyed stately waltzes on the marble floors of the Prince of Wales Club, keeping time to Len Fortier's Orchestra.

Harry Oakes was still the same pit bull of a man, one who didn't suffer fools, flatterers, or panhandlers. He built a wall around his Oak Hall estate to keep out anybody looking for handouts. He wasn't much interested in formal entertaining in his splendid mansion; he usually took his meals in the kitchen rather than at the palatial dining table. Nonetheless, he began to develop the habits of wealth, if not the manners. The perennial itch to reshape his landscape was given full rein: he planted an extensive rose garden and developed an airstrip for himself and friends. He even developed a taste for polo (hardly a popular pastime in small-town Ontario) and laid out a rudimentary polo ground. Whistling tunelessly as he strutted around his estate, he designed a five-hole golf course to suit his own tastes. Infuriated by a particular bunker that kept ensnaring his ball, he ordered his team of gardeners to bulldoze it and relocate the hazard elsewhere. The three-car garage was filled with expensive automobiles, including an elegant black Hispano-Suiza H6B, manufactured in Paris in 1928 with a custom red-leather interior installed in London.

Harry Oakes enjoyed being Daddy Big Bucks for his adopted city, although once again his generosity was always on his terms. He donated trophies for sports competitions, 3 acres for a badminton and tennis club, and 16 acres for a sports ground (Oakes Park Athletic Field), and he also ensured that several parcels of land along the river were converted into parkland. He and Eunice gave to the Boy Scouts, the local hospital, and the sanatorium; Eunice became a fixture at Niagara Falls events, smiling sweetly at ribbon cuttings and presentations while a sullen Harry stood at her shoulder. "This tablet commemorates the public spirit and generosity of Sir Harry Oakes" reads an inscription on the wall of Oakes Garden Theatre, an open-air amphitheatre on the site of the former Clifton Hotel and his most important contribution to the city.

When the Depression hit in the 1930s, he deliberately created jobs when he commissioned the restoration of the road behind Oak Hall, which ran down the escarpment to the falls. Each man who was prepared to wield a shovel for half a day was paid two dollars. Ornery as ever, Oakes insisted that the men be paid in two-dollar bills, which meant that the supervisor had to spend half his time running around town in search of the right denomination. In recognition of his philanthropy, Oakes was invited to join the Niagara Parks Commission in 1933—the same provincial agency that is today housed in Oak Hall. He was also appointed honorary lieutenant-colonel of the Lincoln and Welland Regiment, which has as its motto *Non nobis sed patriae*—"Not for ourselves, but for our country." This motto's meaninglessness for the new officer would become obvious only later.

During the 1920s, Oakes renounced his American citizenship and acquired a red British passport. (A red passport indicated that he was a British subject and Canadian national, but that he was not born British. Only British-born individuals got the more exclusive blue passports.) Perhaps the move was for business reasons; perhaps it was to avoid American tax; perhaps his Australian wife liked Canada's colonial deference better than Yankee brashness. The Oakes family required passports because they travelled extensively, especially in the winter months, when Oakes's asthma and bronchitis bothered him. By the early 1930s,

Harry Oakes spent only a few nights a year in Kirkland Lake, to check up on his gold mine.

Beyond Canada, Oakes acquired real estate in haphazard fashion: a twenty-seven-room "cottage" called The Willows at Bar Harbor, on the Maine coast; two newly built properties, 131 and 151 Barton Avenue, in Florida's sophisticated new resort town of Palm Beach; and the Palm Beach Winter Club, which he converted into a riding stable; plus some tracts of oceanfront property. There were frequent visits to Europe, and the children enjoyed a hit-and-miss education from a series of governesses, tutors, and boarding schools.

Despite the switch in citizenship, Oakes remained loyal to his Maine roots. When biographer Geoffrey Bocca visited Dover-Foxcroft in 1958, he sought out John Clair Minot, who had been Oakes's contemporary at Bowdoin College and who now edited the Portland *Herald*. Minot told Bocca that Oakes had turned up at a Bowdoin class reunion during the 1920s, and was barely recognized by his classmates—word of his fame had not yet reached his birthplace. Nor did Oakes brag about his success to the men who, as boys, had laughed at him. According to Bocca, "The others at the class of 'ninety-six saw only a tough-looking little fellow, quietly though expensively dressed in a Savile Row suit." A committee of his old fraternity, Zeta Psi, was raising money to build a new chapter house, and Oakes was casually asked if he would contribute anything. "Sure," he said, and he stunned the fundraisers by immediately presenting them with a cheque for $50,000. "Don't worry, it won't bounce," Harry laughed. "And if you need any more, let me know." Minot told Bocca that he had flung an arm around Oakes's shoulders and remarked, "You really did it, Harry. You found your gold mine and you took your million dollars out of the earth, just as you said you would. I admire your achievement more than I can say."

Bocca embellished the anecdote with a fictional flourish. "Harry . . . felt inside him an untwisting of his internal muscles, a relaxation, as though for the first time in his life he did not expect the touch of another human being to consist of a fist in the face or a boot in the groin. It was an unusual sensation of happiness." But in Bocca's account of Oakes's life, this was the calm before the storm. The author went on to describe how Oakes

> . . . did not seem to know what to do with himself now or in which direction his fortune should take him. His animal dynamism was as great as ever, but he was driving aimlessly in neutral gear, the engines roaring, the great wheels churning and turning but without meshing, going nowhere. Somewhere there was bound to come a break, a missed connection, a blown fuse which would throw this whole great machine into chaos.

Bocca was probably right that Harry Oakes chafed at the lack of challenges in his life. By 1930, he was fifty-six years old, and photos taken during the Niagara years depict a fit and muscular man, glossy in his well-tailored, fur-collared overcoat, who might find family life and five holes of golf a little tame. With hindsight, as Bocca shows, it is easy to assume that "a blown fuse" was inevitable, and it makes a better story to predict fate unfolding with an angry inevitability. But was it obvious at the time? Hard to know, since Harry Oakes himself left no letters, diaries, or papers from which I can draw such conclusions.

WHEN THE EXPLOSION came, it was triggered by Harry Oakes's least favourite subject: taxes.

During Oakes's Niagara years, Lake Shore Mines became a freight train of an earner. In the twelve months ending mid-1925, bullion worth $1.8 million was produced and $600,000 in dividends was paid. By mid-1931, bullion production had risen to $9.15 million and dividends to $3.6 million. After the 1929 market crash, stocks in most commodities and industries went into a tailspin—except for the mining industry, and particularly gold mining, thanks to gold's perennial appeal as a financial security blanket. Lake Shore bullion production and dividends continued to rise along with the price of gold, and Lake Shore shares (of which Oakes owned 50 percent) jumped from $20 to $35.10. Lake Shore Mines was the darling of the Toronto Stock Exchange, and as the Great Depression bit into other economic activities, Lake Shore and other Ontario gold mines became vital props to the entire provincial economy.

According to one reliable estimate, between 1924 and 1932 Oakes's mining stock earned for him about $10.7 million—or around $25,000 a week. And since Canadians were permitted a 50 percent depletion allowance on all gold stock earnings, even the tax bite on the Oakes's millions was blunted. During these years, Oakes paid personal taxes on only $5.3 million of his earnings. In 1933, the shares earned another $3 million, and he paid just over $1 million in taxes. Harry Oakes's capital kept accumulating, despite his increasingly expensive travel and tastes, his property acquisitions, and his scattered philanthropy in Kirkland Lake and Niagara Falls.

These were fabulous sums within the context of the 1930s, when the Canadian population and economy were much smaller than they are today. In the early 1930s, federal revenues were $300 million, so Oakes's after-tax income of $2 million made him an irresistible quarry for politicians.

First came the party bagmen, hoping for substantial donations to their parties from Canada's richest man. What could they offer as a quid pro quo? Rumours circulated about what reward

Harry Oakes might want, and they have continued to do so ever since. In the run-up to the 1930 federal election, Prime Minister Mackenzie King is said to have offered Oakes either membership in the unelected Canadian Senate or the lieutenant-governorship of Ontario (the monarch's representative) in return for a generous donation to the Liberal Party. When the Liberals then lost the election despite his donation, Oakes saw the power and recognition that he assumed he had bought slipping away. I can imagine that it triggered all his atavistic hatred of smooth talkers who had never got their hands dirty.

Next came the taxman. Washington had recently revalued gold bullion from $20.67 an ounce to $35, resulting in enormous windfall profits for gold producers. In the 1934 Canadian federal budget, the minister of finance proposed a new 25 percent tax on gold, plus a progressive reduction in the depletion allowance on all gold stock earnings. In 1934, Oakes's Lake Shore holdings would once again pay dividends of around $3.15 million. But this time, the tax bite could have been as high as 90 percent, or $2.9 million.

Then Oakes heard talk that the Ontario provincial government planned to hike death duties on large estates. In his view, Canadian tax authorities were about to do what those silk-suited financiers had tried to do during his years of struggle—appropriate the hard-won millions that he had earned by the sweat of his labour and without any help from them.

The fuse blew.

Quite suddenly, Harry Oakes announced he was leaving Canada. He took the train south, to Palm Beach. He stopped being resident in Canada, which meant that, even as the holder of a British passport, he would no longer have to pay Canadian taxes.

The move was for his physical as well as his financial health, he insisted. In a 1938 interview with Gregory Clark of the *Toronto*

Daily Star, he explained that he had been lying in bed in Oak Hall, suffering acute bronchitis. According to Clark, "Congestion had him and double pneumonia threatened. . . . He got up. He dismissed the doctors and commanded the frightened nurses [to leave]. . . .With his [bronchial] tubes stuffed, and smothering, he got up out of his bed and with no nurse or anybody to accompany him, he caught the train via Buffalo to the south."

In Clark's lengthy feature about the "Ontario millionaire," written four years after this dramatic exit, Oakes explained,

> This is what came to me that night I bid Canada goodbye. If I died that night, between Niagara Falls and Palm Beach, at the rates of taxation and other duties existing at the moment, my family would owe the country $4,000,000. Counting all my wealth and subtracting from what was left of my other commitments when duties were paid, I would be leaving my family in the red, not the blue. For years I had been suffering bronchial trouble to such an extent that I couldn't stay in Canada more than 90 days out of the year. I was paying in taxes $17,500 a day to live in Canada.

Oakes's estimate of Ottawa's tax grab is unreliable, but the basic point stands: the tax hike was punitive. In Clark's account, Oakes continued, "Well, I said to myself, that doesn't make sense, in any man's language. True, I had found the pot of gold at the end of the rainbow. And I had found it in Canada." But Lake Shore was already paying corporate taxes, and now taxes on his personal income would jump. He reckoned he would soon be paying 80 to 90 percent in taxes on the gold he had found. "Men don't work for that." Fearing his own imminent demise, and in the interests of securing his own health and his family's future security, he gasped and choked his way out of the country. However, he did not sell all his Canadian real estate.

Biographer Geoffrey Bocca doesn't give much credence to Oakes's rationale about his health. Instead, he suggests that Oakes's breathlessness was triggered purely by the thought of all his money being diverted to Ottawa. The Canadian government's motive for its tax initiatives was founded on malice towards Oakes, he writes, and Oakes's bronchitis was a direct result. "That Oakes's asphyxiation was largely psychosomatic there can be no doubt. The great man lay between his silk sheets, breathing with the greatest difficulty, surrounded by medicaments, guarded by nurses, and contemplated his future with the deepest gloom."

There is no choking exodus to Palm Beach in Bocca's account. Instead, according to Bocca, there was nothing but tight-fisted anger. "For all his toughness and dogged courage, Oakes was basically a run-out man without any sense of responsibility. He had ignored the war even though it caught up both of his two countries, taken up Canadian citizenship as a convenience, and was now quitting when it was inconvenient."

Conservative newspapers and former colleagues publicly deplored the idea that a great philanthropist should be driven out of the country. From his home in Barrie, Bill Wright lined up in solidarity with his mining buddy, and said he, too, might become a tax exile and was considering either the Channel Islands or Bermuda as his next home.

Wright wasn't serious about moving, but he was sympathetic to Oakes's predicament. In fact, he had found his own way to fight taxes. He had finally met a stockbroker he trusted: George McCullagh. McCullagh had sorted out Wright's muddled financial affairs, allowing him to focus exclusively on his stud farm. McCullagh had then persuaded the reclusive millionaire to invest in Toronto's leading Conservative newspaper, the *Globe*, with the argument that the newspaper could wage war on two of Wright's bugbears: income taxes and unions. McCullagh then increased his own—and Wright's—media influence by buying the

Mail and Empire and merging the two papers, installing himself as publisher. Soon the new *Globe and Mail* was regarded as a mouthpiece for gold-mining interests, and the original *Globe*'s subscribers were shocked to discover that, under the new owner, horse-racing results became a regular feature.

But there was also significant public outrage about Oakes's well-publicized departure, reflected in such headlines as "Multi-millionaire Champ Tax-Dodger" and "Heart Like Frigidaire to the Land that Gave Him Wealth." Then as now, clever tax-evasion strategies aroused little public sympathy. Don't tycoons who have made their millions from a country's resources owe any obligation to pay back? Oakes's workforce, back in Kirkland Lake, was dutifully paying taxes; why should he be exempt?

The *Toronto Daily Star* published a reader's poem that summed up the rancour. It began:

Life may be hard and full of grief
For out-of-works upon relief,
But what do those poor devils know
Of all the misery and woe
That drive to exile and despair
The luckless multi-millionaire?

Oakes's reaction to the negative press is not recorded. It wasn't in his character to care what people thought. His family settled into a new and much warmer lifestyle in Palm Beach, and American tax authorities prepared to take their bite. But the family's Florida sojourn was short-lived, because Harry Oakes would soon discover that there were places on the globe where he could get away with paying almost no taxes at all.

CHAPTER 7

Bahamas' Bay Street Bandits

The reason for the sparseness of the population of the Bahamas is the poverty of their terrain. The islands are almost completely flat. . . . This harsh, often almost lunar landscape is moderated by the climate, one of the finest in the world. . . . Well do the islands merit the title given them by a nineteenth century visitor, "the Isles of Perpetual June."

MICHAEL CRATON *A HISTORY OF THE BAHAMAS*

From the minute Harry Oakes stepped onto the noisy wharf in Nassau, he was impressed by the warmth of both the weather and the welcome he received in the capital of the British colony of the Bahamas. But the sixty-year-old multimillionaire was most excited by another aspect of the Bahamas: he could escape taxes here. Death, however, was another matter.

Oakes had already heard about the Bahamian tax regime from the large, rumpled man with startling green eyes and bushy red eyebrows who was now shepherding him through stalls selling fresh fish, mangoes, and sea sponges. Harold Christie was a Bahamian-born real estate agent who had met Oakes in Palm Beach and infected him with his own excitement about the colony's sun-kissed future. He knew that Oakes was looking to park his substantial fortune beyond the grasp of both the Canadian and the American government because he had heard that Oakes was considering a move to the Channel Islands, offshore tax havens in the English Channel. Christie made it his business to go to Florida and meet Oakes, and to explain that in the Bahamas, residents need pay no income tax if they arranged their affairs properly. Even when a man died, Christie told Oakes, the state took only 2 percent of his personal estate, and it didn't touch his real estate. Harry Oakes found this prospect irresistible.

Next, the silver-tongued Bahamian entrepreneur, who had quickly sized up his quarry, hinted that New Providence Island, on which Nassau was situated, offered far more scope for Oakes's raw energies than did the palm-court prissiness of Florida's most fashionable resort. The cluster of islands that made up the Bahamas was wide open, and offered infinite possibilities, Christie suggested, for a man who liked to mould his surroundings. And the climate was ideal for a man with troublesome bronchial tubes.

Although Oakes had met plenty of entrepreneurs and hustlers in his life, he may never have met anybody quite like Harold Christie. Soft-spoken and twenty-two years younger than his new client, Christie had recently elbowed his way into the Nassau colonial elite. This was quite an achievement, given his humble birth and the rigid social distinctions that prevailed in the little colony. Christie owed his membership in the elite to financial success, as well as to a chameleon-like ability to be whatever was necessary to "fit in."

The Bahamas themselves were, in microcosm, similar to too many British colonies: a society in which an impoverished black majority was ruled by a small, arrogant, and reactionary white elite. The governor of the Bahamas, appointed by London, was no more than a figurehead. For more than two hundred years, the islands had been run by a handful of merchant families—the Malcolms, Duncombes, Adderlys, and Mosleys—most of whose predecessors had arrived as Loyalist exiles after the American Revolution. Their offices and stores lined Bay Street, Nassau's main thoroughfare, and they dominated the House of Assembly and its inner circle, the executive council. The "Bay Street Boys," as they were known, were indifferent to the conditions in which black Bahamians lived. In 1934, almost nine-tenths of the islands' 60,000 residents were black, but only a handful of them attended secondary school and almost none met the property qualification to vote in elections for the House of Assembly.

On other Caribbean islands, such as Bermuda, racial barriers were crumbling, but in the Bahamas they were rock hard. Non-whites could not enter the New Colonial Hotel or be members of the Nassau Lawn Tennis Club. Written into sales contracts for one residential development was the stipulation that a purchaser must be a "full-blooded member of the Caucasian race." Jews and Asians were also specifically excluded.

Members of the white elite lived comfortable but not opulent lives, because other than its beautiful beaches and turquoise ocean, the Bahamas had little to offer. Attempts to emulate the sugar and cotton plantations of other Caribbean islands had failed; exports of pineapples, sisal, and sea sponges were generally lacklustre. The Bahamas had only two major claims to fame. The first was that Christopher Columbus's first landfall in the New World in 1492 was probably on one of their seven hundred islands, cays, and rocks. The second was that, since then, Bahamians had developed brutal expertise in a range of criminal activities, including piracy, wrecking, and (during the American Civil War) blockade busting. The most recent and lucrative felonious activity had been the smuggling of bootleg liquor into the United States during the 1920s.

In the decade before Harry Oakes set foot on the islands, the Bahamas had enjoyed a brief but lopsided boom thanks to Prohibition, which boosted the colony's annual revenue from £80,000 in 1919 to over £1 million in 1923. The old merchant families played the major role in this boom (they were renamed the "Bay Street Bandits"), but so did others who only aspired to their exclusive tennis and yacht clubs. At this stage, Harold Christie was firmly in the latter category. Nassau's excellent harbour facilities proved ideal for the movement of liquor, including West Indian rum, English gin, and Scotch whisky. Muscular porters would heave the barrels off the ships, and a small army of women and children would roll them off the wharf, down Bay Street, and into nearby warehouses. From the warehouses, barrels and crates could be loaded onto speedboats that took the cargo to northern islands, mainly Bimini and Grand Bahama, which are close to the Florida coast.

Prohibition profits surged through the colonial capital: churches were renovated, wages for black labourers rose, the harbour was deepened and the wharves lengthened. But little of the new wealth spilled over onto smaller islands, where farmers and fishermen were starving. As historian Michael Craton observed, "It would have been shortsighted indeed if an Assembly of any composition had legislated against such a windfall, but one of the least happy aspects of the Prohibition boom was that it produced an even deeper separation between the 'haves' and the 'have-nots.'"

However, Prohibition had been the making of Harry Oakes's new friend, Harold Christie. Despite his very humble origins, the policy had allowed him both to dream big and to make enough money to begin to fulfill those dreams. And his dreams were all about real estate.

In the words of Bahamas historian Gail Saunders, Christie

started life as a "poor, near-white outsider." One of eight children, he was the son of an impractical poet who would disappear on week-long journeys around the island to preach the Word of God. Christie's mother was likely of mixed race (his father may have been, too, although he "passed" as white), and before the First World War, the entrenched merchantocracy would have spurned the Christies. While still in his teens, Harold left New Providence and went to work for General Electric in Schenectady, New York. He claimed that in 1917 he had travelled to Canada to join the air force, never saw combat, and was discharged at war's end with the rank of cadet. A couple of years later, he returned to the Bahamas and established H. G. Christie Real Estate.

During Prohibition, he acted as a middleman between Nassau's alcohol wholesalers and their law-breaking customers in the United States. But he was smart enough to realize that Prohibition couldn't last, so he looked beyond bonded warehouses and liquor-stuffed speedboats. He had watched Florida's dizzying rise in real estate prices during the Jazz Age decade, as rich Americans made the Sunshine State a winter health resort. Back in the Bahamas, he began to scoop up sizable banks of beachfront properties from poor black farmers at rock-bottom prices, with a view towards reselling them at great profit to expatriate English and American investors.

Next, he persuaded a few wealthy Americans to have a little overseas adventure, and cross the Straits of Florida to inspect the colony's wide beaches, with their powdery pink sand, their coral reefs, and the aquamarine ocean. He was not the only entrepreneur intent on developing the islands' tourism potential. By the end of the 1920s, New Providence boasted two substantial hotels and regular steamship service to New York and Britain. The Bahamas had particularly close links with Canada; several vessels made regular sailings to Halifax and Montreal, and the Royal Bank of

Canada, which had taken over the Bank of Nassau in 1917, was thriving (not least because of the profits of rum running).

If there was one gift that Christie had inherited from his ineffectual father, it was an evangelical streak—although he was a soft-spoken persuader rather than an impassioned tub thumper. Thanks to his salesmanship, mainland speculators purchased his picturesque beaches and isolated cays and started to build elaborate stucco mansions on the waterfront. The real estate entrepreneur was soon a rich man. As historian Saunders puts it, "Money 'whitened.'" He moved his business to a more prestigious Bay Street address, and was elected to the House of Assembly in 1928.

But the good times came to a grinding halt with the 1929 Wall Street crash, followed by the end of Prohibition. Government revenue dropped to less than £200,000 from a high of £1.5 million in the mid-1920s. Jobs dried up, wages fell, prices rose, and the tourism industry wilted.

However, "at least one man," writes historian Craton, "did not lose his faith that the Bahamas would magically regain their lost prosperity." Harold Christie continued to nurture his vision of what the Bahamas might become: a Mecca for global wealth, so gorgeous and luxurious that it would draw the international set away from the Riviera and Biarritz and Palm Beach. He was determined to make the British colony somewhere that millionaires would want to go to mingle with fellow plutocrats.

As soon as Christie met Harry Oakes in Florida, he decided that this fabulously rich Canadian was the man to help him.

The contrast between the two men was almost comical. Oakes was combative, outspoken, and rough mannered. Harold Christie was soft-spoken and, according to a Nassau friend, "would go miles to avoid unpleasantness." At the same time, Oakes was a straight shooter who couldn't stand trickery, while Christie was a wheeler dealer with a devious streak. In photos of the two men, Christie usually has a cigarette in hand and sweat stains on his shirt—a big, affable guy who seduces the viewer with a compelling smile. Oakes, short and stocky, stares at the camera with a pugnacious expression, brow furrowed and fists clenched. Yet they were united in their impatience with protocol and dress codes, and their commitment to the development of the British colony. Over the next eight years, and through extensive business dealings, they became good friends.

Their first meeting on Bahamian soil, during the winter of 1933–34, went well. As Oakes shook hands with Christie, he was likely his usual noncommittal self; only a rich vein of gold ever inspired him to exuberance. And there was no visible gold in Nassau. It had none of the features he had come to appreciate elsewhere—the pioneer friendliness of Kirkland Lake, the dramatic scenery of Niagara Falls, the wealth of Palm Beach. Yet the tiny town centre, only a short walk from the waterfront, had its raffish charm. Donkey carts and horse-drawn drays clattered along the streets, forcing the luxury cars of the island's elite to grind into bottom gear. Shoppers strolled past the shaded store-fronts of Bay Street, which ran parallel to the harbour. On the waterfront, fishermen hawked conch and grouper while farmers from other islands offered mangoes, melons, and papaya.

In the middle of town, pink stuccoed government buildings clustered around a statue of Queen Victoria, known as "Auntie Wikki" (an affectionate contraction of Victoria) to Bahamian natives, who credited her—quite erroneously—with the abolition of slavery. On the hill behind these buildings, stone churches and two-storey wooden houses, with elegant balconies and wooden shutters, lined the streets. At one end of George Street, a policeman in a pith helmet and white tunic directed traffic at the junction of Bay Street, while at the other end, up a flight of steps and past a statue of Christopher Columbus, stood Government

House, a modest building with wide verandas, where the governor lived. Hibiscus and oleanders bloomed everywhere in unclipped profusion, obscuring an encroaching shabbiness.

Government House, and the villas of the colonial elite, faced the harbour, so their white occupants could enjoy sea breezes. Descendants of slaves and free blacks lived on the other side of the hill, in Grant's Town and Bain Town, with buckets for toilets and communal standpipes for water. Barefoot children and feral dogs ran through dirty streets while sweating grandmothers sat outside dilapidated shacks, fanning themselves in the oppressive heat.

Once Christie drove his visitor out of the city, Oakes could see that most of New Providence was an unforgiving landscape of sand and mangrove swamps, speckled with the one-room wooden shacks of former slaves trying to scratch a living out of the sparse soil. As the two men bumped along unpaved roads, there were only brief glimpses of pink beaches and aquamarine ocean. Inland, there were distinct similarities with the worst of Northern Ontario, including vicious mosquitoes, no clean water, and no sewage services. Ironically, the statue of Queen Victoria and the faded Union Jacks hanging limply on flagpoles suggested another similarity with Canada—a continuing deference to the British Empire, and to whichever drawling British grandee was sent out from the imperial centre to act as the Queen's representative. But Canada was now an independent country within the British Empire, with a population of over 10 million and its own laws and system of taxation. Largely thanks to its primary resources, including the gold from Oakes's mine, it was economically independent. The poverty-stricken, underpopulated Bahamas clung to their colonial status and subsidies from Britain, and seemed headed for economic decline.

The absence of income tax might have been enough to persuade Oakes to invest in Bahamian property. But there were other,

Prospectors heading into rugged Canadian Shield country.
ARCHIVES OF ONTARIO (AO) 10022421

The Temiskaming and Northern Ontario Railway opened the bush up for settlers and prospectors. MUSEUM OF NORTHERN HISTORY (MNH)

Kirkland Lake's rough-and-ready Government Road in the 1920s. MNH

The Ojibwa people watched their resources being ransacked. AO 10022409

Roza Brown. MNH

Kirkland Lake miners hefting gold bars at the Swastika station. MNH

Miners worked deep underground without helmets, gloves, or other safety equipment. MNH

Cobalt miners with a 2,614-pound silver nugget. AO 10004672

Bill Wright, one of Kirkland Lake's first millionaires, would later own the *Globe and Mail.* MNH

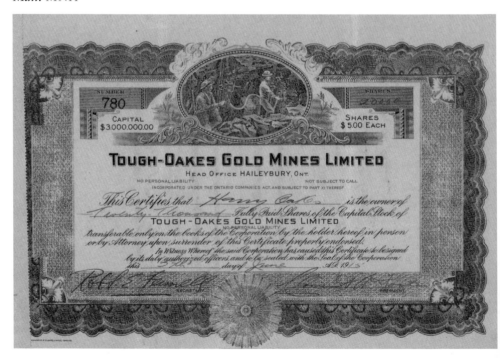

Tough-Oakes was the first producing mine in Kirkland Lake. MNH

It was also the first to produce viable amounts of gold. MNH

Harry Oakes (far left, seated on rail) and a 1922 mine crew, including two cooks, outside the first Lake Shore bunkhouse. MNH

British aristocrat Lord Redesdale, an unlikely and unsuccessful prospector. MNH

T&NO Railway parlour car, where deals could be made in comfort. AO 10020757

Lake Shore in 1929: the largest and most productive Kirkland Lake mine. MNH

Lake Shore bunkhouse. MNH

Some of Lake Shore's 2,000 employees, ready to descend into Number One shaft. MNH

Harry Oakes, successful at last. MNH

The Chateau, the Oakes's Kirkland Lake home and today the Museum of Northern History. MNH

Oak Hall, Niagara Falls. AO 10020290

less risky tax havens available. How did Harold Christie persuade the famously distrustful Harry Oakes that New Providence had enough attractions for a wealthy investor?

When Christie wanted to captivate, he was irresistible. He knew how to inspire others with his vision: green eyes dark with excitement, an enthusiastic grin lighting up his fleshy face, he extolled the glories of his "island paradise." There were other, less attractive sides to this entrepreneur—rumours of Mafia connections that had landed him in trouble with the US authorities in Boston; a careless disregard for the shocking conditions in which most black Bahamians lived. His strategic land purchases displaced many poor black farmers who were ignorant of the value of their beachfront lands. But Oakes recognized a fellow go-getter—a wildly ambitious man who had started with little, but was prepared to achieve his vision at all costs. And Oakes, who never really grasped how the stock market worked, understood the idea of profiting from a tangible asset like land. After spending the past few years amongst men with little of his own or Christie's hardscrabble drive, Oakes decided to trust Harold Christie.

WHEN HARRY OAKES returned to Florida, he contacted his lawyer, Walter Foskett.

Foskett owed his practice to Oakes's patronage. He had been junior partner in a respected Palm Beach legal firm—Wilcox, Winters, & Foskett—when Oakes shambled through the firm's door unannounced in 1931, looking for advice on Florida real estate. The receptionist told this stocky stranger with an abrupt manner that nobody was available to see him, but he could sit and wait if he liked. Oakes was offended by this brush-off, but then Foskett walked through the waiting room and offered his

help. Oakes took Foskett out to lunch to discuss his legal challenges; as the size of Oakes's fortune dawned on Foskett, the
sleek, respectful young lawyer became increasingly eager to
help. The two men, both short in stature and forceful in manner,
quickly bonded. In no time at all, according to a newspaper columnist, "Handling Oakes' business became an avocation as well
as a vocation for Foskett." Foskett left the large firm and set up
his own practice, and made himself indispensable to both Harry
and Eunice Oakes. He was soon helping with personal as well
as legal issues.

By the time Oakes returned from Nassau, Foskett had already
honed a fancy legal manoeuvre to ensure that the Palm Beach
properties would not be subject to stiff American inheritance
taxes if Oakes died. These properties were owned not by him
but by a company called Teadem Inc. (of which Oakes was the
chief shareholder). When the Oakes family occupied any of their
homes there, they were scrupulously careful to pay rent to the
corporation.

Now Harry Oakes asked Foskett to devise similar tax shelters to shield any other assets from tax collectors. Foskett set
up several Bahamian holding companies, such as Caves Co. Ltd.
and Nassoak Ltd., to purchase all of Oakes's Canadian securities,
including the million Lake Shore Mines shares that Oakes personally owned. Oakes then took shares in the tax-free Bahamian
corporations, so that they could pay him, as dividends, what they
received from the Canadian securities. Once Oakes was receiving
dividends from the holding companies rather than directly from
Lake Shore, he was no longer liable to pay income tax on the
income in Canada; instead, as a resident of the Bahamas, he had
to pay Ottawa only a 5 percent withholding tax on Lake Shore's
earnings. Between 1925 and 1939, Harry Oakes's Lake Shore
dividends amounted to $22.75 million, of which the Canadian

tax take was only $1.1 million. That left over $20 million for Harry Oakes to spend in the Bahamas and elsewhere. Such a sum would be worth at least twenty times that amount today, or around $400 million. And this represents only Oakes's Lake Shore dividends; the value of his Lake Shore shares, in today's terms, ran into the billions.

In no time at all, Oakes began to write large cheques to Christie. Within the next few months, he would purchase thousands of scrubby acres in the western part of New Providence, including a 3000-acre stretch running north–south from Cable Beach, the island's most beautiful seashore, to Lake Killarney in the centre. At one point, he would own between a quarter and a third of the entire island.

Soon, the Oakes clan was spending several months a year in the Bahamas. Harry Oakes first built a mansion called The Caves, 12 kilometres outside Nassau, named after the old limestone caves nearby where, it was said, pirates had once hidden their booty. According to the Nassau newspapers, there were twelve bedrooms, picture windows overlooking the white sandy beach, and a swimming pool that held 52,000 gallons of salt water.

Next, Oakes acquired a more modest white-painted residence, Westbourne. This pleasant villa had a veranda along the ground floor and a balcony walkway that was reached by two outside staircases and linked the bedrooms on the floor above. It also boasted a saltwater pool, tennis court, and a separate cottage for staff. From the porch, visitors could watch sparkling breakers slowly unfurl along Cable Beach's 8 kilometres of pearly sands. At the back, only a few clumps of trees stood between the house and the tranquil waters of Lake Cunningham. Vivid red, purple, and pink bougainvillea clambered over the woodwork and around the shutters. Sir Harry's next project was to build a golf course and a country club adjacent to Westbourne. Now none of the island's leaders could afford to ignore Sir Harry Oakes if they wanted to enjoy these amenities.

Eunice and their five children settled into their new life in the Bahamas, alternating between the houses. But while they enjoyed the swimming, sailing, and exuberant social events, Oakes's attention was focused elsewhere. New Providence gave him the opportunity to remodel a virgin wasteland with noisy, powerful machines, and to indulge the affection for trees that he had developed during his Maine childhood. (His activities in Niagara Falls were always constrained by well-established buildings and neighbours.) According to historian Michael Craton, "With the enthusiasm of a young man he threw himself into ambitious projects costing in all over $400,000 and employing many local labourers who had been on the point of starvation."

The colony's new resident became a familiar sight: a dishevelled figure in breeches, muddy boots, and checked shirt, reliving the challenges and excitement of the good old days in Northern Ontario when he was tearing apart the bush to reveal its treasures. He was twenty years older now, but he got the same thrill as he ground the gears on his large bulldozer or snapped at anybody who questioned the destruction. When an employee refused to drive a tractor up a particularly steep slope, Oakes jumped into his Opel car, roared to the top of the hill, and yelled at the driver to follow him up.

In the mid-1930s, Oakes started a farming project at The Caves, growing strawberries and planting thousands of imported coconut trees and citrus plants. Near Westbourne, as well as a golf course, he created a polo field, Five Stones Park. Then he built stables for his polo ponies. On land east of Lake Cunningham, he levelled and paved an area as an airport, to be called Oakes Field. He improved the old highways, inaugurated a mosquito control system, and constructed a botanical garden for the city. Next,

Oakes purchased the New Colonial Hotel, a white elephant that he rescued from bankruptcy, for $1.5 million, renamed it the British Colonial Hotel, and spent half a million dollars redecorating it. (It continued to operate at a loss.)

As the Lake Shore dividends rolled into his Bahamian companies, there was always another impulse to indulge. One winter, he decided to redesign the water mains that piped fresh water downtown to the hotel and augmented the city supply. The city supply used spherical wells, and there was reason to believe that the sea deposited salt on the well pipes and that, sooner or later, the salt would reach the fresh water and contaminate it. Oakes designed a different system that used a network of slit trenches, with perforated pipes above the salt level; this, he decided, would keep fresh water above salt water on the low-lying island. It was never established whether the new system was any more effective than the old one, and visitors continued to report that Nassau water tasted salty.

Another Oakes project was the development of San Salvador, the island on which Columbus first landed. He purchased two-thirds of the 11,000-acre island, at $10 an acre. But then he lost interest.

During the Depression, Oakes's projects were a godsend for Bahamians on his payroll. The Bay Street Boys had little interest in the black population, preferring to leave them to their shantytowns, lilting calypsos, rotgut rum, and poverty. A visiting American reporter reflected Bay Street condescension in his description of the underclass as "a docile people, respectful, courteous and chiefly occupied with fishing, gossiping and attending prayer meetings." He recorded their incessant song in the soft, tropical nights: "Mommy don't want no peas, no rice, no coconut oil . . ."

But Harry Oakes had spent most of his life in far less stratified societies, and his get-the-job-done drive rode roughshod over entrenched racial prejudice. Just as he had selectively looked after his Kirkland Lake workforce, he now improved conditions for his New Providence employees, many of whom lived in Grant's Town. In the mid-1930s and early 1940s, he paid his labourers five shillings a day, one shilling more than the minimum wage, and fed them hot meals at the job site. He organized a bus service through Grant's Town, and he established a school and clinic there. He also provided milk for the children. At the British Colonial Hotel, he insisted that black Bahamians should fill all jobs except the top management positions. When Oakes discovered that there were not enough non-white Bahamians who knew the hotel business, he opened a school to train them.

"Even in his philanthropies," remarks Craton, "Harry Oakes was not guiltless of a certain calculation. By his steady engagement of some 1,500 labourers otherwise unemployed, he became very popular in Nassau." Ruthless self-interest rather than a commitment to racial equality drove Oakes's actions; everything he did was designed to get the most out of his employees. Nevertheless, he did not share the blatant racism of his Bahamian neighbours. He had not been raised in a particularly racist part of the United States (there were few African-Americans in Maine), and he had shown no ethnic prejudices in Kirkland Lake—a pioneer community where the Kaplans and Charlie Chow had thrived. Moreover, he was genuinely appalled by the rampant illiteracy and poverty. His investments proved crucial to Bahamian prosperity in a dark decade. In the opinion of Sir Orville Turnquest, who would serve as the fifth Bahamian-born governor general of the Bahamas, from 1995 to 2001, "Sir Harry Oakes arguably did more than any other person, agency, or government to affect life positively in The Bahamas" between 1934 and 1943.

Still sporting prospectors' breeches rather than linen suits,

Oakes looked more like a truck driver than a multimillionaire as he stomped around his estate, barking orders at gardeners, groundsmen, golf caddies, labourers, and anyone else in his employ. Spurning cocktails at the country club, he preferred to drop into a friend's gas station on Bay Street, sit on an oil drum, and chat. He still had neither small talk nor patience for social niceties; his temper was short and his language could be abusive. Stories about his boorishness quickly spread, just as they had in Canada. He was said to have purchased the New Colonial Hotel in a fit of pique because he had showed up one day in scuffed boots and muddy breeches, and was either denied admittance or served badly. According to local gossip, he stalked out, bought the hotel the following day, and immediately sacked the maître d'hôtel who had humiliated him. There is little evidence that the tale was true, but Nassau society enjoyed spreading it.

Two people never objected to Oakes's manners. The first was his wife, Eunice—now a stately matron, exuding dignity and grace in her pearls and straw hats—who was noted for the warmth of her welcome and for the enormous bouquets of lilies decorating her house. To outsiders, the Oakeses seemed a devoted couple. Madeline Gale Kelly, the Oakeses' housekeeper and wife of their business manager, recalled the occasion when Harry won a rare orchid at a society raffle. Eunice was at the family's residence at Bar Harbor at the time, so Harry's fellow guests expected him to present the orchid to his hostess. Instead, he strode over to Mrs. Kelly, thrust the bloom at her, and asked, "How soon can we get that to [my wife]?"

The Oakeses also gave the impression of being a model family. A formal portrait shows the seated parents, Harry with William on his knee and Eunice with Harry on hers, and the older three children grouped around them. Three good-looking boys in pale linen suits, two girls in ringlets and big smiles, and the parents apparently glowing with well-being and contentment—it is a picture of solidarity and mutual affection. Oakes relied on his wife to raise their children but he was proud of them, particularly his favourite, Nancy, the eldest.

But all the children were kept on a tight leash, and their parents were not lavish with money or love. When Nancy was nine years old, she was sent to boarding school in Switzerland. The three Oakes boys attended St. Andrew's College, a British-type boarding school in Aurora, north of Toronto. The constant moves and separations meant that ties between the siblings were not as tight as the photo made them appear. As Nancy, the most spirited, became a teenager, she started to bristle at the limits on her freedom and her allowance.

The other person who never criticized the millionaire was Harold Christie, who spent a lot of time with his wealthiest client. With his habit of ducking a fight and smoothing over conflict, Christie would simply shrug, "Harry's all right. . . . A rough diamond, that's all."

Christie was doing very well, because, thanks in part to tax exiles like Harry Oakes, Nassau was finally acquiring some cachet. Private yachts crowded into its harbour. Bay Street's buildings had been repaired and painted, and its stores, catering to the steady flow of tourists, offered French perfume, Irish linen, and English china. The Royal Bank of Canada lent the street an aura of stability, while in the bar of its neighbour, the Prince George Hotel, visitors enjoyed rum punches. At night, Bay Street Boys and millionaires mingled in the Porcupine Club or Jungle Club—both billed as "exclusive" (a euphemism for "whites only"). Villas, beach houses, and vacation homes spread along the island's shore.

Another Canadian multimillionaire who had joined Oakes in the Bahamas was Sir Herbert Holt, now chairman of the Royal Bank of Canada, who had built a house that he named

Ballycrystal, after his Irish birthplace. Unlike Oakes, Holt had no interest in the welfare of those less successful than he; if people were poor, it was their fault. During the peak of the Great Depression of the 1930s, while the bank was making extraordinary profits, Holt had announced to some petitioners, "If I am rich and powerful while you are suffering the stranglehold of poverty and the humiliation of social assistance . . . it is foolishness on your part and as for me, it is the fruit of wise administration."

A further recruit to the Caribbean tax haven was a Swedish industrialist, Axel Wenner-Gren, an aloof character with a taste for well-tailored suits and shady deals. Wenner-Gren had amassed a vast fortune by developing and marketing Electrolux vacuum cleaners and refrigerators worldwide; by the late 1930s, he was the largest private employer in Sweden, with interests in newspapers, banks, and arms manufacturers in several countries, including Mexico and Germany. He represented the Krupp family in its international munitions sales and boasted of his friendship with Hermann Göring. The Swedish tax exile owned a 700-acre island, now Paradise Island but then called Hog Island, just off New Providence. His massive steam yacht *Southern Cross*, which he had bought from Howard Hughes for $2 million, was often moored off shore. Harold Christie, Nassau's unofficial ambassador to the rich and restless, was almost as friendly with Wenner-Gren as he was with Harry Oakes.

Christie himself continued to pursue his vision. He was busy developing an area of sand dunes at the extreme western tip of New Providence, called Lyford Cay, where he planned to create an ultra-exclusive community (a place where billionaires could get away from millionaires), and he had landscaped the area with a carpet of grass and fast-growing casuarina trees. However, his ambitions still outpaced his wallet, and he needed Harry Oakes to keep spending too.

—

IN THE MID-1930S, a glamorous British travel writer named Rosita Forbes turned up in the Bahamas after an adventurous career that included a scandalous divorce, a journey across the Sahara in Arab garb, and sycophantic interviews with Adolf Hitler and Benito Mussolini. Tall, elegant, and athletic, she swanned around the islands, noting the coral beaches along the shorelines and the social mores of the country club set. Given her admiration for fascist dictators, I'm not surprised that she was immediately drawn to the most powerful players in Nassau. "At the moment, the Bahamas have at least two geniuses to their credit, one of them indigenous and the other imported," she would write in her memoir, *A Unicorn in the Bahamas*. "It is interesting to speculate on what—in Napoleonic fashion—these two men will do for the islands and to the islands for which they have considerable feeling."

In Forbes's opinion, both Christie and Oakes were Peter Pans: "Neither will ever grow up." Describing Christie as "burned to the golden colour of seaweed on a Scottish beach," the writer marvelled at the businessman's unquenchable enthusiasm and wild imagination as he listed off all the improvements he was making to his hundreds of rocky acres and tranquil cays in order to attract outsiders.

While Christie overwhelmed her with his unstoppable flow of ideas, taciturn Harry Oakes fascinated her because he was a "hard-working visionary with immense interests and limited speech." She was seduced by the raw power of Oakes's determination to remake his surroundings: "His extraordinary tractors tear up the bush and devour it as they go along. . . . His treasure is the earth. He must possess all of it that he can." Charmed by Eunice Oakes's beauty and wit, Forbes was also amused by Eunice's indulgence towards her husband's activities. During one visit to Westbourne, Forbes was surprised to see a bulldozer parked on the front lawn. "What is it doing?" she asked her hostess. Eunice smiled and shrugged. It was making yet another road.

Rosita Forbes developed her own rosy theory about what Harry Oakes was up to in the Bahamas. In his mining days, she speculated, he felt like "an ill-treated servant of the earth, baulked, frustrated, fooled by it until he learned all its mineral secrets and turned them to good account. Now he does what he chooses to the element which once denied him. As a conqueror he disposes of its shape, curtailing, eliminating or creating as he desires. If any debt existed, the earth has been forced to repay."

CHAPTER 8

"Pick, Shovel Man Is 'Sir'"

When a man living in a rented house moves out his belongings, the landlord realizes he is about to lose a tenant. When a person residing at a hotel packs up his trunks and cases, the manager believes he is about to lose a guest. When an Ontario millionaire forms a personal holding company at Nassau, then begins to transfer his assets to it, Toronto and Ottawa treasury moguls get a sinking feeling in the pit of their stomachs. They foresee the loss of another big tax-payer. . . . But as things stand, there isn't a thing they can do about it.

TORONTO DAILY STAR, FEBRUARY 16, 1938

I n 1938, a rather different picture of Harry Oakes emerged in a lengthy feature in the *Toronto Daily Star* by Gregory Clark, one of the paper's most popular reporters. Clark presented Oakes not as a mighty Prometheus reshaping his world but as a jealous Croesus hoarding his gold.

Clark's article was illustrated with a photograph of the Bahamian good life—Oakes, jacket straining over his paunch, watches his Bahamian chef barbecue three-inch steaks, while three friends (the Holts and a bare-chested Harold Christie) look on. In the headline, Clark quoted Oakes's determination to keep "two jumps ahead" of people who were after his wealth. Oakes gleefully explained to the *Star*'s man that it was "the old situation of the 'haves' and 'have-nots.' . . . The 'have-nots' are today completely in command of the situation. Stalin takes it, whole-hog. [Canadian Prime Minister R. B.] Bennett took it all but 15 percent. . . . Pride of possession belongs today to the politicians. You find it. They spend it." This barbecue was the occasion when Oakes explained to Clark that, when he heard that the Canadian government was contemplating a tax on gold profits, he left the country. This is what had triggered his health crisis, he insisted: the thought of Ottawa confiscating his wealth had brought on acute bronchitis and forced him to flee to warmer climes. That's why he was here, roaring around the sunny Bahamas, wielding a machete in the jungle and driving his tractor across abandoned plantations. Wouldn't any sensible tycoon do the same thing?

The tone of Clark's article is exuberant and skeptical, but it's evident that the two men got on well. Eunice was away, and Oakes was bored and ready to be charmed by Clark, a witty and engaging reporter. Oakes even lined up Sydney (clutching a black puppy), Shirley, William, and Harry, all barefoot and dressed untidily, for the camera. The millionaire allowed Clark to hang around for two full days and told him, "You'd never have got pictures of the children if she were here. She has no use for newspapers. Neither have I."

Clark injected a little provocation into all this bonhomie. "What if they introduce an income tax here?" he asked his host. "Just a nice little teeny-weeny income tax of five percent?"

He had hit a nerve. "Five percent," Oakes snarled. "That's the way they all start. Five percent. And the next thing you know it's 10, and then 50, and then 80."

Clark never specified in the article exactly how much the mine owner was reckoned to be worth, preferring to write vaguely of his "countless, fabulous millions," but he made it clear that his host's chief priority—in fact, his only priority—was to protect his fortune. When Oakes spoke darkly of having already made up his mind where he would go if the Bahamas were foolish enough to introduce an income tax, Clark pressed him to reveal his destination. "A beautiful country," said the millionaire. "Guatemala." (This appears to have been a fleeting fancy, as Guatemala was never mentioned again.)

By now, Harry Oakes was the wealthiest and most powerful person in the Bahamas, with massive investments in New Providence, in both his own and Harold Christie's projects. The Bay Street merchants might find his manners and his generosity towards black Bahamians deplorable, but they loved his golf club and his spending habits and they were anxious not to offend him. The idea that Oakes was even contemplating moving elsewhere horrified the Bahamian governing council. If Oakes pulled out of the colony, many developments would come grinding to a halt. Harold Christie was even more alarmed. H. G. Christie Real Estate relied heavily on commissions from buying and selling on behalf of Oakes, and the two men were partners in various schemes. The millionaire's departure would cause trouble for Christie.

Not surprisingly, Bahamian government leaders made every effort to look after Oakes's interests. A request to the Colonial Office from the governor of the Bahamas triggered two "nearly-impossible-to-obtain" seats for the Oakeses at the coronation of King George VI in 1937 because, as the official correspondence notes, he was a "great benefactor to the Colony." Now the white members of the legislature came up with another scheme to anchor Oakes in New Providence. They pressed him to stand for election as a member of the House of Assembly, although Oakes had lived in the Bahamas for less than four years.

Oakes agreed to let his name be listed on the ballot, although he did not take the election very seriously: on voting day, he was not even in the colony. Trusted assistants followed the local custom of buying votes with money, rum, or groceries. The loudest chant at the polling stations was "We'll drink his rum, and have some fun, and vote for Harry Oakes." Voters lined up to declare to polling officials the name of their candidate, while organizers listened carefully so they could ensure that the bribes had paid off. Oakes was duly elected, and the following year he was invited to join the legislative council.

There was a downside to this victory. The seat that Oakes had won traditionally went to a non-white, and his opponent was a popular and well-regarded black merchant named Milo B. Butler, who had assumed that the seat was his for the taking. But Milo Butler hadn't stood a chance. The Bay Street Boys, keen to stay onside with the formidable billionaire in their midst, ensured that Butler's credit at the Royal Bank of Canada was stopped during the campaign, and he was so decisively beaten that he lost his deposit. In the short term, Butler's defeat tarnished Harry Oakes's popularity amongst black Bahamians. The long-term impact was more serious: it aggravated growing discontent about rigged elections and starvation wages. The racial politics of the colony started to simmer.

There were other critics of Oakes's activities and of Christie's reinvention of Nassau as a millionaires' Mecca. One prominent visitor was appalled. William Lyon Mackenzie King, who had succeeded the Conservative Bennett as prime minister of Canada, travelled to the Bahamas in October 1938. King, a Liberal who was steeped in the Canadian distrust of opulence and enjoyed portraying himself as an unassuming man of modest means, recorded his reactions in his diary.

King found the Bahamas morally distasteful. "One feels about

Nassau that the atmosphere of the place is most unhealthy. It has been built up out of excessive money made from rum-running and expenditures of millionaires who have gone to reside there to escape taxation in their own countries." He noted with satisfaction that his revulsion at Oakes's corrupt election was shared by the governor, Sir Charles Dundas. Despite having wangled coronation tickets for Oakes, the governor disapproved of this crude North American and did not like what had happened to Milo Butler. He confided to King his concern about race relations and his determination to defuse the situation by introducing a secret ballot for future Assembly elections.

What really irritated King was that so many of the plutocrats flocking to this tax haven were Canadians. In February 1938, at least 144 wealthy Canadians had established holding companies in Nassau, then transferred most of their assets into them. The list of these tax dodgers "reads like a cross section of Canadian Who's Who of industry, finance and the professions," according to the *Toronto Daily Star*. As long as these businessmen did not spend more than 183 days of a year in Canada, they could claim non-resident status and evade Canadian income tax.

All that lost tax revenue left the Canadian prime minister with a sour impression of the islands. "Sir Herbert Holt has a magnificent residence; he is also erecting a trust company building. These features all related to means of escape from taxation to the State in Canada leave a rather painful impression. Personally, while I thought individual homes were quite beautiful, I did not care for the island itself. The business part, anything but pleasant. The native population a little too numerous and assertive. The developments not at all equal to those in some of the important places in the US."

==

DURING THIS PERIOD, Harry Oakes spent much of each year outside the Bahamas, although he was careful to be in New Providence long enough to claim it as his principal residence for tax purposes.

One sad event that required his presence elsewhere was the tragic death of his sister Gertrude Oakes. Gertrude had continued to spend much of the year in her lodge, Red Pines, near Kirkland Lake, even after Harry and Eunice Oakes had moved south. She was popular in Kirkland Lake; unlike her brother, she was active in community affairs—she sat on the board of the golf club, for example, and handed out prizes at school graduations. At Christmas, before she took off for warmer climes, she sent gifts to the children of Lake Shore employees.

But in the early hours of Friday, January 25, 1935, newsrooms across the United States buzzed with the news that a luxury liner, S.S. *Mohawk*, had been rammed by a freighter off the coast of New Jersey and had rapidly sunk. This was the boat on which Gertrude and a friend, Miss E. B. Gentle, were travelling to Mexico for a holiday. Although most of the *Mohawk*'s 53 passengers and 110 crew managed to scramble into lifeboats, Gertrude Oakes was not amongst them. Her sister Jessie Oakes Ellis made the identification of her body.

Gertrude was one of the few people for whom Harry Oakes had deep respect. He never forgot her loyalty and generosity through his hardscrabble years, and he had come to rely on her judgment on business issues. He trusted her completely because she was not after his money; when Gertrude urged him not to be stingy, he listened. Like Eunice, she had helped to calm his hair-trigger temper and soften his rough edges in public, and her warmth and generosity ensured that the Oakes name was well regarded in Kirkland Lake. Her death was a major headline in the newspaper there: "Miss Oakes Victim of Waves in Wreck of

Liner Mohawk . . . Saturday News Shocks Kirkland Lake . . . Missed as Benefactress."

Harry Oakes travelled to New York City for Gertrude's funeral, and then to their childhood home in Foxcroft, Maine, for her burial. He never got over the loss; in the years ahead, he would miss her steady advice and support. He would also miss her good sense on how to handle the Lake Shore dividends that continued to flood into his numbered companies in the Bahamas.

There were other regular excursions. Eunice Oakes liked to spend her summers in Bar Harbor. The Oakeses still had property in Palm Beach, and they frequently showed up in the social columns there, mingling with other millionaires and described as "English." Harry had remained close to his family (all of whom likely held Lake Shore stock), and he particularly enjoyed visiting his brother Louis in Piscataquis County in Maine and looking up old school friends. He and Louis donated land to Foxcroft Academy and discussed schemes that might bring some employment to the area. Harry continued to be generous to Bowdoin College. A bust of him stood over the mantel in the common room of the Zeta Psi fraternity house, in recognition of his substantial donations. In time, he would lend valuable paintings to the college's Museum of Fine Arts, and the university would award him an honorary degree. At Bowdoin, as in Niagara Falls, Harry Oakes was regarded not as a raging bully but as an eccentric benefactor.

But Harry Oakes's most significant travels in this period were his trips to England.

It is hard to track Oakes's activities in England because of the paucity of sources other than brief newspaper references. At first I assumed this was because he was peripheral to English society, where he was likely regarded as just another rough-mannered colonial parvenu, flaunting his wealth but lacking in grace and education. Sometimes such men managed to insinuate themselves into powerful circles: Harry Oakes's Canadian contemporary Max Aitken, the future Lord Beaverbrook, had demonstrated incredible adroitness in making connections, entering politics and morphing into a press baron. But a more familiar pattern was that encountered three decades later by Rupert Murdoch, the ambitious Australian who also became a press baron in London, but who never forgot the snubs he encountered when he first showed up in the "old country" and was dubbed the "dirty digger."

Harry Oakes certainly did everything expected of a man of his means. In 1935 he acquired a brace of properties that reflected his wealth. His townhouse, 15a Kensington Palace Gardens, was on the capital's most expensive street, which had been known as "Millionaires' Row" ever since the 1850s, when it was developed on the site of the former kitchen gardens of Kensington Palace. Oakes bought the lease on his creamy brick-and-stucco property in West London for £40,000 (the same property today is worth £37 million, or $65 million). With its three storeys, magnificent reception rooms, ten bedrooms, extensive domestic quarters, and echoing garages, it was large enough to house not only his family, but also several Rolls-Royces and a retinue of servants. There were at least a dozen fellow millionaires on the street, including the Marquess of Cholmondeley and the Duke of Marlborough. A guard at the street's entrance from Notting Hill Gate kept out non-residents. Oakes relished this, because he was infuriated by the endless requests for money from strangers who turned up unannounced on his doorstep.

The Canadian millionaire also rented a country estate: Tottingworth Park, near Heathfield on the Weald of Sussex, 85 kilometres south of London. This was a sprawling and rather forbidding late-Victorian red-brick mansion set on the side of a deep valley, with several outbuildings and a walled kitchen garden. The new occupier's first initiative was to give the dour pile a new name: Oak Hall. Next, Oakes added an overmantel to the fireplace in the hall with a personal motto, *Sanguinis et operae virtute non astutia pro patria*, which translates roughly as "By the power of family and hard work, not trickery, serve your country."

The rolling landscape around Oak Hall was rich in the romance of history and the cachet of illustrious neighbours. A few kilometres down the road was Bateman's, the seventeenth-century lodge belonging to the writer Rudyard Kipling. Kipling, now a revered but grouchy figure in his seventies, relished Sussex's woods, bridleways, and streams, telling friends that the whole place was "alive with ghosts and shadows." Kipling loved the "blunt, bow-headed, whale-backed Downs" that he commemorated in his poem "Sussex." He proclaimed that the county was his favourite place on earth.

Oakes had no such sentiments about his 800 acres of thickly wooded land. He was immune to the charms of a landscape so different from those he had known in Maine and Northern Ontario, and so much prettier than sun-scorched New Providence. The usual impulse to remodel his property to suit his own tastes soon emerged. Despite his love of trees, he felled century-old oak trees in order to create a network of walks crisscrossing the valley, then he levelled terrain for a polo ground (by now he was besotted with the sport, and loved both playing and watching it) on the north side and dug an ornamental pond on the south side. Ignoring the native hornbeam and sweet chestnuts, he planted imported bamboo on the pond's artificial island and brought in Canadian redwood trees. Soon he had a dozen locals working as gardeners, including one whose sole duty was to keep the driveway free of leaves. Local lore records the belligerent landlord's expectations of his employees. If Oakes discovered a single leaf on his driveway, he fired the man responsible.

How did the Oakeses spend their time in England when Harry was not demolishing ancient bridleways or training polo ponies? The colonials cropped up at the kind of aristocratic dances, dinners, fundraisers, and other white-glove events at which newly minted North American millionaires, affluent beyond the dreams of many British grandees, were always welcome. In June 1934, Eunice enjoyed being amongst sixteen Canadian women who were presented by the wife of the Canadian High Commissioner to King George V and Queen Mary as part of the London Season. They were frequently mentioned in *The Times*'s social columns. They attended an afternoon sherry party at Lady Londonderry's London mansion. Eunice was at home at 15a Kensington Palace Gardens for the meeting of the Playing Fields Ball, to be hosted by the Earl of Derby. They attended Queen Mary's birthday ball in 1935. Harry attended a dinner at the London Guildhall at which the Duke of Kent was present. In June 1937, the Oakeses were guests of the Duke of Atholl at the "Golden Ball" at Grosvenor House in London; Oakes was described as the "Canadian owner of much property in the Bahamas." In September of the same year, "Mr. and Mrs. Oakes of Kensington Palace Gardens" were amongst the "brilliant assemblage" attending a ball at the close of the Argyllshire Games, in Oban, Scotland.

When Eunice Oakes was in Sussex, she happily filled the same role of local VIP that she had performed in Kirkland Lake and Niagara Falls. She presented the prizes at British Legion sports events, where the legion president noted that the Oakeses had been "good friends to the Legion." Meanwhile, Harry continued to startle observers with his unconventional behaviour. He stuck to old-fashioned breeches and button boots, although these had long been superseded by the wide flannel trousers and soft leather lace-ups favoured by Edward, Prince of Wales. On one occasion, instead of organizing several chauffeur-driven limousines, Oakes hired a down-market motor coach to transport his wife, five children, and two friends from Kensington Palace Gardens to Oak Hall because, as he pointed out, it was much easier to stow all the baggage and passengers in one vehicle. His titled neighbours made no public comment, although they must have wondered whether the occupant of 15a was a diamond or a rhinestone in the rough.

More was happening than these fleeting glimpses suggest. Harry Oakes might enjoy flouting convention from time to time, but he wanted to fit into the society to which his millions had given him access. He made it his business to meet the influential British art dealer Sir Joseph Duveen, who had made a fortune by buying old masters from impoverished European aristocrats and selling them to such wealthy Americans as William Randolph Hearst, Henry Clay Frick, and John D. Rockefeller. "Europe has a great deal of art, and America has a great deal of money," the dapper, smooth-talking Duveen famously declared, and his sales pitch included the implication that buying art also entailed buying status. Duveen must have been happy to acquire the Lake Shore owner as a client, and Oakes was soon in possession of an oil painting by Thomas Gainsborough, *The Woodcutter's Return*, purchased for US$210,000 from Duveen. The Gainsborough had originally belonged to Lord Leigh of Stoneleigh Abbey. Around this time, Oakes also bought several paintings, including a Rembrandt and a Frans Hals, from the Knoedler Gallery in New York.

The biggest surprise came in June 1939, when Harry Oakes was made a baronet in King George VI's Birthday Honours list. Ostensibly, this was a reward for philanthropy. In 1937, out of the blue, Oakes had made a contribution to the refurbishment of London's St. George's Hospital, then situated at Hyde Park Corner. How this happened is not clear, although one explanation appeared in the *Globe and Mail* after his death. "It is said he was riding in Rotten Row [in Hyde Park] one morning when he saw a sign over the hospital which read: 'We need £25,000 urgently to keep going.' Sir Harry is said to have stopped to write a cheque immediately, muttering that the 'ugly sign is spoiling the beauty of Rotten Row.'"

The gift came as a complete surprise to Lord Willingdon, who chaired the rebuilding committee for the hospital. Oakes "must be the shyest man in the world," he told a reporter. "I never even had a chance to meet him and thank him." In subsequent months there were a couple more cheques, amounting to £80,000.

Given that the press continued to refer to the Canadian millionaire as "one of the world's richest men," these were not particularly generous contributions. However, there was more to these gifts than simple philanthropy. Oakes had been taken up by a shadowy web of right-wingers that included both Sir Joseph Duveen and a friend of his, Lord Luke of Pavenham, known as "the Bovril King." Lord Luke had made a fortune from beef extract and had spearheaded several appeals on behalf of London hospitals. However, Luke was a member of the Conservative Party's far-right faction, and an effective fundraiser for more sinister causes than St. George's Hospital. As a passionate supporter of the policy of appeasement towards Germany, Luke also helped finance *Truth*, an anti-Semitic periodical that during these years was widely regarded as close to Oswald Mosley's British Union of Fascists.

Another associate of Luke in these crypto-fascist circles was a more eminent figure: Joseph Ball, a former MI5 officer who ran the Conservative Party's research department. Ball also kept an eye on *Truth*. In Joseph Ball's papers in Oxford University's Bodleian Library, there is some correspondence from 1938 about Harry Oakes—usually referred to as "our friend"—between Ball and Duveen. Sir Joseph Duveen spent a month in Nassau over the Christmas holidays that year, and a possible reward for Oakes in the King's forthcoming Birthday Honours list was obviously under discussion.

Duveen sent Ball a two-page biography of Harry Oakes, plus a list of donations he had made in Kirkland Lake, Niagara Falls, and Nassau, and added a handwritten note marvelling at his host's wealth. "He has an estate here where he lives on 12,000 acres and owns nearly half the island." In the same letter, Duveen praised the appeasement policies towards Nazi Germany that Prime Minister Neville Chamberlain had taken. "The political outlook is improving daily and there will be no war. The PM is a miracle. He will some day be recognized as the greatest PM we ever had."

Ball replied to Duveen that, although the political outlook was "troubling," he had every confidence that the prime minister "will be successful in his efforts to stop a world war." The point of his letter was that "all goes well in the matter of our mutual friend." Harry Oakes was going to be rewarded for his donations.

But some of those donations look questionable. The most mysterious item in the Ball papers is the mention in a handwritten letter from Oakes to Lord Luke of an undisclosed sum to be disposed of: "a) £10,000 to St. George's Hospital b) a sum not exceeding £15,000 to the London Hospitals Street Collection Central Committee's May Day Fund . . . c) any balance to such purposes as may be determined by you and Sir Joseph Ball jointly in consultation with the proper authority." How much was the "balance," and where did it go? None of the many historians who have tracked British fascists in these years has discovered the answer to those questions, or discovered whether there were subsequent donations. But two years after Oakes's initial gift to St. George's, he became Sir Harry Oakes, 1st Baronet of Nassau.

Had Sir Harry Oakes bought his baronetcy by quietly funnelling much larger amounts into the coffers of either the Conservative Party or one of its offshoots? If so, he was certainly neither the first nor the last person to buy a British title. The significance of the transaction is not the purchase itself but the Conservative Party connections he was making. He had evidently been swept up into seedy political circles during the late 1930s, when a motley assortment of politicians, anti-Semitic aristocrats, and pro-German businessmen were working hard to build an antiwar coalition. Joseph Ball, who manoeuvred to secure him the title, was a key figure in the Conservative faction that worked to undermine Winston Churchill, as the latter sounded the alarm about German rearmament. Oakes's sponsor for the baronetcy was no less a person than Prince George, Duke of Kent, the King's dissolute youngest brother, who strongly supported appeasement policies.

Oakes himself never exhibited the anti-Semitism or contempt for the working classes displayed by British right-wingers, but he likely shared their distrust of expensive military adventures and their indifference to the evils of Hitler's Nazi regime. Similar attitudes were common amongst Nassau's tax exiles, and Oakes was already comfortable with men like Axel Wenner-Bren. He welcomed his newfound political friends as his guests in Nassau. His hospitality was enjoyed by not only Sir Joseph Duveen but the iron-fisted Tory chief whip David Margesson, who had supported Chamberlain's policy of appeasement.

In a photo taken on a sunny June day in 1939, there is no mistaking the excitement on the faces of Sir Harry and Lady Oakes soon after the Birthday Honours announcement of the baronetcy. Sir Harry is unusually dapper in a well-cut blue blazer, white shirt, checked tie, and panama hat, while Eunice is her usual stately self in a pastel-coloured suit, white gloves, and wide-brimmed hat. "Pick, Shovel Man is 'Sir,'" read the headline in London's *Daily Mirror*.

Oakes loved how the baronetcy confounded all his critics— not least the wretched Canadian politicians he blamed for driving him offshore. It gave him particular prestige in both the United States and the Bahamas, since both Americans and Bahamians had always loved titles. In Nassau, Harold Christie threw a party and gave a champagne toast to Sir Harry and Lady Oakes.

But a baronetcy was trivial compared to the titles of the couple that was about to arrive in the colony.

CHAPTER 9

"A Pathetic Little Job in a Ghastly Backwater"

When the radio waves brought the news of Your Royal Highness's appointment as Governor of the Bahamas, the Deaf heard, and the Dumb spoke, the Blind saw and the Crippled leaped for joy. Your reputation as a humanitarian and King had preceded you. Surely, we said to ourselves, the Duke of Windsor will not allow us to continue to live amidst social inequities that sap our self-respect and prevent us from attaining our full status as first-class citizens.

DR. CLAUDIUS R. WALKER, NASSAU PHYSICIAN, 1942

TOP PRESS: Former King Appointed Governor of Bahamas!" blared the front page of the *Nassau Daily Tribune* on July 10, 1940, setting off a wave of excitement across the colony. The newspaper went on to acknowledge that the world had not expected such a post for the former King Edward VIII, now the Duke of Windsor, and his duchess, the former Wallis Simpson, the woman for whom he had abdicated the throne. The editor, Étienne Dupuch, quoted *The Times* of London's surprisingly hyperbolic description of the office of governor of the Bahamas as "one of the oldest and most honourable posts under the crown."

The colony's residents, and especially members of its ruling white elite, chose to assume that the forty-six-year-old duke and his American wife were as happy to represent the Crown in Nassau as Bahamians were thrilled to have figures of such international renown in their midst. It had been less than four years since the abdication crisis, and to distant observers, the former King Edward VIII and the former Mrs. Simpson still trailed wisps of romance. The government in London and the duke's brother, the shy, stammering George VI, might be infuriated by the Windsors' behaviour, but as the editor of the *Nassau Daily Tribune* reported some years later, "At the time, the couple were viewed by most—and this was certainly true of ordinary people throughout the Empire—as victims of official stuffiness. . . . Theirs was, indisputably, the romance of the century, according to the wisdom of the day." Already, the telling phrases from the crisis were stuck in the collective memory like the crackling radio broadcast: "Found it impossible . . . to discharge my duties as king . . . without the help and support of the woman I love."

However, the Windsors regarded the Bahamas posting as an appalling fate. While the duke was still mid-Atlantic, he described his new job as "this wretched appointment" in a letter to his London lawyer, adding that he viewed the prospect of "an indefinite period of exile on those islands with profound gloom and despondency." The duchess was even less excited. She considered it a "pathetic little job in a ghastly backwater," the social equivalent of Napoleon's exile to Elba or St. Helena. As far as the Windsors were concerned, the only positive aspect of the Bahamas was the one-hour flight to Florida.

But upper lips were stiff. A month after the official announcement, the heat was stifling when the new governor and his wife arrived in Nassau, which had been freshly painted and decked with bunting for the occasion. Policemen kept enthusiastic crowds behind cordons, and the police band played a welcome as the Windsors walked down the gangplank from the Canadian vessel *Lady Somers*. The duke was in a general's uniform; the duchess teetered onto dry land in a navy-blue silk coat, a simple print dress, and a white cap. The welcoming party consisted exclusively of white officials and their wives, plus other prominent white individuals, all lined up to greet them. Even the little girl who presented the duchess with a bouquet of flowers was white. Everyone else was kept behind barriers. The duke and duchess probably did not notice the racial segregation (both were deeply racist), but they certainly noticed the August humidity. Dark patches of sweat stained the back of the duke's khaki tunic. Still, neither betrayed their discomfort as they were escorted to the House of Assembly by the Bahamian colonial secretary and the American consul.

In the council chamber, the new governor sat glumly under a red canopy bearing the insignia of the Crown in gold. His wife sat one step below him but one step above the seat normally reserved for the spouse of a governor—a position arrived at after an excruciating debate between protocol buffs. Word had arrived from London that the Duchess of Windsor was to be addressed as "Your Grace," and that ladies should give her a half-curtsy rather than a full curtsy. George VI had announced his refusal to grant Wallis the title "Your Royal Highness" soon after his own coronation, and his refusal had already become the irreducible core of the split between the two brothers, never to be resolved. The new governor seethed with rage at this perceived insult to the woman for whom he had sacrificed the crown.

Lieutenant Colonel R. A. Erskine-Lindop, commissioner of police of the Bahamas, read the commission of office. Next, the duke swore his allegiance to the King, his younger brother, and signed the oath of office, as administered by Chief Justice

Sir Oscar Daly. While the duchess merely glowed in the dripping heat, the newly installed governor wiped his brow with a handkerchief before shaking hands with 285 people in the airless, crowded chamber. Then the glamorous couple was ushered to the balcony so that they could perform the required regal wave to the throng below.

If the duchess's mood was not already bad enough, worse was to come. When the Windsors finally arrived at their future home, Government House, Her Grace was outraged. As the duke later wrote to an American friend, it "was in such a filthy state, almost denuded of furniture and having the appearance more of an institution than an official residence, that we refused to live in it after a week until it was reconditioned." The local director of public works admitted that the house was riddled with termites and in need of a major overhaul, whoever the new occupants were. The Windsors decamped to the Nassau mansion of Sir Frederick Sigrist, the British industrialist whose aviation companies were turning out the Hawker Hurricane fighter planes now playing a heroic role in the battle against the Luftwaffe.

The Oakeses may have already met the Duke of Windsor in Britain, especially since it was the new governor's brother, the Duke of Kent, who had recommended Harry Oakes for the baronetcy the previous year. If they had been in Nassau for the Windsors' arrival, they would certainly have been in the official welcoming party. When they heard that the Windsors had not found accommodation that met their standards, they suggested that the governor and his wife move into their own house. Westbourne was larger than the Sigrist property and cooler because, situated right on Cable Beach, it enjoyed sea breezes. The Windsors accepted, and moved in with their entourage, although the duchess disdainfully described it as "a shack by the sea." The Oakes family withdrew to another of their properties.

There was a world of difference between the immaculately tailored and class-conscious former monarch and the muddy-booted baronet. But it was inevitable that the Windsors and Oakeses would see a lot of each other, given their shared political views and the size of Nassau's social elite. They were both very big fish in a very small pool, and the duchess was quickly aware that Sir Harry was the largest landowner and wealthiest man in the colony. She had always had an eye for rich men. In her memoir *The Heart Has Its Reasons*, the duchess observed that this "small but impressive man, with gray curly hair . . . affected a scorn for the conventional niceties . . . in spite of his great affluence."

And Lady Oakes loved to entertain; the Oakeses gave lavish dinner dances in their various residences, sometimes for three hundred guests. In 1941, a society page reported: "This year even the Oakes purse feels a proportionate pinch, and there is the shadow of war to dim too much display. However, the comings and goings at Westbourne [and] their Caves Point villa kept it about as quiet as 42nd St. at high noon." In the absence of much other excitement, the Windsors graciously accepted their invitations.

There was little personal chemistry between Sir Harry and the duchess, despite their shared American birth. For all his riches, Oakes did not appeal to the fiercely snobbish duchess, who privately sneered that he was "our Charlie Chaplin." But the duke, whom she described as "always attracted to the pioneering type," was fascinated by Sir Harry's eagerness to fill swamps and clear land. Besides, Oakes could offer the governor something he dearly wanted: the chance to play golf. The duke wrote to the same American friend to whom he had complained about Government House that the course Sir Harry had laid out close to Westbourne was "flat and very uninteresting . . . but at least one can exercise." The governor played regularly with Oakes and another man who was very keen to cultivate His Royal Highness's friendship: Harold Christie.

Meanwhile, the Government House renovation ground on. The upgrade reflected both the duchess's Parisian tastes and her determination to enhance her husband's job. She summoned a well-known New York designer and gave him carte blanche. He threw out dilapidated wicker chairs, oil paintings of Queen Victoria and Queen Mary, and much of the termite-ridden mahogany furniture, and brought in painters to redo the pale pink stucco exterior, and craftsmen to patch damp-stained ceilings, flaking plasterwork, and crumbling woodwork. A heavy oak door, fabricated in Wales and presented to the duke for his investiture as Prince of Wales in 1911, was installed at the main entrance; a capital *E* and the insignia of the Order of the Garter were emblazoned in gold leaf in a glass panel. Rustic French wallpaper (in smoke grey and banana yellow) and pastel drapes softened the impact of the formal reception rooms, which included a large drawing room and a state dining room with a twenty-six-place dining table. (Purpose-made of Honduran mahogany for the house, it escaped the duchess's purge.) Upstairs, five bedrooms with adjacent sitting rooms were thoroughly refurbished. Rattan furniture was purchased for the duke's bedroom/study, and his possessions carefully unpacked: a rack of fifty pipes, a box made of wood from Nelson's ship the *Victory*, a midshipman's dirk. A new three-storey west wing was added to the building to accommodate the duke's personal staff.

The Nassau House of Assembly had voted a sum of $8,000 to restore Government House; the final cost of the renovations came to $20,000. With some reluctance, the House of Assembly footed most of the bill. The result didn't diminish the duchess's displeasure. "I hate this place more each day," she wrote to her

Aunt Bessie in Baltimore. "We both hate it and the locals are petty-minded, the visitors common and uninteresting." The company of people like Oakes and Christie, and evenings spent at the Bahamas Country Club, were no substitute for the salons of Paris or the Côte d'Azur. The couple appeared to have been almost oblivious to the large majority of the population, black and mixed-race Bahamians, although the latter expressed their welcome in a separate celebration a week after the Windsors set foot in New Providence. Black musician Blind Blake Higgs wrote a hugely popular calypso:

It was love, love alone
Cause King Edward to lose de trone . . .
I know King Edward was noble and great
But it was love that cause him to ablicate [sic]
It was love . . .

THE DUKE OF WINDSOR'S appointment as governor of the Bahamas was indeed a form of exile. Immediately after his abdication, he had expected both a generous allowance from the Civil List (the annual grant from Parliament to the royal family) and a serious job, either within or outside Britain. A senior ambassadorship, he thought, would be an appropriate role. But since the abdication in 1936, his brother had made it clear that the Windsors were unwelcome in Britain. Queen Elizabeth was adamant that the former Wallis Simpson not establish a rival royal court around the former King Edward, because it would inevitably be much flashier than her husband's.

The British government had been increasingly concerned by the former king's Nazi sympathies and admiration for Germany. Wallis Simpson's rumoured premarital affair with the German ambassador in London, Joachim von Ribbentrop, didn't help. (There were countless rumours about Mrs. Simpson, some of them sexist and misogynist, but some undoubtedly true.) From the Windsors' 1938 visit to Hitler's Third Reich, made against the advice of the British government, to their network of friendships with dubious financiers, they were in conflict with government policy. At best, they were appeasers (along with much of Britain's aristocracy and several cabinet ministers); at worst, they were potential traitors, illicitly keeping open channels of communication with the Nazi high command.

The Windsors exacerbated these suspicions. With the onset of war, they fled first to their house on the French Riviera, then through Spain to Portugal. In Lisbon, they had been guests of Ricardo Riberio do Espírito Santo Silva, a well-connected Portuguese banker with both British and German contacts. By now, the duke was a lightning rod for speculation: had he already agreed to be reinstalled as Hitler's puppet on the British throne if the Nazis won the war, with Queen Wallis at his side? Immediately after the Dunkirk disaster, for example, when much of the British army's most modern equipment had been abandoned on Normandy beaches, German diplomats suggested that the Duke of Windsor might mediate peace talks because the Führer trusted him. In official German documents, he was described as the only Englishman who might be "the logical director of England's destiny after the war." There were the beginnings of a German plot ("Operation Willi") to kidnap the duke, and Prime Minister Churchill was warned by one of his ministers that the former king "is well-known to be pro-Nazi and he may become a centre of intrigue."

Eager to remove this potential fifth columnist from the Continent, Winston Churchill chose the Bahamas as the best place for the duke because Churchill regarded it as one of the most distant and insignificant colonies in the British Empire. Even shipping the Windsors to Nassau had been fraught. Unhappy about the posting, the ducal couple announced they would spend a few days in New York City en route, shopping and seeing friends. They were brusquely told that such a stopover was impossible because the Americans were in the midst of a presidential election campaign. The real reason the visit was forbidden was that Churchill didn't want the former king to make mischief with his defeatist attitude and support for a negotiated peace while the British government was pressing the United States to enter the war. So the Windsors bypassed New York and sailed to Bermuda, where they stayed with the governor. After dinner on their first evening there, when the men made their way to the library for brandy and cigars, the duke blurted, "If I had been King, there would have been no war."

So, the reason for the Duke of Windsor's move to the Bahamas was quite different from Sir Harry's motive in settling there, but there was plenty for the two men to talk about. Both belonged to the network of wealthy and titled men who deplored Anglo-German hostilities. And both were obsessed with their finances. Oakes was convinced that everyone was after his fortune; the duke was convinced he had been unfairly robbed of his personal inheritance and was running out of money. By abdicating, he had lost access to royal funds that he had taken for granted as heir apparent and then monarch. Had he remained king, he would have received £425,000 from the Duchy of Lancaster and £2.4 million from the Civil List, and he would have been entitled to a life interest in Sandringham and Balmoral, the two residences that belonged to the royal family and were worth at least £5 million. But there were no provisions, no precedents, for a former king.

The financial negotiations around the abdication had proved more poisonous than anticipated. Before he left the throne,

Edward insisted that his brother should pay him £25,000 a year in return for releasing the two houses to him. He was horrified to discover that he would no longer receive the income from the Duchy of Cornwall and that, as former king, he could not expect anything much from the Civil List. He was still a wealthy man. By 1937, he had amassed from the Duchy of Cornwall, which yielded an annual income of at least £364,000, an estimated £1 million worth of investments and property. His private investments included a substantial portfolio of stocks, managed by the Rothschilds, and his ranch in Canada, with a large herd of shorthorn cattle. But he now found himself cut off from his investments except for the Canadian ranch (which he sold), with an extremely expensive wife and an income far more limited than expected. His salary as a colonial governor was £5,000—a pittance by royal standards. For the rest of his life, he was obsessed with money and remarkably tight-fisted.

ONCE INSTALLED IN Nassau, the Duke of Windsor settled down to the demands of his new job and was good-humoured and enthusiastic in public, despite his exasperation with the triviality of his duties. (He was not alone in this observation. His critics within the Royal Navy joked that he was the only man ever to have gone from being First Lord of the Admiralty to third mate on a tramp.) His most important function was to preside over the weekly meetings of the executive council, which ran the government.

Council members did not impress the new governor, as he made clear in a dispatch back to Westminster. He described his government leader as "sly," the chair of the Development Board as "inarticulate," and a member-at-large as "one of the outstanding crooks both politically and commercially and is universally mistrusted." One of the few men on this all-white body who won his admiration was Harold Christie, of whom he wrote, "A remarkable man having built up a big real estate business from nothing and, by faith that the future of these Islands lies in development by private enterprise, has had the vision to buy up large tracts of land . . . a great proportion of which he has succeeded in persuading wealthy Americans and others to buy." Christie struck the duke as a savvy operator, despite his limited education. "Although Mr. Christie is illiterate as well as inarticulate, and next to useless in the House of Assembly, he is, from contacts with big business in America and as a member of the Development Board, a useful link between my Council and foreign private enterprise, which is so valuable an element in The Bahamas."

In his remarks about race relations, the duke demonstrated the deeply ingrained bigotry of many British aristocrats. He insisted that he himself had no particular prejudice against non-whites, but that the rigid discrimination was "a fence that must not be rushed." This was not a man who intended to challenge the status quo, let alone take such a drastic step as inviting a non-white to join his government. In a dispatch to a senior official in London's Colonial Office, he wrote that "any suggestion of the appointment of a coloured member to Executive Council would not only be unwelcome but meet with the utmost hostility." A large part of the problem, he explained, was that a black member of the council would have to be invited to social functions at Government House, and then his wife would have to be invited too. That would never do. "White Bahamians will not allow their wives to sit down to dinner with coloured people. . . . No one in their right senses would ever be so tactless as to invite coloured people to meet American guests at dinner." During the duke's governorship, no black person was ever allowed through Government House's heavy oak front door. The only blacks allowed in the house were members of the domestic staff, about whom the duchess complained regularly.

By the time the Windsors arrived in Nassau, the British Empire had been at war for nearly a year. To their surprise, they found a way of life almost untouched by the conflict; American tourism had been unaffected, and their own arrival caused an upsurge in wealthy visitors eager to meet them. Residents like the Oakeses, Wenner-Grens, and Sigrists continued the seasonal rounds of cocktail parties, sailing races, and tennis matches; thanks to Sir Harry's polo ground and ponies, polo became a popular specta-tor sport. Various celebrities arrived to relax under the hibiscus and party at the Jungle Club, including Greta Garbo (a guest of Wenner-Gren) and Lorenz Hart, fresh from the success of the Rodgers and Hart Broadway hit *Pal Joey*. The white population's ranks swelled thanks to a motley collection of Europeans eager to sit out the war: aging aristocrats from Central Europe, wives of Royal Air Force (RAF) officers, the young students from Belmont School, Sussex, to whom Sir Harry Oakes lent accommodation.

Under pressure from the Colonial Office in Westminster, the Bahamas government had made generous contributions to the war effort in the form of gifts and loans, and had issued war savings certificates and stamps. Étienne Dupuch, owner and editor of the *Nassau Daily Tribune*, had organized a campaign to send war materials to Britain. Cannons from ancient fortifica-tions and rusting relics from the cotton, salt, and sisal industries were smelted, then shipped east. Sir Harry Oakes underwrote six Spitfires to contribute to the air war waging over Britain. But for most Bahamians, the war was a long way away.

Once settled back in Government House, the new governor and his wife graciously took on roles within the community. Photographs of the duke, in a double-breasted suit, and the duchess, in pearls and white gloves, appeared regularly on the front page of the *Daily Tribune*, as they smiled, shook hands, and presented cups or medals. The duke became patron of the Bahamas Central Branch of the newly established British Red Cross Society, and the duchess became its president. The society met in a building owned by Sir Harry. The duke became the first Bahamian governor to broadcast regularly on the radio, projecting a firm image of a benevolent ruler. He expressed concern at the level of poverty, particularly on the smaller islands, while the duchess established two infant welfare clinics in Nassau's poorer neighbourhoods.

This humdrum tranquility was shattered when the Japanese attacked Pearl Harbor, and the United States entered the war in late 1941. Suddenly the Bahamas, and specifically the island of New Providence, assumed strategic importance for the British and American governments. A year earlier, Harry Oakes had constructed the Oakes Field airstrip, which he then donated to the government. When New Providence was chosen as a base to train US military airmen, an American construction company arrived to develop both Oakes Field and a larger site at the western end of the island that would be a military airfield.

The Pleasantville Construction Company shipped bulldozers, tractors, and building materials to the island to construct and complete the two airfields. The company then brought in white foremen (they stayed in Sir Harry's British Colonial Hotel), appointed two white local contractors to deal with the local workforce, and advertised within the Bahamas for labourers to clear pine forest, grade the runways, and construct airport buildings. Men from all over the Bahamas flocked to New Providence when they heard the promise of jobs, jobs, jobs.

Trouble began almost immediately. Black Bahamians hoped that, since Americans were running "The Project," as it was known, wages would be higher than the subsistence rates paid by local employers. The going rate for unskilled workers in the United States was three dollars a day, and Bahamian labourers expected the equivalent—which, in Bahamian currency, would have been twelve shillings. Instead, they learned they would receive *one* dollar a day—four shillings. That was barely a living wage. Sir Harry Oakes had already upset local contractors by paying his workforce five shillings a day, and the Bay Street Boys were not prepared to allow similar slippage. There were rumours that the Pleasantville Construction Company had been prepared to pay two dollars (eight shillings) a day, but that the two Nassau-based building contractors had nixed that suggestion because it would upset the local economy. The company withdrew its offer.

Outrage erupted at the unfairness. Within days of The Project's start, hundreds of men downed tools. They began a noisy march towards Nassau along the highway linking the two airfields—a road that had been named Burma Road, after the recent British retreat to Burma from China. Police watched the boisterous crowd, with its stentorian battle cry: "Burma Road declare war on de Conchy-Joe." "Conchy-Joe" was slang for white Bahamians, and referred in this angry chant both to the two white building contractors and more generally to the colony's ruling class. Once in Nassau, the crowd slid out of control. Using bottles from a Coca-Cola truck as missiles, young men surged up and down Bay Street, attacking police, breaking windows, and looting the luxury stores. Gold jewellery, Chanel perfumes, and cashmere sweaters were borne off in triumph. Napoleon McPhee, a local stonemason, destroyed a Union Jack. When asked later about his behaviour, he explained, "I willing to fight under the flag, I willing to die under the flag. But I ain't gwine starve under the flag."

The demonstrations and violence continued for three days in early June. Three people were killed during the Burma Road

Riot, and two more died later from wounds. Government officials and Bay Street merchants panicked and demanded a crackdown. Peace was restored only after the Duke of Windsor proved more sympathetic than the merchants to the strikers, and negotiated a free midday meal and a shilling-a-day increase for the Bahamian labourers. Their wages were still less than half those earned by white employees for the same work.

A delegation of three local black leaders arrived for an audience at Government House. It was led by Dr. Claudius Roland Walker, a member of the House of Assembly who had received his medical degree in the States. A short, bald, genial man with protruding eyes, Walker was held in great respect by Bahamians on both sides of the racial divide. During these years, black Bahamians were invariably addressed as either "boy" or "nigger" by whites, regardless of age. But Walker was "Doc" to everybody. Because the delegation members were black, the duke met them in the Government House annex rather than the main drawing room. Undeterred, Dr. Walker told the duke about the misery of Bahamians who were "poorly housed, poorly fed and poorly educated."

Walker radiated dignity as he quietly but forcefully explained how people like Harold Christie had ripped off Bahamians by buying their property cheaply, then selling it at vast profit to North Americans like Harry Oakes. "Many years ago, England and American missionaries walked amongst us intent on souls to save and bodies to enslave, until one day one of my ancestral brothers was forced to remark, 'Fadder, when firs' you come to Bahamas, you had da Bible and we had da land. Today, Fadder, we gat da Bible and you get da land.'"

The Duke of Windsor admired Dr. Walker's oratory but took no steps to alleviate the hopelessness and despair of the labourers. Instead, he reported back to Whitehall that the riot was a clash between the reactionary policies of "certain sections of Bay

Street" on one hand, and "negro agitators" on the other. In private, he paraded his blinkered prejudices by dismissing the leaders of the uprising as "mischief-makers—communists . . . [and] men of Central European Jewish descent, who had secured jobs as a pretext for obtaining a deferment of draft." No evidence supported this claim.

The riot, triggered by poverty and racial tension, foreshadowed growing pressure from the black majority for a greater say in the way the colony was run. Gradually, political parties, including a Progressive Liberal Party and a United Bahamian Party, would emerge. But it would be the 1960s before the Bahamas achieved their first real taste of democracy. Meanwhile, by the end of 1942, jobs were drying up as construction of the airfields neared completion. The Duchess of Windsor wrote to her aunt: "The negroes are busy complaining now that the base is nearing completion and some of them are being laid off. I should not be surprised to see more trouble—but this time one is somewhat prepared and there is enough fire-power on the island to deal with the situation."

Sir Harry Oakes played no role in the Burma Road Riot or its aftermath, although he had a great deal more sympathy for the rioters than for the government. Given that New Providence was already baking in the summer heat, I suspect that the entire Oakes family had followed its customary practice of decamping to their Bar Harbor mansion to enjoy cool Atlantic breezes.

Moreover, Sir Harry was starting to have troubles of his own. For the first time in his life, he turned to the bottle to help him deal with them.

CHAPTER 10

Don Juan from Mauritius

Sir Harry was alone, bored, restless, cranky. He would stay a day or so at The Caves, then a few nights at Westbourne, or in his suite at the British Colonial Hotel. . . . He was a funny old bird [and] clearly troubled. He feared, above all, that the colonial government could not be trusted—that they were about to impose some sort of income tax. Another worry gnawed at him; if something wasn't done soon to improve the lives of the blacks, a terrible rebellion was coming. Nassau was a tinderbox, waiting for a match.

ALFRED DE MARIGNY, A CONSPIRACY OF CROWNS

W herever Harry Oakes went, his reputation as "the man who owns a gold mine" preceded him. At its peak, the Oakes fortune was widely rumoured to have reached $200 million, although this was the total value of Lake Shore shares, of which he owned only half. Yet this latter-day Midas made little effort to learn how to manage his fortune, other than in tax-avoidance schemes. Like his friend and fellow mining millionaire Bill Wright back in Canada, he continued to regard almost everybody who wanted to be either his friend or his financial adviser as on the make. Instead, he left most of his substantial dividends to accumulate in his Bahamian holding companies. Only his new friends Harold Christie and Walter Foskett had somehow earned his trust, and now Oakes and Christie used the Bahamian companies as piggy banks for property deals on New Providence.

While Oakes tore around a minor British colony on a tractor, the young country of Canada had emerged as one of the most important sources of metals in the world. Toronto was still a dreary city dominated by thin-lipped WASPs, but it was becoming a global leader in one niche: mining stocks. The Toronto Stock Exchange's predominance in that sector enabled it to blow past its glitzier Montreal rival. The city's financial district filled up with the industry's corporate headquarters, plus offices housing mining consultants, lawyers, and engineers. At a time when sky-high unemployment and the complete collapse of the wheat market pushed much of the rest of the continent into despair and the Depression, mines were a bright light in the Ontario economy. The profits and production of goldfields in Northern Ontario were barely dented by the 1929 crash, which devastated every other sector of the stock market.

In the following grim decade gold did even better, as speculators began to hoard it. Oakes's fortune got an unforeseen boost when President Franklin Roosevelt raised the price of gold in order to devalue the dollar during the Depression. For decades, the price of an ounce of gold had been fixed at $20.67, but by 1935 it was $35 an ounce, and Harry Oakes's annual dividends had skyrocketed. No wonder he had been able to buy one-quarter of New Providence Island. No wonder that, back in Canada, there had been another surge of development in Kirkland Lake. In 1937 the seven Kirkland Lake mines paid out $20.26 million in dividends and bonuses.

But every mine gets worked out, and Lake Shore was no exception. Its manager had instructed engineers to keep digging farther and farther down, and some shafts were now more than 2 kilometres deep. However, despite 160 kilometres of underground workings, the mine's output had peaked in 1934. Now profits were nosediving, from $7,732,417 in 1937–38 to $2 million in 1942. The payouts that arrived each quarter in Oakes's account at the Royal Bank of Canada's Nassau branch were still substantial, but they were shrinking at an alarming rate. They contracted further in 1942 when Ottawa declared that gold mining was not an industry essential to the war effort. This meant that Lake Shore Mines could no longer get supplies or compete for men and materials with mines producing essential metals. Lake Shore's workforce shrivelled to fewer than a thousand older workers.

As the latter-day Midas saw his fortune dwindle, he became more obsessive than ever about protecting his wealth. Ever since the outbreak of war, Sir Harry had foreseen trouble. All British subjects were required to declare their holdings in foreign property or securities so that these might be mobilized if exchange ran short. Would the British government lean on its colonies for additional support for the war effort, or on British subjects living abroad for foreign exchange? In either eventuality, as a British subject, Sir Harry Oakes would end up at the mercy of the British tax collector.

Oakes's lack of financial sophistication meant that his portfolio was incoherent. He distrusted the stock market far too much to have invested much of his fortune there; he preferred tangible assets like real estate. His residences in England and Florida remained good investments, but the money he had used to buy property in the Bahamas, encouraged by and often in partnership with Harold Christie, was speculative—and now locked up in the Bahamian corporations he had set up. He was said to have kept a portion of his immense wealth in the form of napoleons, sovereigns, and other gold coins, giving rise to constant rumours in England, Canada, and the Bahamas that he had buried his fortune somewhere. Oakes had already talked about pulling out of the Bahamas and moving to Central America, out of reach of tax collectors. Would the war accelerate his plans?

Sir Harry Oakes was not the only person in New Providence who was thinking about his investments. The war had already damaged the financial empire of another Bahamian tax exile: Axel Wenner-Gren.

Wenner-Gren is one of those individuals who haunt the margins of history, because during their lifetimes their considerable wealth gave them access to power. Like Oakes, he had been attracted to the Bahamas by the absence of income tax, and he had made himself welcome in the colony by investing in seafood and fishing businesses on the island of Grand Bahama, and by developing his 700 acres on Hog Island, just off Nassau. But his close connections to German businessmen and politicians had been tracked carefully for years. The FBI had a fat file on him, and various senior Americans, including Under Secretary of State Sumner Welles and President Roosevelt's close adviser Harry Hopkins, were convinced that he was close to the German high command and, in Hopkins's words, "violently pro-Nazi."

Did this access translate into influence? He had offered unsolicited advice during the 1930s to British, American, and German officials on how to secure peace, and he cast himself as a high-class middleman between governments. But his impact is uncertain. His "friend" Field Marshal Hermann Göring wrote in his diary that Wenner-Gren was a "meddling Swede." And British diplomats in Sweden scoffed at the American allegations; in their view, Wenner-Gren was "generally disliked and regarded as a pompous ass, but not guilty of any worse offences than extravagance, attempted social climbing and tax dodging."

Nevertheless, the rumours about Wenner-Gren's sympathies fuelled wild conjecture in the Bahamas concerning his activities on Hog Island. He had hired hundreds of labourers to excavate a network of canals across the island, as well as a safe harbour in which vessels might shelter from tropical hurricanes. A whisper campaign suggested that these waterways were intended to shelter a fleet of German submarines, and that Hog Island might become a U-boat base. By 1942, U-boats were active in the Gulf of Mexico and off the eastern coast of the United States. After the war, this chatter was dismissed as ridiculous (the canals were too shallow for submarines), but it helped ratchet up the surreal atmosphere of wartime Nassau as well as the distrust of the Swedish tycoon.

Axel Wenner-Gren had met the Duke of Windsor briefly in Paris, before the war, and during their first months in the colony the Windsors were happy to socialize with this charming and cosmopolitan European. The Swedish multimillionaire put his large yacht, the *Southern Cross*, at their disposal for a trip to Miami, and he and the duke enjoyed long conversations. "In many respects we share the same opinions," Wenner-Gren noted in his diary, in a likely reference to their pro-German views. So it came as a shock to the governor when he received a warning from Westminster that Wenner-Gren was an unsuitable companion. Prime Minister Churchill himself advised the duke that the Swede was "a pro-German International Financier with strong leanings towards appeasement, and suspected of being in communication with the enemy."

The duke demanded evidence to support this assertion, but none was forthcoming. So he and his wife continued to enjoy cocktails at Wenner-Gren's home, and outings on the *Southern*

Cross, until their host was abruptly blacklisted by both the United States and Britain in April 1941 and fled New Providence to avoid arrest. His assets in the Royal Bank of Canada were frozen, and he was banned from dealing with brokers or bankers, and forbidden to return to the Bahamas during the war. He retreated to his house in Cuernavaca, Mexico, and continued to run his financial empire from there and stay in touch with the Windsors. This confirmed British suspicions. Although Mexico was nominally neutral, the British regarded it as very unfriendly (the country had appropriated all British oil interests there, with no offers of compensation), and diplomatic relations had been severed.

A month before Wenner-Gren's departure, the Duke of Windsor had already committed a diplomatic blunder when he received a sixteen-person delegation from Mexico at Government House. The delegation included a sinister business associate of Wenner-Gren's: General Maximino Ávila Camacho, governor of the Mexican province of Puebla, brother of the president of Mexico, and a man with a murderous reputation.

Camacho had been welcomed to Nassau by none other than Harold Christie and Harry Oakes. A photo of the three beefy middle-aged men, taken just after the general had stepped out of a private plane, shows that this was a serious occasion—all three wore shirts, ties, jackets, pressed pants, and dress shoes, despite the heat. Camacho was a guest of Oakes at the British Colonial Hotel, and Oakes (who had already talked about moving his fortune outside British territory, so likely wanted to get to know this influential politician) took him to Government House.

There was another person present at that meeting: Montgomery Hyde, then an MI6 officer quietly engaged in counter-espionage work, who was in Nassau to discuss security with the governor. Hyde realized that the meeting concerned a scheme to transfer funds from Nassau to Mexico City—although this contravened British foreign exchange controls that applied to all Bahamian residents, including the governor. Shocked by the blatant illegality of this initiative, Hyde arranged for an immigration officer to check the passports of the Mexican visitors. One of Camacho's colleagues turned out to be on the FBI blacklist, wanted for un-American activities.

The complicated web of connections between the Duke of Windsor, Wenner-Gren, Christie, and Oakes, plus General Camacho, would lead to speculation about illicit transfers of currency and gold designed to put them beyond the reach of the British government. Philip Ziegler, biographer of the Duke of Windsor, brushes off talk of the duke's involvement as "nonsense." Since there is no reliable evidence, he argues, "there is no reason to believe anything so picturesque." Ziegler also argues that the Duke of Windsor's relationship with Axel Wenner-Gren was entirely innocent, and that the duke was misused.

But this defence of the Duke of Windsor is disingenuous, if not dishonest. The duke, anxious as always about his finances, had already made the outrageous demand to London that he should be exempt from the British requirement to register his holdings in foreign property or securities. And for Sir Harry Oakes, any scheme that put his money out of reach of the British taxman had a powerful appeal. Gossip about shady financial dealings between these men was not too far-fetched.

AROUND THIS TIME, it appears that Sir Harry Oakes had begun to drink. Given that he had been a teetotaller for the first four decades of his adult life, he didn't have much tolerance for alcohol. But his wobbling fortune was not his only worry; there was another family matter that might have prompted him to reach for the bottle. In 1942, two days after her eighteenth birthday, his eldest daughter, Nancy, had eloped with a man nearly twice her age: "Count" Marie Alfred Fouquereaux de Marigny, who had already accumulated two ex-wives. Tall, dark-haired, and athletic, with a gleaming smile and suave manner, Freddie de Marigny was everything that Sir Harry despised. To a man whose callused hands proved how hard he had worked for his wealth, Freddie was an insolent playboy and fortune hunter. And the man whose social manners had been honed in Kirkland Lake's frontier society had little experience dealing with such a racy charmer, who openly sneered at the millionaire's lack of class.

De Marigny had first arrived in the Bahamas in the late 1930s, hoping to escape scandal. His own background is hard to track because he gave wildly divergent accounts of himself. The memoir he published in 1946, *More Devil Than Saint*, is repeatedly contradicted by a second memoir that he published in 1990, *A Conspiracy of Crowns*. Both state that, soon after his birth in 1910 into a grand French-speaking family on the British island of Mauritius, in the Indian Ocean, his mother (from whom he inherited his title) deserted his father for another man. Young Freddie apparently suffered both the resulting social stigma and his father's bitterness. Depending on which account a reader believes, he went on to attend school on the island and then in Paris, or he was educated in Normandy and went on to study at the University of Cambridge. In the 1946 account, he mentions his first wife, a young French woman, but by 1990 she has vanished from the story.

Why de Marigny felt the need to rewrite his life story is not of concern: if, as I've mentioned, a skilful selection of facts is crucial to biography, memoir is even more malleable. Memoirs tend to be idealized versions of their writers' lives, in which all decisions are retroactively justified and motives are scrubbed pure. Manipulating the impression we make on readers is a very human impulse, especially when, as in this case, the author probably suffered significant insecurities after an unhappy childhood. The significance of de Marigny's behaviour here is that it explains why people hesitated to trust him. He was a little too slippery with the truth.

Both of de Marigny's memoirs agree that in London, his debonair figure was a fixture at society and sporting events in the early 1930s, and that he established a formidable reputation as a yachtsman. In those days, as he recalled in his 1990 memoir, "London was a paradise for a bachelor. Money, a good address, and a Savile Row tailor were considered the essential assets." He began to dabble in business, and did well. Next, de Marigny moved to New York, where he embarked on an affair with Ruth Fahnestock, the wife of his stockbroker. Soon, Ruth had divorced her husband and married what a New York gossip columnist described as "a Don Juan from Mauritius." The couple moved to a house on the Bahamian island of Eleuthera, but the marriage soon went downhill and the de Marignys divorced. They continued to occupy the same house for a period in 1940, but Freddie spent most of his time in Nassau.

In the Bahamian capital, de Marigny invested in real estate (thanks to Harold Christie), built and sold a beachfront apartment block, bought a grocery, and started a chicken farm, where he worked alongside his black employees as they built henhouses and fences. He owned a Star-class yacht, a challenging 6.9-metre keelboat that he loved to race, and he named it *Concubine* (a name, he bragged, that raised "a few eyebrows at the stuffy Royal Nassau Sailing Club"). He was soon winning trophies throughout the Caribbean, and fist pumping with triumph for the benefit of press cameras. Accompanying him on many of these adventures was his cousin, Georges de Visdelou-Guimbeau, who radiated the same air of aristocratic entitlement. In Nassau, the two men shared a home on Victoria Avenue, a palm-lined street of old-fashioned wooden houses close to the harbour, where they partied hard.

Few of the other wealthy expatriates in Nassau warmed to Freddie de Marigny. The colony's English-speaking white elite were appalled by this handsome newcomer with a French accent. He broke too many rules. They didn't like the fact he had Jewish friends, to whom he rented apartments. They disapproved of the way that he and his cousin, both in their thirties, liked to date teenage girls. (There was talk that they drugged them, then raped them.) They disapproved of his familiarity with his black employees. They were confused by the way he delivered chickens to their kitchens in the morning, then sat down to eat the same chickens at their tables in the evening. They found his devil-may-care attitude irritating. (His motto was *Loué par ceci, blamé par cela. Me moquant des sots, bravant les méchants, je me presse de rire de toute peur d'être obligé d'en pleurer.* Praised here, scolded there. Disdaining the fools, defying the rogues, I am forced to laugh for fear I might be obliged to weep.)

Perhaps most shocking to anglophilic Bahamians was de Marigny's undisguised contempt for the governor, of whom he had once remarked loudly, "He is not my favourite ex-King of England." There were various run-ins between the two men, and de Marigny took pride in coming out on top. In his second memoir, he insisted "it was not true" that he never missed a chance to taunt the duke, "but most of the episodes clearly ended in [my] favour." After a fire at a Nassau liquor store, for example, de Marigny swiftly made arrangements with the owner to buy five rescued cases of Hennessy Five-Star cognac, which had come from occupied France and which he knew the duke himself had planned to acquire. The duke sent his aide-de-camp, George Woods, over to ask if de Marigny could spare a couple of cases.

Captain Woods made it clear that the governor expected the cases as a gift. De Marigny laughed at such an idea, but suggested an outrageous price if the duke was so interested. Captain Woods responded, "I have never heard such rubbish," and took his leave.

Despite such behaviour, de Marigny had his charms. He was wealthy, he had a title (a courtesy title unmentioned in the *Almanach de Gotha*, but it still gave him a hint of blue blood), and his sailing skills were much admired. His wolfish grin and sense of fun proved irresistible to the younger nightclub set.

In subsequent accounts, both Freddie de Marigny and Nancy Oakes enjoyed casting their relationship in storybook terms—the maiden who conquered a Casanova. By 1942, Nancy Oakes was a slim, attractive teenager, red-haired and long-limbed, with her mother's height and her father's square jaw, and a reckless determination to escape from her protective parents. Since her mid-teens, she had watched Freddie de Marigny sailing to victory in the *Concubine* and dancing at the British Colonial Hotel with the island's most glamorous women. She developed such a crush on him that she learned everything she could about him: the trophies he had won, the properties he owned, the names of his ex-wives.

At first, de Marigny had been oblivious to this lanky, freckled youngster. But then he began to notice that her eyes were constantly following him. What could be more flattering? Soon they were clinking champagne glasses, and de Marigny had decided she was "like a filly who needed taming." Nancy was attending school in New York, and Freddie followed her there. On a breezy spring day, May 19, 1942, they walked together to a Bronx attorney's office, where they were married. Afterwards, the third Mrs. de Marigny telephoned her parents and told them her news. Her mother was in Niagara Falls at the time, and her father was in Nassau. The storybook romance theme did not cut much ice with either of them. "We were frightfully upset," Lady Oakes would recall. "She was only a child, she was still at school. We knew that Alfred was divorced." But they loved their daughter and at first they tried to make the best of things.

The newlyweds were invited to the Oakes summer property in Maine so that de Marigny might be formally welcomed into the family. In Bar Harbor, Freddie met Nancy's three younger brothers—Sydney, William, and Harry, now aged fifteen, twelve, and nine. He taught them and their thirteen-year-old sister Shirley how to sail. He assured his father-in-law that he had sufficient means to keep his new wife in appropriate style. Sir Harry took his new son-in-law to Foxcroft, showed him his birthplace, and introduced him to his brother Louis, now a prosperous timber merchant. Conversations were cordial; in fact, Sir Harry appeared to like Freddie's energy and disregard for rank. De Marigny records Sir Harry as saying, "Frenchie, you and I think alike. We both have a hell of a temper, but that's a good thing."

But the relationship soon hit some very jagged rocks. The de Marignys decided to travel to Mexico for a prolonged honeymoon, and while they were there, Nancy first developed typhoid fever and then severe gum disease. Her head was shaved and her mouth required extensive surgery. When she had finally recovered sufficiently to rejoin her family in the Palm Beach house, her parents were horrified to discover that, despite her continued frailty, she was pregnant. Lady Oakes decided that Marigny had forced himself on his wife while she was still recovering from dental surgery. Over de Marigny's protests, they insisted that their daughter have an abortion because her health was endangered. They may also have felt de Marigny's marital track record made him unfit to be a father. Nancy caved, and agreed to abort the pregnancy. De Marigny was furious. In his second memoir, he explained his conduct in lofty terms: "My Catholic training asserted itself. . . .

I saw the issue then as a moral one . . . and a test to see who controlled my young wife."

There were further rows. De Marigny would later claim that he asked the lawyer Walter Foskett, whom his wife called "Uncle Walter," to intercede with Sir Harry on his behalf. But Foskett responded that he was "nothing but a skunk" who had no business marrying a woman so much younger than he. Foskett had in his possession a disturbing letter to Lady Oakes from Ruth Fahnestock, Nancy's predecessor, which had arrived at Foskett's Palm Beach office. The letter suggested that de Marigny's capital all came from his second wife, which confirmed Sir Harry and Lady Oakes's suspicion that their new son-in-law was a fortune hunter. Fahnestock also claimed that she was pregnant by her former husband even as he was in the throes of getting married to Nancy. (There is no evidence of a birth.) Foskett refused to show de Marigny the letter, and he also withheld the letter from Lady Oakes, although he told her its contents over the phone.

De Marigny could see that Foskett would give him no help. Tired of being rebuffed, he stormed away and flew back to the Bahamas. Nancy followed a week later.

That fall, once everybody was back in Nassau, there were attempts to patch over the tensions. But both Sir Harry and Freddie de Marigny were proud men who needed to win every battle. Nancy's obvious affection for her husband, and Eunice's concern for her daughter, got lost in the clash of male egos. One evening, the Oakes family and the de Marignys were invited to a cocktail party at the governor's mansion, but Freddie and Nancy did not turn up. Sir Harry went straight from the party to de Marigny's house to find out why they hadn't attended. Insouciant as ever, de Marigny simply shrugged, "Aw, to hell with the duke." His father-in-law flew into a fury. According to de Marigny, Sir Harry started screaming in the street, "That's the whole trouble with you stupid young fools! You'll never learn, will you, that in a small place like this you can't go around saying, 'The hell with everybody.' You've been doing that sort of thing too long around here, God damn you!"

There were other incidents, all of which would be endlessly rehashed in the months ahead. Some of the clashes smacked of melodrama. Sydney Oakes told his brother-in-law that once, as Sir Harry drove away after bellowing insults at de Marigny, he told him, "Not a bad sort, de Marigny. You have got to get to know these Frenchies." On other occasions, Sir Harry was suspected of being drunk when he banged on his son-in-law's door. One time, it was five o'clock in the morning when he arrived to demand that his son Sydney, who was spending the night with his sister, get dressed and come home. De Marigny appears to have shrugged off the rough treatment, but he made no conciliatory overtones. And Sir Harry Oakes, who adored his eldest child, had no idea how to heal the breach by being more conciliatory. As a man who had made his fortune entirely through his own efforts and single-minded determination, he had never mastered the art of negotiation.

Nancy de Marigny was in the worst position, under constant pressure to choose between husband and father. Although it was widely assumed that de Marigny had married her for her money, both he and Nancy always insisted that this was never part of the attraction. De Marigny noted in his 1990 memoir that he had turned down offers from his father-in-law of both a home and a 1,000-acre plot of land, ready for development. A year after her marriage, Nancy told her mother in a letter that she was sending back a gift of £2,000 in British War Loan bonds that Eunice had given her, unless her family accepted her husband.

THE GOSSIP AND family dramas were trivial when compared with the wartime tragedies and losses that thousands of other families were absorbing. On the other side of the Atlantic, the conflict had reached a grim stage by early July 1943. Allied troops were completing the North African campaign, in which 400,000 Allied and Axis troops were killed or injured, and they were preparing to invade Italy. The headlines in British and American newspapers spoke of the impending troop landings in Sicily and hinted at tensions between President Roosevelt and Prime Minister Churchill over strategy. It was nearly four years since war had been declared, and in the words of Eugene Dupuch, assistant editor of the *Nassau Daily Tribune*, the little British colony was "no longer an international playground. It was just a grim and distant outpost of an empire at war." The tourist trade had come to a standstill, and Bay Street was half-deserted in the heat.

Unlike her husband, Lady Oakes had fallen out of love with the Bahamas, and she preferred to spend both summer and winter months at their other properties. She had not set foot in New Providence since the late spring of the previous year. There was speculation that the Oakeses' marriage was in trouble; they were frequently apart, and Nassau observers had noted Sir Harry's wandering eye and increasing thirst. He had promised to join Lady Oakes in Bar Harbor for the month of July, admitting that Atlantic breezes were preferable to Nassau's hot, sticky summer. However, first he had some business to complete.

By June, Nancy de Marigny had followed her mother off the island; still recovering from illnesses contracted during the Mexico honeymoon, she had enrolled in a summer dance course with Martha Graham at Bennington College, the expensive liberal arts college in Vermont. Her husband, like her father, remained in Nassau; de Marigny was busy with his chicken farm.

Sir Harry's latest project was to make New Providence more self-sufficient in food. He had recently discovered a flock of hardy sheep in Cuba and imported 1,500 of them. Golfers on Oakes's course next to Cable Beach were not happy about this new scheme, since the sheep were grazing on the course. A poem appeared on the front page of the *Daily Tribune*:

> *There seems a lot of grumbling from the golfers by the sea,*
> *Who follow little pilules round the course at Cable B.,*
> *They criticize the livestock browsing quietly on the*
>   *green;*
> *When putting, curse the cards they leave which scarcely*
>   *can be seen.*
> *The players call them Oakes acorns . . .*

The animals turned out to be infected with screw-worm fly, and eventually all died.

On the first Wednesday in July, the sky was so overcast that everyone knew a thunderstorm must be on its way. Drained by the humidity, Nassau's residents went about their business in slow motion. Sir Harry had already confirmed his ticket to leave the island the following day and travel to Bar Harbor to spend the summer there with Eunice, teenagers Sydney, William, and Shirley, and ten-year-old Harry. This would be Sir Harry's last full day in the Bahamas for several weeks.

In the early afternoon, he dropped into Harold Christie's real estate office on Bay Street to suggest that his friend come and admire his sheep the following morning, before his departure. Christie, always happy to oblige his friend and best client, and perhaps hoping for improved publicity for Sir Harry's latest scheme, suggested that they invite someone from the *Daily Tribune* to join them. Both Étienne Dupuch, the editor, and Raymond Moss, a reporter, were keen. Dupuch agreed to appear at Sir Harry's house the next day.

Next, Sir Harry and Christie drove back to Westbourne, the Oakes residence, where the two men played mixed-doubles tennis with Christie's young niece Sally Sawyer and her friend Veronica McMahon. For all his expanded girth and advancing age, Sir Harry could still serve an ace. Guests arrived for cocktails: Charles Hubbard, a Woolworth executive who had retired to Nassau and was Oakes's neighbour, and Mrs. Dulcibel Henneage, wife of a British Army officer, who was rumoured to be having an affair with Harold Christie. After gin and tonics, the two younger women left; Sir Harry suggested that Hubbard and Mrs. Henneage, nicknamed "Effie," stay for dinner.

Freddie de Marigny was also hosting a dinner party that night, at his house on Victoria Avenue. He had returned home from the yacht club in high spirits, after a windy sail in *Concubine* and then a drink at the Prince George Hotel. Oblivious to the dangerously sullen clouds and threat of a tropical storm, he invited several guests to dinner at his house, including Alfred Ceretta, an American engineer involved in the airport construction. At the Prince George bar, de Marigny had discovered Ceretta enjoying cocktails with Dorothy Clarke and Jean Ainslie, wives of RAF officers, who were promptly added to the dinner party. Eventually, eleven people would sit down at de Marigny's table, including his cousin Georges de Visdelou (his friends usually omitted Guimbeau, the final part of his name) and Georges's lively blond girlfriend, Betty Roberts, the seventeen-year-old cashier at the local cinema.

Although de Marigny himself rarely drank, he had a reputation as a generous host, and as the wind rattled windows and blew palm fronds down the street outside, his butler, Harris, was kept busy filling everybody else's glasses with excellent wines. When the electric lights failed towards the end of the evening, Harris quickly brought in two candles and some hurricane lamps. There was laughter as de Marigny reached to light them, and inadvertently singed his hand on the flame.

A deluge of tropical rain had begun by 12:50 a.m., when most of the guests departed. Ten minutes later, the host and the two remaining stragglers, the RAF wives, got in his car for the short drive back to their rented cottage on Cable Beach, just beyond Westbourne. They left de Visdelou, who said he would take Roberts home later, although he was already complaining of a cold. De Marigny swished off in his Lincoln Continental through the storm, which was now approaching hurricane force, with Clarke and Ainslie next to him on the front seat, peering at the road as the windshield wipers battled the downpour. He would later describe how he dropped the two women off just after 1:20, then drove home and went straight to bed because he knew he had a busy day on the chicken farm the following day. But his sleep was disturbed, he would report, first by the sound of his cousin Georges de Visdelou driving off in his Chevrolet to take Betty Roberts home, and then by Georges's return. Georges's cat had been playing with the blind in de Marigny's bedroom, and de Marigny shouted at his cousin to take the cat away. De Visdelou obliged.

Sir Harry Oakes's party was more subdued. After a quick dinner, he and his guests settled down to a couple of games of Chinese checkers. His guests could all hear the wind blowing outside, the rain pelting down, and the sea pounding on Cable Beach. Around eleven o'clock, Hubbard offered to drive Mrs. Henneage back to her house in Nassau, where she lived with her three children and their nanny, before the storm worsened. Harold Christie, a frequent visitor to Westbourne, asked his host if he might spend the night there. Sir Harry likely just shrugged; Christie had slept there the previous night, too, and Mrs. Ellis, the housekeeper, left a guest room prepared for him. By 11:30, all the Westbourne domestic staff had gone home, leaving Oakes and Christie alone in the house as the rain drummed on the flat roof.

Both men went up to Sir Harry's bedroom on the second floor, where Christie settled down with a whisky to chat with his host. However, Oakes put on his pyjamas, climbed into bed, pulled the mosquito netting around him, and turned on the radio to show he wasn't interested in conversation. Christie knew his friend's habits well. He picked up the latest issue of *Time* magazine and said, "Good night." Leaving his friend's bedroom by the door leading to the upper porch, he darted through the gusts of wind and rain squalls, past the door to another bedroom, and then into the bedroom at the far end of the building. It was close to midnight. Later, he would recall that he had a wakeful night, disturbed first by mosquitoes that had got inside his netting, and then by the thunderous rainstorm.

Sheets of sibilant summer rain hissed across Cable Beach, pockmarking the white sands, roaring through Westbourne's tall casuarinas and palms, and slithering in gurgling rivulets over the soggy ground. The literary term pathetic fallacy, which means ascribing to nature a link to human behaviour and emotion, might have been invented for the night of July 7 on the island of New Providence. As the storm raged, somebody murdered Sir Harry Oakes by cracking open his skull with a square-tipped hammer, and then searing his flesh with flames.

PART THREE

LOSING
IT

CHAPTER 11

Suspect Number One

Today's sitting in the preliminary investigation into the charge of murder against Alfred de Marigny opened with a dullness in keeping with the sultry weather, but gradually developed a rumbling crescendo and finally exploded with a flourish of legal ballistics. . . . The sweltering audience sat entranced.

NASSAU DAILY TRIBUNE, AUGUST 17, 1943

B y the time Sir Harry's cook arrived to prepare breakfast the following morning, the storm had blown itself out and Westbourne's lush garden steamed from the overnight drenching. Around seven o'clock, Christie padded along the upper porch to Oakes's bedroom. His intention, he would later explain, was to wake his host and remind him of their meeting with the *Nassau Daily Tribune*'s editor and reporter.

An appalling sight lay behind the bedroom door.

"I went into the room and saw some smoke," Christie testified later. "Then I rushed to the bed and found Sir Harry with his clothing burned off. There were several raw spots on his body. 'For God's sake, Harry,' I shouted, and shook him. The body was still warm. I lifted his head and put a pillow under it, took a glass of water and put some in his mouth. I got a towel and wet it, wiped his face, hoping to revive him. I thought him still alive."

But Sir Harry Oakes was dead. Very dead. His body was battered, bloody, and unmoving. There were four puncture marks behind his left ear, and three of them had fractured his skull. A smoke-smudged Chinese screen near the bed was splattered with drops of blood, and there were blood spatters on the carpet, and streaks of blood on the bedroom and hall walls. An inflammable fluid, probably kerosene, had been splashed on the bed and the carpet: the perpetrator had then set it alight and turned on the electric fan, presumably to fan the flames. The fan had also scattered feathers from a torn pillow; many had settled on the charred corpse.

Christie later described how he rushed out onto the porch and yelled for help. Nobody responded. Next, he ran downstairs to the telephone and began making frantic calls—to a neighbour, to his brother, Frank, and to Colonel Erskine-Lindop, commissioner of the Bahamas' small police force. When he put the receiver down, the phone rang immediately. The *Tribune*'s Étienne Dupuch was on the line, wanting to confirm that 9 a.m. meeting. Christie blurted out the news. Sharp-eyed, dark-skinned Dupuch had newspapers in his blood: his father had founded the *Tribune* with a small treadle press and one case of type forty years earlier. Étienne, who had begun his own career at the age of five, selling his father's papers, managed an adroit balancing act: he appealed to both the Bay Street Boys and native Bahamian readers by combining excellent reporting with progressive views. Now his professional instincts kicked in.

"This is a very big news story, Mr. Christie," he said. "And I'm a journalist."

At Westbourne, a succession of officials and friends turned

up all morning. Amongst the first to arrive was the local physician, Dr. Hugh Quackenbush, who had been summoned by Madeline Gale Kelly, wife of Sir Harry's business manager, who lived in a cottage on the Westbourne estate. (Newell Kelly was away on a fishing trip that week.) The doctor went straight to Sir Harry's bedroom and took note of the thin pall of soot everywhere, a small patch of mattress that still smouldered, and the charred remnants of the frame for the mosquito net. After sticking his index finger into the most severe head wound, he announced that the skull had been fractured at the spot. Sir Harry had been killed between 2:45 and 5:15 a.m., he estimated, and went on to state that some of the burns on his face and body had been sustained before death because they had left blisters on the skin. He pronounced Oakes dead.

Meanwhile, Colonel Erskine-Lindop had called Major Herbert Pemberton, deputy commissioner of the colony's police, and told him to get to Westbourne immediately. Then the colonel made a more delicate call, to Government House, and asked to speak to the governor. When the Duke of Windsor heard the news of Sir Harry's death, he made an instant decision that, in retrospect, was unwise—the latest in a lifetime of ill-advised decisions by the former king. Assuming that the case was beyond the capacity of Nassau's police resources (four officers and 140 constables), he looked elsewhere for help. The appropriate source of sophisticated expertise for a British colony was the criminal investigation unit at London's Scotland Yard. Given the distance and the wartime circumstances, there might have been a case for turning to the Federal Bureau of Investigation in Washington. But the governor does not appear to have considered these options. Instead, he placed a quick call to the Miami Police Department. On his recent visit to Florida, he had been escorted by a local detective named Captain Edward Melchen, whom he had found to be a very good fellow. He asked the chief of Miami's police force to send Captain Melchen over to Nassau.

The duke then announced that no word of Sir Harry's death should leave the island. Too late: Étienne Dupuch had already telegraphed the Associated Press in Miami, and the sensational story was winging its way around the world. The brutal death of the Canadian multimillionaire was on front pages from Miami to Manchester, New York to Sydney. Bulletins from Sicily and Italy, where the Allies were battling Axis troops, had to compete against the police photos of Oakes's corpse, which Dupuch had somehow got hold of, and speculation about the identity of the murderer. In Britain, where newsprint was rationed and *The Times* was down to four pages, the story displaced war news in the headlines. In the United States, where there was no rationing, the coverage was extensive.

Thousands of kilometres to the north, the newspaper in remote Kirkland Lake reprinted every item the editor could find about its most famous mine owner. The *Northern News* mourned his death, and deplored the way he was being belittled as a symbol of "autocratic wealth." In the North, wrote the paper's editor, "the courage of this man who surmounted innumerable obstacles to bring his mine into production will live on and serve as an example to other men facing similar problems." But there was little hope of such fond memories warming up other accounts of Oakes's life. The crime had all the elements of the perfect international tabloid story: a brutal killing, the involvement of a member of the British royal family, a glimpse into the world of plutocrats, and despite the lack of an obvious suspect, much gossip about motives. Within hours, reporters were on their way to Nassau.

—

DURING THE TRIAL three months later of the only suspect who was ever tried for the murder, the details of events after the discovery of Sir Harry's charred body were described in court by various witnesses. This makes it easy for a biographer to track how July 8 unfolded. The presiding judge, Chief Justice Sir Oscar Daly, wrote everything down, by fountain pen in black ink, in two leatherbound volumes, which I and several others have thumbed through in the Nassau Archives. (He was a slow writer, which meant the hearings took a long time.) Far easier to follow than the judge's handwriting are the accounts that appeared in the *Nassau Daily Tribune* each day, which were subsequently published in book form in 1959. Étienne Dupuch and his son Eugene covered both the preliminary hearing in front of a magistrate and the subsequent murder trial in front of Justice Daly. Both men evidently had excellent shorthand skills, and they conscientiously transcribed both statements and cross-examinations.

Reading the Dupuchs' accounts, it is obvious that Westbourne rapidly turned into a circus on July 8, 1943, and confusion amongst the shocked officials ensured shoddy police work. The attorney general, the commissioner of the police, three local detectives, and Harold Christie all tramped along the porch and through Sir Harry's bedroom, taking photos of the corpse and of the blood spatters. There was blood on the door handle of Harold Christie's bedroom, but no indication of how it got there. At first, entry to the second floor of Westbourne was unrestricted, so various friends and neighbours also arrived to gape at the crime scene, disturbing the evidence as they speculated in hushed tones about what had gone on. Bloody footprints were obliterated, while visitors left their fingerprints on lamps, chairs, doors, and windows.

Next to arrive at Westbourne was Freddie de Marigny. He had been driving into Nassau from his chicken farm when, he claimed, an acquaintance had shouted at him, "Have you heard? Harry Oakes is dead." De Marigny went immediately to Westbourne. He did not go upstairs, but he did go across to the Kelly cottage, where Mrs. Kelly told him what had happened. A couple of hours later, the corpse, wrapped in a bedsheet, was carried out of the house and transported by ambulance to the hospital. Meanwhile, de Marigny sent a cable to his wife in Vermont, telling her to contact her mother. Harold Christie called Lady Oakes in Bar Harbor to confirm the dreadful news. De Marigny then took the receiver and passed along his sympathies, according to his 1946 memoir: "She was upset, but pleasant and cordial."

In the afternoon, Captain Edward Melchen, the Miami detective summoned by the governor, arrived at the airport, along with his colleague Captain James Barker, a fingerprint expert. In theory, the two Americans had impeccable qualifications for this assignment. Fifty-year-old Melchen, a short, broad-shouldered man with a chubby face and wire-rimmed glasses, stomped off the plane, radiating confidence. He was chief of Miami's homicide bureau, and during the course of five hundred homicide investigations, according to the *Miami Herald*, had handled "confidence men, pickpockets, cases of burglary, forgery, arson, robbery, counterfeiting and postal violations."

Barker, taller, fitter, and ten years younger, outdid his colleague in terms of swagger because he worked on the leading edge of forensics: fingerprint evidence. Fingerprints were as crucial to case building in the 1940s as DNA evidence is today. And Barker had expanded the library of fingerprints in Miami's identification laboratory, which he headed, from 1,100 sets to 72,000 over the past fourteen years. His bureau also contained "a complete scientific laboratory for identification of firearms, handwriting and typewriting, hair analysis and all branches of photography." But none of these forensic skills were as developed by 1943 as fingerprint evidence, which had been accepted in British and American courtrooms for nearly four decades.

The standard police method for gathering fingerprint evidence at that time was to cover the surface of an object or piece of furniture with special powder, so that any prints would be revealed. The prints could then be photographed *in situ*, or lifted off with sticky tape. The particular patterns in each print—the ridges forming arches, loops, and whorls—could then be carefully compared to the patterns in fingerprints taken from suspects. As everybody's fingerprints are unique, a match between an individual's prints and a telltale print at the crime scene was considered conclusive. Because several sensational cases in the 1930s had hinged on fingerprints, a few criminals had begun to take steps to eliminate the evidence. In 1933, Handsome Jack Klutas, leader of a gang known as the College Kidnappers, had tried to avoid future identification in court by filing down the ridges on his fingertips. Klutas's fellow gangster John Dillinger obliterated his fingerprints with acid, and a couple of other Chicago gangsters, Alvin "Creepy" Karpis and Freddy Baker, got a mob physician to hack off their skin. These attempts at self-mutilation all proved irrelevant: Klutas and Dillinger were both killed in police shootouts, while the scars left on Karpis's and Baker's hands were even more distinctive than their prints. Meanwhile, the FBI had established that telltale ridges reappear during healing, and palm prints are also unique to individuals and can be used for identification purposes.

Melchen and Barker's expertise sounded irreproachable. In practice, the Miami lawmen (who came from a force notorious for corruption) had neither the ethics nor the skills for their new assignment. They carried only elementary equipment—Barker had a microscope, but not a specialized fingerprint camera—that was ineffective in the tropical temperatures of summertime Nassau, where the humidity caused fingerprint evidence to deteriorate rapidly. They had no knowledge of British law. But Melchen and Barker loved the limelight. Shouldering the Bahamian officials aside, they took charge.

WITHIN A FEW hours of Sir Harry's death, the two Miami detectives had a suspect. So far, they had found no murder weapon, lifted no fingerprints, and failed to discover the source of the fire. But they had decided that Freddie de Marigny was the murderer. Melchen had questioned de Marigny closely about his movements the previous night and, after examining under a magnifying glass his hands, arms, and beard, triumphantly announced that they had found burned hairs. De Marigny told the detectives he hadn't seen Oakes for three months and hadn't set foot in Westbourne for two years. The Mauritian displayed his usual casual arrogance, making it clear that he had no respect for the dead man, dismissing his father-in-law as a "stupid fool" who was bitter about his daughter's marriage and could not be reasoned with.

On Captain Melchen's orders, police seized several items of clothing from their suspect (de Marigny said he couldn't recall which shirt he had been wearing the previous evening) and assigned a Scottish-born Nassau detective, Lieutenant John Douglas, to stay overnight in his house with him. De Marigny regarded Douglas as a friend and, according to Douglas, confided that "the old bastard should have been killed anyway," since he was so mean. De Marigny later denied making this statement, but he did not deny asking if a murder suspect could be convicted on purely circumstantial evidence if no weapon had been found. His blithe nonchalance ("[I] still felt no alarm, sensed no threat") would do him no favours in court. Even today, as I read these statements that Lieutenant Douglas would conscientiously repeat in court, I cannot help wondering what de Marigny was thinking. After all, this was the heyday of American crime fiction, with Raymond Chandler pumping out short stories and novels such as *The Big Sleep* and *Farewell, My Lovely.* The cinema (whites only) on Nassau's Bay Street regularly screened Hollywood's favourite genre at the time, "film noir," featuring hard-boiled detectives such as Sam Spade, the hero of *The Maltese Falcon.* De Marigny's careless indifference added to the pulp-fiction atmosphere on the island. He seemed a convincing villain, which reinforced the detectives' certainty and the ghoulish delight of the crowds to come.

The following morning, the victim's son-in-law was summoned to Westbourne to be questioned further by Melchen, and then, in his own account, taken upstairs for "a strange interlude . . . involving a drinking glass and a pack of cigarettes." De Marigny would later describe how Melchen continued to question him without taking notes; instead, he urged a glass of water on his suspect, taking the glass from de Marigny's hand as soon as the latter had taken a sip. Next, he tossed a cigarette pack across the room at him, which de Marigny nimbly caught in his right hand. Although these two actions were not particularly hostile, both felt contrived. De Marigny's sublime self-confidence began to wobble.

In court, Captain Melchen would deny that this exchange ever happened.

At this point in the crime-scene narrative, an event occurred that has intrigued all subsequent writers. The Duke of Windsor appeared at Westbourne, asked to see Barker, then had a private twenty-minute conversation with him in the bloodstained bedroom—a room very familiar to him, as the Windsors had slept there while Government House was being renovated. Was the governor simply checking on progress? Was he urging a quick resolution? Was he offering his own speculation on the identity of the murderer? There is no record of what was said.

Two hours later, de Marigny was arrested and charged with the murder of Sir Harry Oakes. The duke was quick to send a telegram to the Colonial Office, congratulating himself on the quick result achieved through his decision to secure the services of Melchen and Baker. They had rendered "most valuable service by their relentless investigations, which have in a large measure resulted in the arrest of the accused."

The accused man was driven to the Nassau prison, and the barred door of cell number two slammed behind him. De Marigny found himself in a room that measured three metres by four metres, brilliantly lit and furnished with a folding cot, an enamel basin sitting on a small wooden stool, a pitcher, and a large gal-vanized bucket that served as a toilet and was emptied three times a week. Fifty years later, he would recall how he "curled up on the cot, the light directly in my eyes. . . . The veins of my head throbbed, and I wanted to scream. I grabbed my hair with both hands and pulled as hard as I could, forcing myself to concentrate on the pain. It helped me to take a grip on my mind . . . . I was an innocent man in the custody of the English Crown, waiting to be tried by my peers, and I would live like an animal for the next 124 days." Under British law, bail is rarely granted in a murder case.

By now, de Marigny had realized he needed a lawyer. The Nassau legal community was small, and he was told that his first choice, his friend Alfred Adderly, was unavailable: he had already been retained by the Bahamian attorney general, Eric Hallinan, to help prosecute the case. De Marigny's legal team would con-sist of two London-trained lawyers: Godfrey Higgs, a tall white man in his early forties whose practice was largely in corpor-ate law, and Ernest Callender, a younger Nassau native with a

British Guyanese father. Higgs wore a sombre dark suit to court; Callender, who had a deep, vibrant voice and an actor's sense of timing, wore a much flashier double-breasted white suit. Both of these men were widely respected on the island, but neither had much experience in criminal cases.

The deck was stacked against De Marigny, as he himself vividly described in his memoir. He was "the one person who could be safely accused, who could be hanged without dividing the island. I was a foreigner, I had quarreled with Oakes, . . . I had married his daughter, years younger than I, without asking his consent; I had been less than discreet in certain public comments about the Duke of Windsor." The speed of his arrest, within two days of the murder, spread the impression of his guilt. New Providence was convulsed with gossip—that Oakes had been killed in a voodoo ritual involving chicken feathers, that the de Marignys had hosted "naked orgies [featuring] perversion, lesbianism, and worse." Alfred de Marigny was outraged that the stories, all of which reached his young wife's ears, were "written, printed and broadcast by irresponsible, scandal-mongering professional purveyors of pap for the lecherous mouths of the public."

The preliminary hearing before a magistrate, to establish whether there was sufficient evidence to pursue the case, was scheduled to begin in mid-July.

SIR HARRY OAKES's family had been notified by phone of his ghastly death, and Nancy Oakes de Marigny had flown from Vermont to Maine to be with her mother. Lady Oakes was devastated. Together they prepared for Sir Harry's funeral and burial in the Dover Cemetery, on the outskirts of Dover-Foxcroft, where he had spent his childhood. The funeral, which was attended by

Sir Harry's brother Louis and his sisters Myrtice and Jessie, was a small affair. The Newell Kellys had accompanied the body on its journey from Nassau, and the Duke of Windsor had sent a representative. There was a small delegation from Kirkland Lake: the managing director and chief engineer of Lake Shore Mines, along with the local physician. Because of wartime restrictions, each had to apply to the Foreign Exchange Control Board for a permit to take currency into the US. Back in Kirkland Lake, Roza Brown donned a black armband.

The funeral was conducted by the local minister, the Reverend Gordon Reardon, who had known Sir Harry since childhood. In his brief eulogy, he traced with admiration the dead man's extraordinary resilience, and the family's belief in him. "Few will ever know the disappointment and defeat which discouraged his adventuresome spirit. Men of lesser courage would have given up." However, the minister went on, "He had the confidence in himself . . . and he possessed the greatest asset that a man can possess—his mother's confidence."

There had been a curious hiccup in the dead man's journey from Nassau to Maine. When the aircraft carrying the coffin was already airborne, it was instructed to return to the hospital in Nassau. There Major Pemberton opened the coffin, ostensibly so that the corpse could be rephotographed. Captain Barker later explained that the photos taken of the corpse at Westbourne were unusable because light had got into his camera. However, the Westbourne photos are available and have been widely reprinted. The broken journey was yet another mystery in the murder story, and would give rise to speculation that the police had decided the autopsy was inadequate and wanted to re-examine the body in case they had missed significant facts—were the head wounds caused by bullets, for example? But no additional details emerged.

The day after the funeral, Captains Melchen and Barker flew to Bar Harbor to visit the distraught widow, who had returned to the Oakes home there and taken to her bed. They told Nancy Oakes de Marigny that she could not enter her mother's bedroom, and then proceeded to give Lady Oakes a graphic description of the murder. Lady Oakes was so horrified that she insisted that Nancy join them and hear the appalling story that the two detectives had told her. According to Nancy, they said the murderer had taken a pointed stick from a pile in the Westbourne garage, crept into Sir Harry's bedroom, struck down his sleeping victim, then sprayed his body with insecticide and set the bed on fire. Barker described how the sixty-eight-year-old baronet had staggered into the hall, his pyjamas aflame, gripped the railing, and tottered against the wall before being overtaken and dragged back into his room. During the struggle with his attacker, his blood was smeared on the walls and screen. He died in terrible agony, Barker announced solemnly. Lady Oakes sobbed with shock and grief.

The *coup de grâce* of this melodramatic account came when the younger detective announced that, in his fingerprint search two days after the crime, he had found three or four of de Marigny's fingerprints at the scene. Everything else in this version of the murder was purely speculative and circumstantial: the murder weapon had not been found (it never was) and nobody had seen de Marigny at the scene of the crime. But the fingerprints were damning. The family was not alone in its gasps of horror. Barker's senior colleague, Melchen, turned to him in amazement: although the two detectives had been working closely together for days, Barker had not mentioned this discovery to his partner.

Lady Oakes had originally promised her daughter all the financial help required to clear her son-in-law's name. But as de Marigny's lawyer would write to a Toronto physician who was an Oakes family friend, the "lurid details of the suffering which Sir Harry underwent before he was killed" had so horrified the widow that she reneged on her promise. Godfrey Higgs told Dr. W. P. St. Charles that "Lady Oakes became terribly upset and refused any aid to Nancy." In desperation, Higgs explained, Nancy (who "is completely convinced of her husband's innocence . . . I completely share her views") was now turning to Dr. St. Charles for help. "I am sure she will reimburse you later and you will be doing a truly humane act."

Nancy Oakes de Marigny's belief that her husband was incapable of such a brutal, clumsy killing never wavered. In addition to getting Higgs to ask Dr. St. Charles for financial help, she decided to hire her own detective. On her way from Maine to Nassau, she stopped in New York City to engage the services of a colourful private sleuth named Raymond C. Schindler, who had a distinct resemblance to Alfred Hitchcock.

This "portly grey-haired ace investigator," as the *Nassau Daily Tribune* described him, was a celebrity in his own right, having recently been profiled in a three-part *New Yorker* series. Schindler had begun his career as an insurance expert, investigating false insurance claims made after the San Francisco earthquake, and had quickly realized that wealthy clients paid the highest fees. Now he was a regular in Manhattan's most expensive clubs and restaurants, where he picked up clients, tips, and gossip, and he lived on the estate of railway developer Jay Gould, whose daughter had turned to him after a jewellery theft. The Oakes murder was just the kind of high-profile case that Schindler liked: it would keep his name in the news. For the next few months, Schindler would drop tantalizing hints about fresh evidence that would exonerate his client.

—

NANCY DE MARIGNY was back in Nassau for the first day of
the magistrate's preliminary hearing in mid-July. As the hearing
dragged on through August, continually interrupted by adjourn-
ments, the daily lineup outside the courtroom of reporters,
tourists, and locals eager to get a seat grew longer. The *Tribune*
reporter watched three Americans "persuade" three locals to sur-
render their seats to them for two shillings each—half a day's
wages for a black Bahamian. At this stage, most locals were convinced that the Mauritian had murdered their benefactor, and the
local police feared their suspect might be lynched by a black mob.

Sir Harry's death burnished his reputation for philanthropy
because it reminded Nassau residents of his contributions to New
Providence. At a memorial service held in Nassau's Christ Church
Cathedral the same day as his funeral in Maine, Oakes was recalled
as "a benefactor and a generous employer . . . [who] had taken his
full share of public life in the Colony." Nassau's white elite was
out in force. Amongst the prominent citizens in attendance were
the Duke and Duchess of Windsor, Chief Justice Sir Oscar and
Lady Daly, the Honourable W. L. Heape, colonial secretary, and
Mrs. Heape, and almost all the members of the Nassau House of
Assembly. Nevertheless, the grief demonstrated by this group was
perfunctory. As noted in the local paper, "The very simple service
at the cathedral lasted approximately twenty-five minutes."

Two weeks later, there was a longer, more emotional service at the community hall in Gambier village, where Sir Harry
had built a school. The following week, a large crowd of black
Bahamians gathered at Nassau's Southern Recreation Grounds
to mourn the murder victim. A fund was opened at the Nassau
branch of the Royal Bank of Canada to establish a monument to
the dead millionaire, now tagged as "the working man's benefactor in this colony." Oakes had morphed into the most popular man on the island, while at this point de Marigny was being

painted as a haughty and malevolent interloper. The image of Oakes's son-in-law was further sullied when he began his defence with the supercilious statement, "It is a ridiculous charge as I have no reason to do it."

During the preliminary hearing, the outline of the prosecution case became clear. Alfred de Marigny had frequently and publicly quarrelled with his father-in-law; Sir Harry had made clear his disapproval of the way that de Marigny treated Nancy; de Marigny was struggling financially and needed money; the hair on his hands, arms, and face was singed or burned; his fingerprint had been found on the Chinese screen in the bedroom.

The fingerprint evidence was going to be crucial, since the rest of these arguments were either dubious (the burned hairs on de Marigny's arms) or circumstantial—the Oakeses were certainly not the only wealthy family to have tempestuous squabbles. Barker took a whole day to present the fingerprint evidence, explaining that it had been hard to obtain because of the intense humidity. He described how, from 11 a.m. onwards on the day after his arrival, he had spent two hours examining the Chinese screen for fingerprints; out of the fifty to seventy prints he found, only six to ten were legible. He finally found one legible print (not three or four, as he had reported to Lady Oakes) that matched the right little finger of de Marigny. The screen had been brought into the court, and Barker marked the spot, on the extreme top of an end panel, where he had found the print. Fingerprinting, Barker assured the court, was "the only infallible medium of identification ever discovered."

Several details troubling to de Marigny's lawyers emerged during the preliminary hearing. The two RAF wives who had dined with de Marigny on the night of Sir Harry's death confirmed that, after he had driven them home, he must have been in the neighbourhood of Westbourne during the time frame of the murder. When Harold Christie was called to the witness stand, he provided a motive for de Marigny: he told the court that the Mauritian had asked him to sell his property on the island of Eleuthera because he had considerable expenses to meet. Another witness, John Anderson, who was managing director of the Bahamas General Trust Company, also spoke of de Marigny's financial difficulties. In particular, he mentioned that Ruth Fahnestock de Marigny, the count's second wife, who had been living on the Eleuthera property, was suing de Marigny for $29,000. Nancy Oakes de Marigny's inheritance would evidently have been a very welcome windfall for her husband.

As if opportunity and motive weren't enough, lurid details about toxic family relations kept coming. A neighbour, Thomas Lavelle, described a very public row between de Marigny and his father-in-law earlier in the year. Sir Harry had yelled at him, "You'd better not write any more letters to my wife. You're a sex maniac." John Douglas, the Nassau police officer who had spent the night after the murder keeping an eye on de Marigny, repeated the accused's remark that "the old bastard should have been killed anyway." And Walter Foskett, the Oakeses' family lawyer, reported to the court that Sir Harry and Lady Oakes so distrusted their son-in-law that they had changed the provisions of their will. The object was to keep their millions out of de Marigny's reach.

The most affecting witness called by the prosecution was Lady Oakes, who, as the *Nassau Daily Tribune* headline put it, "Bare[d] Story of Family Breach. Sobbing Widow Tells Why Sir Harry Changed Will." Dressed in black from head to foot, her eyes invisible behind dark glasses, Lady Oakes was treated with extraordinary deference by court officials. Her lawyer turned his fan around to give her its full benefit, and she was allowed to speak from the lawyers' enclosure rather than standing in the witness box. In the middle of her testimony, an orderly tiptoed off and returned with a fresh glass of ice water. The forty-four-year-old widow frequently dabbed her eyes with a handkerchief and sipped medicine from a bottle held by her lawyer. Her son-in-law, who was only eleven years younger and was seated a metre away, stared solemnly ahead. Despite her tremulous state, Lady Oakes was unequivocal about her own and her husband's refusal to accept de Marigny into the family. "I considered him completely irresponsible in his care of Nancy and I knew he was trying to ingratiate himself with Sydney and trying to alienate the child from us."

There was only one detail that jarred from all the testimony. Captain Melchen insisted that de Marigny had not been allowed upstairs in Westbourne between 11 a.m. and 1 p.m. on the Friday, while his colleague Barker was lifting fingerprints from the Chinese screen. It wasn't until after 3 p.m. that he had taken de Marigny upstairs and interviewed him in one of the other bedrooms. Two local policemen corroborated Melchen's statement. But it was contradicted by another witness, Lieutenant Douglas. To the discomfort of the prosecuting counsel, Alfred Adderly, Douglas told the court that he had not been with the accused all Friday morning. Between midday and one o'clock, Melchen had taken de Marigny upstairs for about forty-five minutes. If true, this not only meant that Melchen and the two local constables had lied, but also that de Marigny might have touched the screen before Barker had finished examining it for prints.

Higgs and Callender, de Marigny's lawyers, called only one witness to appear at the preliminary hearing. Dr. Ulrich Ernst Oberwarth was the medical officer at the prison where de Marigny was being held, and he had examined his prisoner when he first arrived. He testified that there was not a trace of fire on the accused that could be detected by the naked eye—no burns, scalds, or singed hairs. He wanted his testimony on record now because he would be out of the colony in October.

But this wisp of a defence had no effect on the magistrate's decision. "From the evidence, I am satisfied that a prima facie case has been made out against you," he informed de Marigny on August 31. "I order you to stand trial at the Court of Sessions in October." The trial would begin on October 18, in front of the chief justice of the Supreme Court of the Bahamas.

De Marigny strolled out of the courtroom and lit a cigarette. Inside, he had lolled in his chair, winking at friends and stroking his stylish Vandyke beard. His nonchalance exasperated his wife and lawyers.

The *Tribune* reported breathlessly that foreign newspapers were planning to carpet Nassau with reporters. "This case will, undoubtedly, be the biggest criminal trial in the history of the Bahamian Courts. . . . Both sides are getting set for the titanic battle." Bay Street storekeepers and Nassau hoteliers jacked up their prices in eager anticipation of the rush. For the duration of the trial, commerce would be as good as in the days of Prohibition. Bookies started taking bets on the outcome of the trial. The chief justice commissioned a larger table for his courtroom, to accommodate the influx of scribblers. The Hearst newspaper chain had already announced it was sending Erle Stanley Gardner, who had created the fictional detective Perry Mason for Hollywood in the 1930s and would go on to use the same character in a long-running radio program, and then in a television series.

FOR THE NEXT six weeks, de Marigny stewed in his cell while his legal team prepared his defence. Paranoia had replaced the blithe unconcern about his vulnerability. In his self-serving account of the whole episode, *A Conspiracy of Crowns,* he would write,

"I had finally begun to see myself as surrounded by peril." He brooded over who had a motive to kill Sir Harry Oakes. According to the 1990 memoir, which benefited from almost half a century of rationalization and hindsight, his thoughts quickly settled on somebody who, in the weeks following the murder, had attracted little suspicion: Harold Christie. He decided that the wounds that had killed Oakes must have been bullet wounds, although there was never any proof of this. Since anybody sleeping only two doors away would have heard four gunshots, Christie must have been lying on the witness stand when he insisted he had heard nothing on the night of the murder.

De Marigny also claimed that, as he paced his prison cell, he recalled a showdown he had witnessed between Sir Harry and Christie over the contracts for the new Allied air base. Oakes was known to want to build the base on his land, under his supervision, as a patriotic gesture to the British Empire. Instead, according to de Marigny, "Christie diverted the contract to an American company for a fat fee, which was to be split between himself and the Bay Street Boys." De Marigny convinced himself that Oakes was so furious he intended to call in his loans to Christie.

When de Marigny was not playing mind games about who the murderer was, and speculating on conversations that he is unlikely to have witnessed, he was thinking about his wife. The reporters already loved nineteen-year-old Nancy, as she tossed her red hair with Rita Hayworth panache and alternated between the roles of loyal wife and grieving daughter. Her visits to the jail to see her husband were opportunities to flaunt her fashion sense and for reporters to gush about her outfits—the full-skirted flower-patterned dress, the elegant straw hats, the white gloves. Her husband observed her transformation into a teenage celebrity. "In a visible way, she seemed to have thrived on the tragedy and scandal. . . . That she had my interest at heart I never doubted, that the role excited her was also obvious." He was appalled at the cost of retaining Schindler, who was an expensive investment. Nancy's appeal to Dr. St. Charles back in Canada for help had been turned down, as she learned from a cable addressed to her. "Would do anything in the world to help you personally but cannot assist in your husband's defence," he had responded. "As a friend of your late father I could not consistently offer help to a man suspected of his murder. Love, W. P. St. Charles."

Schindler was certainly enjoying himself. He spent his evenings socializing with the press and with Nassau's fast set at the British Colonial Hotel. One night, the stout, silver-haired sleuth stunned the crowd by starring in an impromptu rhumba competition in the waterfront bar of the Prince George Hotel.

As the days dragged by, de Marigny fell into despair. At night, his only relief was the gentle lilt of Bahamian ballads coming from a nightclub in Nassau's black neighbourhood. "I would stand on my tiptoes and peer out the tiny barred window at the top of my cell, trying to locate the sound. The music had become important to me, something to cling to in the midst of madness." His sleep was plagued with nightmares about a noose tightening around his neck. This was no idle fear. A rope had already been ordered from a local chandler for a judicial hanging.

Meanwhile, before the trial opened, the Duke and Duchess of Windsor left the Bahamas for a two-month trip to the United States.

CHAPTER 12

The Trial Opens

Visualize a play in which every member of the audience knows each character on the stage, some well, some by sight. But on any day, there is the chance that they will pass one another on the street. Such was the nature and intimacy of Nassau.

ALFRED DE MARIGNY

D ay after day, the *Tribune* carried one juicy item after another. No angle on the biggest story ever to hit their island slipped through the busy fingers of editor Étienne Dupuch and his son Eugene. In mid-August, during the preliminary hearing, readers learned that "the pretty young heiress Mrs. De Marigny" was convinced of her husband's innocence. "In the eyes of many people," she told the paper just before her return to Nassau, "I suppose I am just the hysterical wife trying to save my own pride in defending my husband. But it is much more than that. I have always believed that Freddie could not have done this terrible thing."

A few days later, readers learned that Lady Oakes had now arrived with her Palm Beach lawyer, Walter Foskett, and was staying with the Honourable A. K. Solomon, Nassau lawyer for the Oakes estate, and his wife. The paper ran a photograph of Eunice Oakes looking poised and impeccably groomed, with arched brows and a double strand of pearls. But the widow shared a sense of drama with her daughter. When she appeared in the magistrate's court a couple of days later, "a pall of gloom settled over the crowded little courtroom," and her face was "lined with the imprint of stark tragedy."

One day, a headline proclaimed, "Handwriting Expert Enters Oakes Case." The next day, the *Tribune* revealed, "Mrs. De Marigny Says Police Force Way into House"—apparently, on the hunt for handwriting that the expert might examine. (The possibility of handwriting evidence was never heard of again, inside or outside the court.)

A drumroll of bold print featured special investigator Raymond Schindler, usually accompanied by a photograph of his fleshy face and basset-hound jowls. Schindler "Tells Press He Has Clue," read one news item, although Schindler refused to disclose anything more than that "a prominent man in Nassau had given him certain information." The next thunderbolt was "Schindler Returns with 'Lie Detector.'" The Hitchcock lookalike had got hold of a newly developed polygraph instrument and brought it—and its inventor—to Nassau. "We can't say anything now," Schindler taunted the paper's readers, "except that we found some very interesting things." These "things" were never divulged, but Schindler successfully raised doubts about his client's guilt.

Nassau was agog. Amongst the barefoot fishmongers along the wharf, and over fruit punch in the whites-only nightclubs, rumours blossomed and spread. Beyond the tight little Bahamian world, there was said to be more interest in the case than in the kidnapping and murder of the Lindbergh baby eleven years earlier. Star reporters flew in, amongst them Ruth Reynolds of the New York *Sunday News* and Elizabeth Townshend for the *New*

York Post. The Dupuchs were also filing stories for London newspapers, including the *Daily Telegraph* and the *Daily Express*, as well as the *Toronto Daily Star*, Reuters, and the Canadian Press. The Nassau police, now largely under the direction of Melchen and Barker, were happy to accommodate a request from the press corps for a tour of Westbourne. Erle Stanley Gardner, the bulky, bespectacled crime novelist, caught sight of the Chinese checkers board on which Oakes had been playing with his guests on the night of the murder. His exchange with his police escort was soon part of Oakes lore.

Gardner pointed his pipe at the board and noted that the board remained "just as it was on that fateful evening." The policeman apologetically corrected his celebrity guest: the board had been in constant use ever since the murder, because the police who had been on duty in the house enjoyed Chinese checkers. "Don't let it worry you, Colonel," replied Gardner. "Facts will never spoil a Hearst story."

Meanwhile, under the headline "Oakes Will Still a Secret," the *Tribune* announced that "one of the world's most intriguing secrets is locked in a safe here," and predicted that the will would not be read and filed for probate until after the jury had rendered its verdict on Alfred de Marigny. It could be months. How rich was Nassau's wealthiest man? Had Nancy de Marigny been cut out of the fortune? Only two people knew the will's contents, affirmed the paper: Lady Oakes and her lawyer, Walter Foskett.

But only a few days later, on October 3, Sir Harry Oakes's will was published, and it proved to be a damp squib. It did not deal with the disposal of the largest item in the deceased's estate, his shares in Lake Shore Mines, which were parked in Bahamian holding companies. The will apportioned Oakes's personal property, which amounted to $14.686 million. Lady Oakes would receive a third of the estate, and each child a share of the remainder as she or he reached their thirtieth birthday. Until then, each was restricted to an annual allowance. Nancy de Marigny had not been dropped from the will, but for the next eleven years, she could expect only $12,000 a year. This would barely cover Schindler's fees for a month, and would do nothing to solve her husband's financial crisis. But if she wanted to petition for more, she would have to ask her father's executors: Lady Oakes; her husband's Nassau business manager, Newell Kelly; and the Palm Beach lawyer Walter Foskett—a man who had nothing but scorn for Alfred de Marigny.

Two days later, the *Tribune* had another scoop: "De Marigny Shaves Beard." Apparently, the "Imperial beard and moustache which has been given such widespread publicity in the US and Canada" had gone. Since burnt hair would be such a vital piece of evidence in the trial, the accused had had to obtain permission from the attorney general to shave. The *Tribune* noted that the clean-shaven de Marigny looked particularly debonair and youthful.

Finally, after this cascade of titillating details, the trial of Alfred de Marigny on a charge of murder opened in the Supreme Court of the Bahamas on October 18, 1943.

MURDER TRIALS, as Erle Stanley Gardner knew better than anyone, lend themselves to dramatic writing. Crime can appeal to the voyeur in all of us as we relish the suspense and the squalid details that are revealed in court. With its rules, pageantry, and public seating, the courtroom itself rivals an old-fashioned theatre for atmosphere.

Like most plays, trials follow a predictable arc: first, an exposition to acquaint participants with the situation and setting; then, conflict; finally, resolution—making the journey an emotionally satisfying one. Half the cast of this particular drama wore costumes: lawyers for the prosecution and defence and the judge were all clad in sweeping judicial robes and white horsehair wigs—standard dress for lawyers at London's Inns of Court, and based on the fashions of late-seventeenth-century England. Variations on these outfits were worn in courts all over the world where British law was administered, but most colonies had adapted the dress to their respective climates. However, the Bahamas had stuck to the full rig, despite its oppressiveness in Bahamian heat.

As I explored the de Marigny trial, I found myself fighting the impulse to overwhelm stark facts with colourful adjectives and judgmental prose. I could see that others—witnesses as well as reporters during the trial itself, and subsequent writers and filmmakers—had felt the same impulse, and often succumbed to it. But lurid writing can caricature horrific deeds.

This trial, already dubbed "the Trial of the Century" by Gardner (who never met a cliché he couldn't embrace), was guaranteed to spark sensational headings, given the brutality of the murder and the seedy glamour of the dramatis personae. Crowds waited for the curtain to rise on that sultry Monday morning in mid-October. Outside the yellow colonial building that housed the Supreme Court, people had begun lining up at dawn; by 8:30, a long queue stretched from the courthouse's neoclassical porch, past the war memorial on the green outside, and around the square itself. Many of Nassau's wealthier residents had sent servants to keep a place for them in line. When the doors opened at 9 a.m., 105 people crowded into the small courtroom to grab seats on one of the five benches allocated for spectators if they could, or park themselves in the "standing room only" space at the back. As the minutes ticked past, voices rose and handkerchiefs were pulled out to mop sticky hands and brows. Policemen in pith helmets, gleaming white jackets, and red-striped blue woollen trousers stood stiffly by the doors. The stage was set.

At 10:30, the court crier thumped his staff on the floor and Chief Justice Sir Oscar Bedford Daly entered the room, slowly ascended the dais, and stood at his desk, facing the lawyers at the bar. A broad-shouldered sixty-three-year-old who walked with a cane and rarely smiled, Justice Daly was an Irishman who had fought at the Somme and Ypres during the First World War, for which he had received an MBE (Member of the Most Excellent Order of the British Empire). Since then, he had bobbed around the Empire. After working as a barrister in another British colony, Kenya, he had been appointed chief justice in Nassau in 1939 and knighted a couple of years later. As a member of the whites-only Bahamas Country Club, which was owned by Sir Harry Oakes and sat next to Westbourne, Justice Daly fit comfortably into Nassau's cozy little plutocracy and knew most of the people ensnared in this case. In his wig and scarlet robes, he looked like a character out of a Gilbert and Sullivan operetta to American reporters, who were accustomed to a less formal system of justice. This morning, after acknowledging the respectful bows of the lawyers at the bar, he took his seat.

To the left of the chief justice's desk was the dock, a wooden cage raised above the ground—a structure that was no longer used in England but was still supplied to all colonies for murder trials. Here sat the prisoner, impeccable in a grey double-breasted suit, blue-striped shirt, and blue tie. De Marigny was physically uncomfortable—three months of sleeping on the thin prison mattress had produced a carbuncle—and he frequently leaned forward and rested his forehead on the mahogany bars. But otherwise, he was as insouciant as ever, chewing on a match, waving to friends, and winking at his wife. It was left to observers to decide whether this was the behaviour of an innocent fool convinced that truth would triumph or an arrogant murderer thumbing his nose at fate.

The trial opened with the court registrar turning to the accused and solemnly asking, "Are you guilty or not guilty?' In a steady voice, de Marigny responded, "Not guilty."

To the right of the chief justice was the long mahogany pew on which the jury would sit. Jury selection now began. From a pool of thirty-six men, twelve were chosen—all white, and most of them merchants or clerks who were married, regularly attended church, and, if not related, at least knew each other well. They included a baker, three accountants, the owner of a stocking shop, an ice house manager, an insurance agent, and a sponge farmer. The foreman, James Sands, was the island's leading grocer. His father had been a prominent politician. As de Marigny's lawyers, Godfrey Higgs and Ernest Callender, must have recognized, this jury would not warm to a thrice-married fortune hunter with a funny accent who had insulted the governor. Public opinion around New Providence was still firmly against de Marigny, and the community expected to see him swing for his father-in-law's death.

The trial would last for twenty-two days, during which jury members were sequestered in the modest Rozelda Hotel to maintain their isolation. However, Chief Justice Daly secured a few outings for them. On the afternoon of the first day, they all piled into taxis to Sir Harry's Westbourne estate so they could examine the scene of the crime. Another day, along with their police guard, they were allowed to attend a spy movie, *Above Suspicion*. British wartime propaganda at its worst, the film's improbable plot featured a tweedy band of Oxford scholars who thwart Nazi intentions and rescue a pouting Joan Crawford from torture. The following week, jurors were allowed to spend Sunday at the beach. One of them objected to the movie and beach outings on religious grounds, but he was dragged along anyway because the twelve men had to stay together at all times. I'm not sure how the objector resisted the movie's imperial hype, but at the beach, he sat under a palm tree and read his Bible.

After the jury had been sworn in, the barrister Alfred Adderly presented the Crown's case. His address to the jury, which lasted nearly two hours, mingled grisly details with Old Testament allusions, Shakespearean quotations, and hints of new evidence about the murder of "a good man . . . [who] loved this Colony and became . . . a Bahamian Citizen, beloved and respected by all." Adderly condensed the "why" of de Marigny's guilt into three snappy motives: satisfaction, for his "burning hatred"; revenge, for contemptuous treatment; and gain, for a share of the Oakes millions to solve his own desperate financial needs. The absence of any sign of robbery and the burning of the body indicated that this was a crime of hate, he argued. He pointed to the timing of de Marigny's trip past Westbourne, after delivering his two dinner guests home, to answer the "how" that any successful prosecution requires. The murder of Sir Harry had taken place "when his hating son-in-law was at his very gates." The day after the murder, when de Marigny had asked Lieutenant Douglas whether a man could be convicted in a British court on purely circumstantial grounds if no murder weapon were found, clearly pointed at his guilt, reasoned Adderly. "How can any innocent man ask such a question at such an early time after the murder? The Assailant is the only person who knew at that time that the weapon could not be found."

The case would be clinched, the lawyer went on, with fingerprint evidence from the Chinese screen that had stood in Sir Harry's bedroom. Even today, in our more skeptical era, any evidence that smacks of scientific expertise is regarded with particular deference: human memory is fallible, goes the common assumption, but science never lies. Now, in the corner of the Nassau courtroom, shrouded in a sheet, stood the six-panel screen, waiting to do its duty. Who could dispute an inanimate witness?

"Murder is murder, and a life is a life," Adderly boomed at the jury, "but this murder is, as Shakespeare, the immortal Bard, says in one of his sonnets, 'as black as hell and as dark as night.'" Erle Stanley Gardner was enthralled, describing the Crown counsel's address as "masterly . . . as able a courtroom speech as I have ever heard."

Adderly's oration was undoubtedly compelling. However, he included one detail that was new to observers, and it perplexed many of them. Captain Edward Sears of the Bahamas Police Force had made a statement that, at midnight during the torrential rain on the night of Oakes's death, he had seen Harold Christie being driven by a white man through the centre of Nassau in a station wagon. This statement was clearly at odds with Christie's statement that he had never left Westbourne that night. Adderly implied that Sears might have been mistaken, and urged the jury not to be diverted from its focus on the guilt or otherwise of the accused into questions about the credibility of Harold Christie. The Crown was clearly trying to pre-empt anything that the defence might make of this contradiction. What had Oakes's business partner been up to?

The following day, Harold Christie spent nearly four hours in the witness box. Those who knew him always described him as affable and soft-spoken, but today, exhaustion and anxiety seemed to have drained his easy charm. He was at pains to explain that Sir Harry Oakes was one of his closest friends; he had stayed with Sir Harry not only in New Providence but also in Bar Harbor, Palm Beach, Mexico, and England. When Sir Harry was in the Bahamas, the two men spent half their time in each other's company. Christie described how, on the night of the murder, he had been wakened briefly by mosquitoes and the heavy rainstorm, but had then slept until daybreak. He could not explain why the cries of his best friend, bludgeoned and set on fire only twenty-five metres away, had not disturbed his sleep. Then he traced his movements from his initial shock at discovering Sir Harry's battered body to the point at which he had called for help.

When the senior defence lawyer, Godfrey Higgs, began his cross-examination, the sweating Christie visibly wilted, along with his baggy linen suit. As *Time* magazine's correspondent put it, "de Marigny's defense chief kept his big guns trained on Christie."

Higgs clearly wanted to do exactly what the Crown had feared: divert attention to the issue of whether Christie was telling the truth, and (by inference) whether he knew more about the murder than he had admitted. He pressed Christie on whether he had left Westbourne that night. Christie insisted he had not. Yet Captain Sears, who had known Christie since boyhood, had said he saw him around midnight, being driven through Nassau. Christie flushed. "If Captain Sears said he saw me out that night I would say that he is very seriously mistaken and should be more careful in his observations."

Harold Christie was equally uncomfortable on the third day of the trial, when he was back in the witness box for a further hour and twenty minutes. Higgs now focused on Christie's behaviour when he discovered his friend's corpse. Given the state of the body, how could Christie ever have thought Oakes was still breathing? Higgs showed a photo of the battered corpse to the jury, and asked scornfully, "Does this look like someone who is alive?" Then he turned back to Christie. How did he not notice that the mattress was still smouldering? Where did he get the towel to wipe Sir Harry's face? Given that water is bad for burns, why did he wipe Sir Harry's face anyway? Why were there blood-stains on the door of his bedroom?

An agitated Christie did not have clear answers to this barrage of questions, so he ended up looking evasive. When Higgs asked him which end of the towel he had used to wipe the dead man's face, he gripped the rail in front of him and exploded, "For God's sake, Higgs, be reasonable." This did not impress Erle Stanley Gardner, who wrote in his column that Christie's evidence had not been convincing. Yet Detectives Melchen and Barker never followed up on the anomalies in Christie's statements.

A parade of Crown witnesses occupied the court's attention for the next couple of days, each confirming details already established in magistrate's court about Sir Harry Oakes's death and subsequent events. Madeline Kelly, wife of Oakes's business manager, described how de Marigny had appeared at their cottage on the Westbourne grounds and announced, "This is terrible. This is terrible. I think I'm going to be ill." His manner struck her as "very theatrical," particularly since he had not yet seen the corpse, and she told him to take hold of himself. But if this put de Marigny in a bad light, another of her responses cast doubt on Christie. She knew that Sir Harry was dead as soon as she hurried over to Westbourne and saw his body, which made Christie's description of his desperate attempts to revive him look suspicious.

Next came Charles Hubbard and Effie Henneage, who had joined Sir Harry and Harold Christie for dinner on July 7, and who now corroborated Christie's account of the evening. They were followed by the two doctors who had pronounced Oakes dead: Dr. Hugh Quackenbush, who had been summoned to Westbourne after the body was discovered, and Dr. Lawrence Fitzmaurice, the acting chief medical officer of the Bahamas, who had carried out the post mortem. They described the brutal head wounds and extensive burns, and agreed that the victim had been struck while in bed and was probably already unconscious and close to death when he was set alight. Both said he probably never got out of bed.

As the details piled up, the narrative got confused. Captain Melchen had insisted that, the day after the murder had been discovered, he had not taken de Marigny upstairs at Westbourne until the afternoon—after Barker had finished examining Oakes's bedroom and its contents for fingerprints. But Dorothy Clarke, the dark-haired wife of an RAF officer, who had been at de Marigny's dinner, said she saw him go upstairs between 11 a.m. and 1 p.m. She and her dinner companion Jean Ainslie had rushed over to Westbourne as soon as they heard of Sir Harry's death and congregated with all the other curious onlookers in the downstairs sitting room. Ainslie followed Clarke onto the witness stand, and also said that she had seen de Marigny taken upstairs that morning by Melchen. During the preliminary hearing, Lieutenant Douglas had said the same thing.

It was a tough call for the jury. Perhaps Clarke and Ainslie, the two vivacious RAF wives, were overly sympathetic to de Marigny. (Since Nancy Oakes de Marigny had returned to Nassau, she had invited them to dinner several times.) But John Douglas was remarkably even-handed; he also mentioned once more that de Marigny had remarked to him that "the old bastard should have been killed anyway." Jury members had to decide whether witnesses were simply confused or Captain Melchen was lying.

As the days went by, the fans turned listlessly in the stuffy courtroom and Chief Justice Daly's pen scratched on and on. Court officials regularly sprayed under the judge's and lawyer's desks to keep mosquitoes at bay. At noon each day, dozing spectators were jerked awake by the sound of a siren outside—signal for the wartime prayer service to begin outside, on the green.

In the evenings, many of those involved in the trial—witnesses, reporters, Nancy de Marigny, and her best friend, Marie af Trolle, wife of Wenner-Gren's private secretary—found themselves on the same restaurant balconies, parsing the day's proceedings as they enjoyed the cool breezes.

Every day, there was more gossip—that Westbourne's two night watchmen had mysteriously disappeared the day after the murder, that Schindler had a surprise up his sleeve, that the Oakeses' marriage was over and Sir Harry had been playing around. There were whispers about his relationship with Madeline Kelly, a glamorous American who had been a singer at his British Colonial Hotel before marrying his business manager. Mrs. Kelly had flown to Maine for Sir Harry's funeral and then on to Bar Harbor.

One story about Harold Christie was so persistent that he gave an interview to the *Miami Herald* to deny it. He "denounced as unfounded the rumour that he was shielding some woman when he testified last week in the trial of Alfred de Marigny," wrote reporter Jeanne Bellamy. "He admitted that his testimony sounded implausible but declared that he could not help that, because it was the truth." He was particularly worried that the "smear" would damage his reputation as the Bahamas' self-appointed ambassador in "New York, London and Canada." He declared, "You might as well bury me as take my life work away from me. Nassau is my hobby and my livelihood." He was afraid, he said, that these events "would stigmatize me among international people that I know."

This heartfelt denial must have triggered smirks in New Providence. It was an almost open secret that Christie, a bachelor, was having an affair with Effie Henneage, who lived in a cottage on Cable Beach close to Westbourne, where she had dined with Oakes and Christie on July 7. Henneage was the perfect femme fatale in the Oakes story. According to author James Owen, whose grandmother was a friend of Henneage in Nassau, the leggy blonde was a former dancer and lion tamer's assistant who had married an admirer with a castle in Scotland and a house near Ascot. However, her husband's real estate didn't compensate for his drunken outbursts, and the war had given the lovely Effie an excuse to scoop up her three daughters and move to Nassau. A photo taken at the time shows a shapely young woman in a skimpy beach dress, surrounded by adorable little girls with ribbons in their long, curly hair. In the free-and-easy atmosphere of this tropical refuge from bombs and torpedoes, there were plenty of beautiful, fancy-free women drinking Tom Collins cocktails amongst the hibiscus, but Effie Henneage must have stood out from the crowd.

So FAR, THE exchanges in court had been pretty straightforward. The Crown had established the facts of the case and produced its arguments for de Marigny's guilt; the defence had tried to undermine the credibility of the prosecution's arguments and witnesses. But the second week was different. Both sides knew that the fingerprint evidence was crucial to seal the case against the Mauritian, so when Captain Melchen took the stand on Monday morning, spectators leaned forward, de Marigny sat up straighter in the dock, and reporters stopped doodling.

Prompted by prosecution lawyer Alfred Adderly, the American detective described at length his examination of the murder scene, particularly the strange pattern of burns and scorch marks in Sir Harry's bedroom. He suggested there had been two sources of fire, although he could identify neither the inflammable material used nor the reason the fire had been set. Then he spoke of the scorching on de Marigny's arm, hand, and beard that he had detected with his magnifying glass, and the fact that de Marigny had never produced the shirt he had worn on the night of the murder. This omission, he implied, was decidedly fishy.

Captain Melchen then tried to repair some of the damage he had done in magistrate's court, when he said that he had taken de Marigny upstairs on the Friday afternoon. Now he shrugged off his statement as a mistake. In the face of evidence from three other witnesses, he admitted that "he had made a mistake; his memory was at fault." Callender, for the defence, was withering. "What a mistake! What a coincidence that you and the constables should make the same mistake!"

Melchen's chubby self-assurance initially made a good impression on the jury—hardly surprising, after his years of practice in sending murderers down in American courtrooms. When Callender rose to cross-examine him, the policeman continued his sturdy recitation of facts, batting away any doubts that the defence lawyer raised. Chief Justice Daly began to get irritated at Callender's line of questioning, and asked him to stop wasting the court's time.

Callender finally got some traction when he turned to the fingerprint evidence. Melchen explained that he did not know that his colleague Captain Barker had found de Marigny's fingerprint on the Chinese screen until Barker announced this finding to Lady Oakes in her bedroom at Bar Harbor. He admitted that he and Barker had been working on this case for eleven days by then, and had travelled together to Maine, but in their discussions of the case, no mention had been made of the fingerprint.

Callender expressed astonishment. Wasn't the discovery of a fingerprint at the scene of a crime a most vital piece of evidence? An unhappy Melchen agreed that it was. Callender drilled on: Yet Melchen had heard nothing about this until he and Barker met Lady Oakes? Melchen admitted he had not.

Even Sir Oscar Daly's busy pen had fallen silent by now, as he leaned forward and locked eyes with the witness. "Captain Melchen," said the chief justice in his clipped Irish accent, "isn't it strange that Captain Barker did not mention the print during the journey?" The Miami detective's self-assurance faltered as he admitted that yes, it was.

The two prosecuting lawyers, Hallinan and Adderly, realized that their star witness's admission had shaken the careful story they were constructing to prove de Marigny's guilt. Adderly quickly put Melchen back in the witness box. Melchen suddenly "remembered" that, after collecting fingerprints at the Westbourne crime scene, Barker had gone straight to the island headquarters of the Royal Air Force to process some of the prints in the photographic section, after mentioning to his colleague that he thought one of the prints belonged to the accused.

Sir Oscar Daly frowned. "That is very different from what you said yesterday," he pointed out. "Don't you know the very great importance of this piece of evidence? Have you a good memory?" Melchen offered a feeble excuse, given his experience in such situations: "I guess I was tired."

The Florida detective had started to look unreliable, and the chief justice's irritation was noted at the press table. But Melchen's shiftiness related only to when he himself had heard about the fingerprint evidence, not to the evidence itself. However, there were more surprises to come when the Crown called its next witness.

CHAPTER 13

The Chinese Screen

I purposely absented myself and the Duchess from the Colony during the de Marigny trial to avoid adverse publicity. I didn't want to be dragged into sordid and vulgar daily newspaper reports . . . [and] there was a morbid interest in America.

DUKE OF WINDSOR TO THE SECRETARY OF STATE
FOR THE COLONIES

T he evidence presented in court by Captain James Barker during the next two days occupies more than forty pages in the *Tribune*'s careful reporting of the trial, and much of it is laid out on the page like the dialogue of a play. It would yield a royal flush of tense *Tribune* headlines. The first came on October 27: "Defense Springs Surprise in Murder Trial, Asks Judge to Throw Out Fingerprint Evidence." Next day, readers learned that "De Marigny Case Developing into Battle of Experts." This was followed up with "De Marigny Fingerprint Origin Questioned. Defence Suggests It Did Not Come from Screen." After Barker's final day in the witness stand, the headline was blunt: "Defence Suggests Evidence Fabricated."

Let's cut to the chase here. Instead of a blow-by-blow commentary on the courtroom exchanges, let's look at the defence's strategy. In any trial, the defence's job is to cast doubt on the Crown's case; it doesn't have to prove the defendant's innocence, let alone come up with an alternative suspect. Higgs and Callender began the trial with two arguments. The first was that the only piece of evidence linking the accused to the scene of the crime was a single, contested fingerprint. They contended that the two American detectives had manipulated this print, then based their whole narrative of the crime on it in order to convict de Marigny. The careful story that the Crown had built to establish de Marigny's guilt had been undermined by Captain Melchen: the defence lawyers produced an equally compelling narrative to suggest that, far from being the murderer, de Marigny had been framed. Their second argument (which reinforced the impression of police incompetence) was the unreliability of some witnesses.

Captain Barker strode into the courthouse, a handsome young American star in the relatively new field of fingerprint science who had given fingerprint evidence in "several hundreds of cases" and who was now confident that he and Melchen had nailed de Marigny. Two days later, they had been revealed as clumsy liars by two adroit lawyers in a ramshackle British colony.

Godfrey Higgs's first line of attack against Barker was the unreliability of the single print of the accused's pinkie finger on which the Crown had based its case. The lawyer had assumed, he told the chief justice, that the fingerprint photograph entered into evidence had been taken from the Chinese screen. However, he had since learned that the print had been photographed *after* it had been lifted off the screen, and there was no evidence it had ever been on the screen. None of the scrollwork design that was on the screen was visible in the photograph, although it would have been hard to avoid the background pattern if the print had been lifted from the screen, as Barker claimed. Captain Barker then had to admit that he had not photographed the print on the screen because he had not brought the appropriate camera with him from Miami. He also had to admit that, since the screen was easily moved, it hadn't been necessary to "lift" the prints off the screen anyway; he could have taken the whole screen to a facility with the right equipment.

Barker appeared particularly incompetent in one exchange. In the preliminary hearing, he had marked with a blue pencil the heavily smoked area of the Chinese screen from which he had removed the print. Now, twelve weeks later, he said he could not say for sure that the print had come from there. He could only say that it had come from the top part of the panel. Higgs suggested he look more closely at the screen. Barker then made a curt announcement. "I wish to inform the court," he said, "that the blue line I now see was not made by me. There has been an effort to trace a blue line over the black line that I made on August 1 in the presence of the Attorney-General. That blue line is not my work."

At the lawyers' bar, Hallinan, Adderly, Higgs, and Callender looked astonished. Jurors stared at each other in confusion; spectators were spellbound, fascinated by this bombshell. A buzz erupted when the chief justice broke the spell by rising to his feet, stepping down from the dais, and walking heavily across the courtroom to join Barker by the screen. Abruptly, Barker blurted out a retraction. "I wish to withdraw what I said about the alteration. I find my initials where the blue line is."

The fingerprint evidence was starting to wobble. It was not certain where the print of de Marigny's pinkie had come from, and if it had come from the screen, Barker had been so sloppy that he couldn't even identify its exact source. He also had to admit that he had not bothered to dust for fingerprints the headboard of Sir Harry's bed, the thermos on the nightstand, or the railing of the staircase. Of all the people who had been coming and going from Westbourne the day after the murder, he had fingerprinted only Major Pemberton, deputy commissioner of the Bahamas Police; Dr. Quackenbush; Harold Christie; and Alfred de Marigny. He had not fingerprinted Effie Henneage, Madeline Kelly, Frank Christie, the housemaid, Mr. Hubbard, any of the police officers, or Colonel Erskine-Lindop, although several had been in Sir Harry's bedroom while the corpse was there. There was another surprise: Barker had not found a single print from Harold Christie anywhere in Sir Harry's bedroom, although Christie had been in and out of the room before and after the murder.

By expression and body language, Godfrey Higgs indicated that he thought this so-called fingerprint expert had been less than thorough. The implication was that the Florida detectives had fallen victim to a common affliction amongst police officers: tunnel vision. Having decided that de Marigny was the murderer, they hadn't bothered to consider any other suspects or scenarios.

Next, Higgs took his cross-examination in a new direction that indicated an alternative narrative. First, the lawyer questioned Barker about the visit to Lady Oakes in Bar Harbor immediately after Sir Harry's funeral during which, according to Nancy de Marigny, Barker and Melchen had painted a blood-curdling picture of the murder. Higgs asked Barker if they had said that the "assailant had entered the garage and picked up a stick from a pile of railings, crept upstairs and struck Sir Harry on the head with it and sprayed the bed with insecticide and set it afire and that Sir Harry was revived by the flames and tried to fight off his attacker and that Sir Harry had been in great agony until his assailant finally killed him."

Barker vehemently denied this report, but Higgs continued.

Had Barker not mentioned to Lady Oakes that he had already examined the Chinese screen "and found several hand and finger-prints of the accused on the screen"?

Again, the sweating detective denied the charge . . . and the next one: "I put it to you that you or Captain Melchen did say these things to arouse Lady Oakes' hatred of the accused."

And now Higgs laid out the defence's version of events, which revolved around what had happened during Captain Melchen's interview on Friday, July 9, with de Marigny, which had taken place in a second-floor bedroom at Westbourne. The questions previously asked about this interview had focused on the possibility that de Marigny had touched the Chinese screen while he was upstairs, when Barker was still looking for finger-prints. Now the questions concerned what had happened during the interview itself because, Higgs casually dropped into the cross-examination, it was after that interview "that you claimed to have discovered his print, was it not?"

Barker agreed that the timing was correct. But when Higgs suggested that he and Melchen had "deliberately planned to get the accused alone in order to get his fingerprint," Barker snapped, "No sir." However, Higgs pushed on relentlessly with a volley of questions about the untrustworthiness of the vital fingerprint. Barker couldn't explain the three small circles that were identifiable in the photograph's background, or where they might have come from. For those who had listened carefully to the exchanges, Higgs's final assertion in the cross-examination could have come as no surprise. Barker sagged as Higgs leaned forward, stared at him, and said, "I suggest that in your desire for personal gain and notoriety you have swept away truth and substituted fabricated evidence."

The American detective emphatically denied this, but the suggestion had been planted in jurors' minds.

The Crown struggled to regain the upper hand. The attorney general produced a fingerprint expert with seventeen years' experience in the New York Police Department. Frank Conway confirmed that Captain Barker's methods of fingerprinting conformed to "good practice," and that the fingerprint produced in court definitely belonged to de Marigny. However, he was unable to confirm that the fingerprint came from the screen, which did nothing to restore Barker's credibility.

Next, Hallinan tried to bolster the Crown's argument about de Marigny's motive for murdering Oakes by calling a handful of witnesses who had seen angry exchanges between the two men. One repeated the evidence that, in a fierce row in front of the de Marigny residence, Sir Harry had accused his son-in-law of being a "sex maniac." Another recalled de Marigny threatening to "take his big foot" to his father-in-law. But the defence team didn't even bother to cross-examine these witnesses about the ugly insults. Instead, they waited until they could put de Marigny himself in the witness box to elaborate on their theory of how the fabrication had been achieved.

YEARS LATER, Alfred de Marigny would describe in his second memoir the elation he felt as the Crown closed his case. He thought that Godfrey Higgs and Ernest Callender had dismantled the Crown's case magnificently: "I saw Barker as a creature to be pitied, not hated." But, to his dismay, he discovered that reporters did not share his confidence that he would walk. "Members of the press were making bets on whether I would hang or go free, and there was more money against me than for me."

It was always going to be a competition between two narratives, given under oath: the one constructed by the Crown, and the one that the defence was now sketching out. But who had more credibility: the American detectives or the accused? Erle Stanley Gardner was particularly impressed by the evidence given by Harold Christie (who had almost certainly given Gardner his celebrity tour of New Providence) and by Captain James Barker, with his movie-star looks. Now Gardner was spreading the word that the accused's chances were slipping away, and it was Barker, not de Marigny, who was being framed. Perhaps, Gardner mused, a third party had slipped an example of de Marigny's fingerprint into Barker's office while he was in Maine, visiting Lady Oakes, and this accounted for the muddle over the fingerprints. This speculation would have made a delicious Perry Mason plot, but there were no facts to substantiate it in court.

"It was like spectators at a boxing match, rooting for one fighter or another, arguing over the quality of the punches, no one appearing to see the fight," de Marigny would write. For weeks, while he had been confined to his squalid, claustrophobic cell, his name had been tossed around in cocktail conversations, and his character dissected by strangers, enemies, friends, and amateur psychologists. Was he a wicked philanderer, a congenial sportsman, an amoral sponge, a charming Frenchman, a loving husband, a selfish manipulator, an untrustworthy foreigner, or an imaginative entrepreneur? For the past fifteen court days, he had heard thirty-three witnesses testify in support of the Crown's charge that he had murdered his father-in-law. He had been allowed to utter only two words: "Not guilty."

Now he would finally be allowed out of the medieval mahogany prisoner's cage. Standing in the witness box, he could remind people who he really was as he told his story.

Competition for seats in Nassau's crowded little courthouse was particularly intense on the day that the defence was due to open its case. Within minutes of the doors opening, the benches were filled, the aisles were packed, and there were crowds outside the double doors, trying to press forward. Several spectators had brought their own wooden, camp, or cane chairs; others squished themselves in, two to a seat. The most avid had packed lunches, preventing others from grabbing their seats if they left for refreshments. White pith helmets bobbed amongst the heads, as the police tried to control the numbers and keep the entrances clear.

Both *Time* and *Newsweek* carried regular bulletins about the trial during these weeks. The *Newsweek* correspondent did not stint on melodrama as he described de Marigny's appearance in the witness box. "Once he had been debonair and reckless, winking at witnesses and waving to his friends from the wooden prisoner's cage. But on Nov. 4, when he stood to testify under oath, de Marigny was a solemn, tight-lipped man, fighting for his life. And on Nov. 5, when the Crown began hammering at his alibi defence, he grew even paler and more subdued."

The defence lawyers were probably relieved by their client's uncharacteristic behaviour; arrogance is never a good look in a courtroom. During his four and a half hours on the stand, de Marigny remained on his feet, gripping the rail in front of him with both hands, and speaking clearly and unemotionally. Under questioning from Higgs, he described the course of his romance with Nancy, and the slow buildup of hostility he felt from her parents. "Sir Harry was very impulsive and moody and would be friendly one day and not the next." Nevertheless, he continued, Oakes had offered him some land for his chicken farm. But relations had deteriorated after both men returned to Nassau in the spring, culminating in a row one night when de Marigny told his father-in-law, "Sir Harry, you must be either drunk or insane."

Next, de Marigny described his dinner party on the night that his father-in-law was killed and the events of the following two days. Most of this testimony repeated information already given by other witnesses, but it was now presented in a version that put de Marigny in a better light. Once he began describing his interview in one of Westbourne's upstairs bedrooms on the morning of Friday, July 9, the attention of spectators and reporters visibly perked up.

According to de Marigny, Captain Melchen had begun the interview by enquiring if Harold Christie was indebted to Sir Harry Oakes, or had any grievance against the landowner. "I told him Mr. Christie was one of my best friends and Sir Harry's best friend and he could get the information from Mr. Christie himself." Melchen had then batted a few bland questions about his Mauritian childhood to de Marigny before abruptly asking, "Did you see any light at Westbourne last night?" Then the detective pointed his finger at de Marigny and said, "Didn't you want to get quits with Sir Harry and came here to see him and had an argument with him and hit him?" Addressing the jury, de Marigny described how he had told Melchen that if he had wanted to speak to Oakes, he would do it during the day, not in the middle of the night.

The next part of de Marigny's testimony was crucial to the defence case. The accused man described how

> . . . there was a table on the left of me and Melchen was sitting opposite me. On the table was a tray with two glasses and a pitcher of water. He had offered me a number of cigarettes from a pack of Lucky Strikes he had. He asked me to pour him a glass of water. I poured one for him and one for myself. . . . We talked about other things that didn't make heads or tails. Captain Barker put his head in the door and asked, "Is everything okay?" Melchen replied, "Yes." Soon afterwards, Captain Melchen and I left and went downstairs.
>
> At 6:15, I was arrested and charged with the murder of Sir Harry Oakes.

Godfrey Higgs concluded the day by asking his client, "Did you kill Sir Harry Oakes?"

Alfred de Marigny shot back, "No, sir!"

Erle Stanley Gardner and his colleagues scrambled for the door. That night, the staff at Nassau's telegraph office transmitted a total of 18,750 words about de Marigny's testimony from all the newspaper correspondents covering the trial—more than twice the number that had been cabled to various newspapers after the Duke of Windsor was inaugurated as governor in 1940.

The following day, de Marigny was back on the stand to be cross-examined by the Crown. His dignified, straightforward performance under Higgs's questions had swayed public opinion in his favour. Although most Bahamians had initially been happy to accept that de Marigny was the guilty man, they were now beginning to turn. The idea that the colony's white elite had ganged up to nail an unpopular outsider triggered some of the discontent lingering from the previous year's riots.

But now the accused faced Attorney General Eric Hallinan, who was determined to rebuild the Crown's case. De Marigny was forced into a series of damaging admissions—that he had lived with his second wife on Eleuthera for several months after their divorce, that he had received large sums of money from both Ruth Fahnestock and Nancy Oakes de Marigny, that he had lied to Ruth about his finances, that he had married Nancy only two days after her eighteenth birthday without the knowledge of her parents. He acknowledged that Oakes had accused him in a Nassau street of being a "sex maniac."

De Marigny looked like a money-grubbing predator, and Hallinan had successfully brought the court's attention back to the motive for de Marigny's alleged murder of his father-in-law. However, he could not break down de Marigny's insistence that he had been at home in bed at the time that Sir Harry was being beaten to death.

The defence then called a parade of witnesses who went over ground that had already been covered. Georges de Visdelou-Guimbeau, de Marigny's cousin, and Georges's girlfriend, Betty Roberts, confirmed that de Marigny had been in his Victoria Avenue house at 1:30 a.m. on the night of the murder. Captain Sears once again testified that he had seen Harold Christie being driven through Nassau on the fateful night; Christie repeated his testimony that he had never left Westbourne.

But the tension had left the courtroom. For the first time, there were some empty seats, and an atmosphere of anticlimax. The Crown lawyers barely bothered to cross-examine the defence witnesses: Hallinan and Adderly could feel their case slipping away. The credibility of their chief witnesses, the two Miami detectives, was damaged.

The final blow to the Crown's case came when the defence team resorted to a common but effective courtroom tactic—summoning an expert witness whose evidence contradicted that of the Crown's expert witness. Hallinan had produced Frank Conway from New York; Higgs called to the witness box Captain Maurice O'Neil, who had served as supervisor of New Orleans' Bureau of Investigation for the past eighteen years. Captain O'Neil gave his opinion that there was no evidence that the fingerprint around which the Crown had built its case actually came from the Chinese screen in Sir Harry Oakes's bedroom.

Perhaps the moment at which this trial came closest to being a theatrical production was when Godfrey Higgs, exuding the self-assurance instilled during his private-school education in Britain, casually asked O'Neil what might have caused the small circles that were in the background of the fingerprint photograph. Like a magician with a rabbit, O'Neil reached into his jacket pocket and produced a drinking glass with a design of red circles.

An indignant Hallinan jumped to his feet to protest this surprise. "If the Defence were going to produce that glass, I should have had an opportunity to ask the Accused whether the glasses allegedly used by the Accused and Captain Melchen in the north-west bedroom had such a design!"

He had inadvertently jumped the gun. Higgs had asked only a general question about what might have caused the circles. The chief justice himself intervened to say, "But the Defence are not suggesting that it was taken from a glass." But Hallinan knew that no member of the jury could have missed the connection. "Oh yes," was his bitter rejoinder. "That suggestion has been made all along."

Godfrey Higgs sailed on. "No, we didn't suggest that," he said, going on to point out that he had also asked Captain Melchen about ashtrays and other objects. Then he asked O'Neil if he had anything else that might be used in a demonstration of how particular designs might intrude onto fingerprints. O'Neil obligingly put his hand in another pocket and pulled out a glass cigarette case that also had a pattern of circles. Higgs invited James Sands, foreman of the jury, to put his finger on the cigarette case. Captain O'Neil dusted and lifted the print. The lift showed the circles as well as the print. Higgs had subtly connected all the dots in his defence argument. The science of fingerprinting carried weight in this court, but not on the side of the Crown.

Bookmakers were now quoting odds of 4–1 for an acquittal of de Marigny.

Nancy de Marigny knew how to make an entrance.

She was the last witness to testify in her husband's murder trial, and she would spend an hour in the witness box. Press pencils scribbled furiously when the nineteen-year-old heir-ess appeared at the courtroom doors; reporters noted the styl-ish black dress, the jaunty white beret and white gloves. "Mrs.

De Marigny hesitated at the door, threw one brief glance at the gaping audience and then walked straight ahead, looking neither to the right nor the left," wrote the *Tribune* reporter. This was Nancy's first appearance in court; as a future witness, she had not been permitted to hear other witnesses presenting evidence, lest it influence her own (although she could read about it in all the newspapers every night, and chat about each day's proceedings with her friends over a cocktail.)

Her voice was almost inaudible as she took her oath; jurors strained forward to hear her. Prompted by Godfrey Higgs's gentle questions, she described her marriage to Alfred de Marigny and the rupture it had caused in her family. When she went on to talk of her father's death, her eyes filled with tears and her lips quivered. Then she described how, a couple of days before her father's funeral, Captain Barker had told her over the telephone that "there was no question as to who the guilty party was." As she spoke, she closed her eyes, gripped the rail of the box, and swayed. The attorney general quickly suggested she might be allowed to sit on a high stool. Once seated, she continued, "He said it was my husband." A few days later in Maine, she heard them give their gruesome account of her father's violent death to her mother.

Still speaking softly, Nancy recounted her memory of the Melchen–Barker version of Sir Harry's murder. She had been sitting with her mother and sister as the two Florida detectives gave their dramatic account of an assailant who had gone up the outdoor staircase to her father's bedroom, struck Sir Harry over the head, poured insecticide over his unconscious body, and set the bed alight. "My father, they said, had been revived by the flames and had attempted to fight off his attacker."

Nancy had asked the detectives to continue their explanation of the murder in another room, because her mother was so hysterically upset. There, she was told that the assailant had knocked over the Chinese screen during the struggle, then picked it up again so that the fire should not be seen from the road. "They said they therefore examined the screen for fingerprints and handprints and they had found fingerprints of my husband. I understood them to say that they had found several fingerprints or handprints. I got the impression they had prints of the whole hand. . . . They were emphatic in stating that either my husband committed the crime or was present when it was committed."

Detective Barker had specifically denied telling any such story on his visit to Lady Oakes. But few people in court that day were prepared any longer to accept anything that Barker said.

Nancy gave a final polish to her husband's reputation by insisting that he was not a fortune hunter. No, she assured the court, he had never asked her for money. In fact, he had offered to sign a document that waived his claim to anything she might inherit. Both she and Freddie knew that her parents had altered their wills earlier that year, but prior to her father's death, she didn't know what was in it. And no, she had never heard her husband express any hatred towards her father.

Attorney General Hallinan could not have enjoyed his final challenge of cross-examining an attractive young wife who was defending her embattled husband, especially when he knew she had the court's sympathy. He read out a letter that Nancy had written to her mother, saying that if her parents could not treat her husband with more respect, she could no longer love them. In particular, she accused their lawyer, Walter Foskett, of poisoning their attitude towards de Marigny. Mr. Foskett, she had written in the letter, had deliberately turned her parents against her husband by making accusations "based on fantastic and flimsy evidence."

Trying to paint Nancy de Marigny as a heartless young woman, Hallinan asked, "That's a pretty hard letter for a girl to write to her mother, don't you think?"

Nancy replied, "Not if you were feeling as I was." However, she added, she was not trying to sever her relationship with her parents. She simply wanted them all to talk about this together.

But Harry Oakes had never been a man who could discuss his feelings, let alone anyone else's. During his prospecting years, he had lost most of his social skills and made few friends, and affluence had not softened the edges. It wasn't in his nature to show forgiveness or offer conciliatory gestures. When life wasn't going his way, the gruff, suspicious loner resorted to anger. And before there had been a chance for his beloved daughter to diffuse his temper, he was dead.

THE CLOSING STATEMENTS from both the defence and the Crown were models of their kind—clear summations of the evidence that fit their versions of what had happened, and rejections of evidence that contradicted them. Neither Godfrey Higgs nor Attorney General Eric Hallinan was going to waste this opportunity to perform before the international press, so both spoke for nearly three hours. But for anyone who had already sat through three weeks of trial, there was little new to be learned.

Higgs had shredded most of the circumstantial evidence the Crown had collected against his client, and even the Crown's proposed motive for de Marigny had fallen apart during the trial. There was no evidence to substantiate the claim that the accused was after the Oakes millions, and if simple hatred had driven de Marigny to kill his father-in-law, why had he waited so long to do it? They hadn't even seen each other for more than three months.

Most important, Higgs and his colleague, Callender, had made the fingerprint evidence the centre of everybody's attention, and then depicted it as too flimsy to be trusted. Nothing else mattered, argued Higgs, because the focal point of the Crown's case was worthless. Higgs did not even bother to raise red flags about other suspicious behaviours that the court had heard about—Harold Christie's mysterious movements, for example, or whether Sir Harry Oakes's body had been moved. He didn't need to. Pulling himself to his full height and holding the lapels of his legal gown, Higgs turned to the jury. "And now gentlemen, I will detain you no longer but remind you that before an accused person can be convicted the Prosecution must prove its case beyond all reasonable doubt. . . . I feel that the evidence which has been placed before you during this trial proves conclusively that Alfred de Marigny never killed Sir Harry Oakes and I believe, gentlemen, you can return only one verdict—and that a unanimous one of 'Not Guilty.'" To condemn the prisoner to be hanged simply on the grounds of prejudice would, he argued, "be a greater crime than the slaying of Sir Harry Oakes."

For his part, Hallinan patiently rebuilt the circumstantial case that Higgs had swept aside. He reminded the jury that de Marigny was an extravagant man who had proved financially deceitful, who had married Nancy Oakes without her parents' knowledge, and who had insulted his father-in-law. He suggested that Nancy's evidence was not entirely trustworthy, and that her parents were right to worry about her future. Sir Harry had realized that "he didn't have an honest, hard-working son-in-law but a parasite."

The Crown's argument was that de Marigny had been in desperate financial straits, and he had murdered Sir Harry on July 8 because the latter planned to leave the island the following day to join his wife in Maine. De Marigny's alibi (his cousin had testified that he was back home by the time the crime was committed) was shaky; his inability to produce the shirt he wore on the night of the murder was suspicious; the burnt hairs on his arm were damning. And the fingerprint evidence was reliable. The two American detectives were well-respected officers, although "the Defence had thrown dirt at these men" and "were prepared to ruin [their] careers. It was ridiculous to suggest that they were conspiring against the accused."

Halfway through this recitation of arguments for de Marigny's guilt, there was a commotion. Nancy de Marigny jumped up, then stormed her way through the crowd to reach the square outside. "I could not bear to sit there and hear him say such filthy things," she told reporters the next day. A wave of sympathy for the prisoner's sensitive and loyal young wife swept the court.

But Hallinan never paused. He acknowledged that this murder was "so foul that it had attracted the fascinated gaze of millions beyond these shores." He described de Marigny as "a cad, a thief and a liar." He was sure that the jury would discharge their painful duty with honour—and they would not allow unfounded charges of conspiracy and fraud to cloud their judgment.

The attorney general bowed to the chief justice, then sat down.

The court rose.

CHAPTER 14

"Freddie Is Not a Stupid Person"

His Honour, in opening, said that the united nations were now fighting a war for liberty—and one of the most cherished principles of liberty was the guarantee that in the British Empire no man could be condemned except by a verdict of his fellow men. The jurors empanelled in this case had been selected for their high integrity and . . . he was sure they appreciated the fact that they were discharging a duty that sprang from a privilege of free peoples.

REPORT OF THE CHARGE TO THE JURY BY CHIEF JUSTICE
SIR OSCAR B. DALY, NOVEMBER 12, 1943

Over the course of the trial, Chief Justice Daly had laboriously written five hundred pages of notes. But he barely glanced at them as he embarked on his charge to the jury. Instead, he took off his glasses and, speaking softly and deliberately, reviewed the testimony of the past three weeks and instructed the jury as to how to assess it for themselves. For five hours the heat and suspense in the crowded courtroom rose as his soft, measured tones continued, interrupted only once by a brief recess.

He began by reminding the twelve men that every man who came into a British Court of Justice was presumed innocent, and that the jury's verdict should reflect only the evidence produced in court. Jury members, he stressed, must ignore all the rumours and speculation that had galvanized Nassau ever since one of the colony's most esteemed citizens had been battered to death. (This was a tall order: before jury members were sequestered at the start of the trial, they could barely have avoided salacious gossip about the state of the Oakeses' marriage, the sleaziness of de Marigny's past, and the carnage at the scene of the crime.) Daly also reminded them that they could pronounce the accused guilty *only* if they were convinced of his guilt "beyond reasonable doubt." He cautioned the jury to treat with very great reserve any evidence of hatred or strained relations. "Jurors probably knew from experience that relations between married people and their families of the previous generation were not always pleasant." The Crown's case, he continued, was "purely circumstantial. There was nothing to show what weapon was used, how the assailant entered the house, or how he committed the crime."

Jury members listened intently to the chief justice as he reassured them that they didn't have to heed all his suggestions. "A Judge is really a thirteenth juror," he explained. He was there, he said, only to advise them in the law and to discuss the case with them in the same way that they would discuss it amongst themselves. It was, however, entirely a matter for the jury, not the judge, to decide.

Daly's assurances were sly, to put it mildly, since he went on to explain that the Crown's case was deeply flawed. He described Captain Barker's failure to follow accepted practice for fingerprint evidence as "incomprehensible" and characterized Captain Melchen's admission that he didn't know about the fingerprint evidence until he heard Barker describe it to Lady Oakes as "extraordinary." Although the judge cautioned that there was no evidence the two Florida detectives had fabricated evidence, he suggested that both the police evidence and the expert evidence should be treated skeptically. Sir Oscar also deplored the mistakes and contradictions offered by the Nassau police witnesses, and hoped that a thorough departmental investigation would be held. The jury must decide whether the police "were trying to make the facts fit their theories."

The chief justice concluded his lengthy address to the jury by telling them that there were no circumstances to justify the charge being reduced from murder to manslaughter. Jury members had only two choices: guilty or not guilty. To find the accused guilty, the verdict must be unanimous. To find him not guilty required a majority of two-thirds. Sir Oscar hoped that, whatever the verdict, it would be unanimous.

Led by their foreman, James Sands, the jurors shuffled out of the jury box at 5:25 p.m. and climbed the stairs to the jury room for their deliberations. They had been sequestered for twenty-five days, and were eager to get this trial over with and see their families. The sun was setting, and doves cooed softly in the giant silk-cotton tree outside. Some spectators went home, assuming that there would be no verdict until the following day and relieved to escape the crowded, sweaty courthouse into the cool November breeze. But the majority of court watchers remained glued to their chairs, and a crowd started to gather outside in the square. Soon, a line of pith-helmeted policemen was summoned, in case of disturbance.

Most of the reporters had already written their descriptions of the trial's final day, and had a choice of telegrams ready to dispatch—GUILTY or NOT GUILTY. The lawyers clustered at the front of the courtroom.

Alfred de Marigny joined his attorneys at their table, and, he would insist fifty years later, he "felt a cheerfulness in sharp contrast to the unhappy and worried looks worn by Higgs and Callender." Higgs was obviously exasperated by his client's jaunty humour. "Fred," he remarked, "this is a very serious moment for all of us, and you in particular. Are you not fearful of the verdict?" With characteristic overconfidence, de Marigny assured him that he wasn't. In his memoir, de Marigny would write that he entertained his lawyers with a breezy anecdote. "You remind me of the priest who visited Maximilian, the Emperor of Mexico, in his cell just before his execution by a firing squad," he claimed he told his lawyers. "The priest walked out of the cell with tears in his eyes and said to the people waiting outside, 'I came to comfort him, and instead he comforted me.'"

But such bravado came with hindsight. At the time, the *Tribune*'s Eugene Dupuch reported that de Marigny was escorted out of the courthouse to the Central Police Station, where he paced the floor, smoked cigarette after cigarette, and periodically stared across the square at the lighted windows of the jury room. Nancy Oakes de Marigny, barred by regulations from sitting with the accused man, sat one floor above, wringing her hands as she gave an interview to a reporter. "Freddie is not a stupid person, and the crime was stupid and clumsy."

At 7:20 p.m., the court official announced that the jury was ready to come down. They had been gone less than two hours— was this a good or a bad omen? Empty benches in the courtroom quickly filled, and Nancy de Marigny, her fists clenched, slipped back into her seat. As a police guard briskly returned de Marigny to the prisoner's cage, the crowd jostled with excitement. Next, the jurors filed in, their faces expressionless, followed by the chief justice, who limped up to his desk and sat down heavily. In one of the drawers of his desk was the square of black cloth that he would place on his head if the jury returned a verdict of guilty and he was obliged to pronounce the death sentence.

Once again, the rituals and tension made the process feel like a theatrical performance. The ticking of the large clock on the north wall seemed as loud as gunshots. The court registrar solemnly approached the jury box and asked the twelve white men, "Gentlemen, are you agreed on a verdict?"

Foreman Sands answered, "Yes, we have."

The registrar stuck to the script. "How say you? Is the prisoner guilty or not guilty of the offence with which he is charged?"

Sands replied, "Not guilty."

THERE WAS IMMEDIATE uproar. The *Tribune* noted, "Women sprang to their feet and cheered. The police shouted, 'Order!' but the bedlam was unabated. Finally they threatened to clear the court."

With each subsequent retelling of this pivotal moment, the drama of the verdict became more exaggerated. One of the most colourful accounts came sixteen years later, from Oakes biographer Geoffrey Bocca, although he had not been in Nassau at the time. "An ear-splitting cheer came from the court and was echoed outside and all along Bay Street. . . . Never perhaps in a British court of law were there such fantastic scenes, so many cheers, so many tears of emotion shed, so many backs thumped, so many hands wrung, so much hysterical laughter."

Reporters rushed to the telegraph office, eager to dispatch the news. The verdict made headlines internationally. "Triumphant Playboy Celebrates Acquittal in Oakes Murder Case," read the *Newsweek* headline. Godfrey Higgs was celebrated as the "obscure Nassau attorney before his part in the de Marigny case gave him worldwide publicity."

Once Sir Oscar Daly had told the prisoner he was discharged, the latter sprang out of the prisoner's cage towards his wife. After an exuberant embrace, Freddie de Marigny walked out into the square with Nancy's arm around his waist. Police had to use a fire hose to keep the mob under control. The freed man was hoisted onto the shoulders of a diverse throng singing, "For he's a jolly good fellow! And so say all of us!" The couple blinked as a barrage of flashing cameras exploded in the tropical night. The de Marignys managed to extricate themselves and dive into a car that sped them towards their white bungalow on Victoria Avenue. One glance at the unruly crowd there persuaded them to continue on to the house of defence lawyer Godfrey Higgs to toast the victory. De Marigny happily supplied cavalier quotes to the press. "I was tried ten percent for the murder of Sir Harry, and ninety percent for marrying his daughter," he told one reporter, before announcing to another that he had found the trial "boring."

Elsewhere, according to de Marigny's recollections, celebrations continued far into the night. "The hotels and bars of Nassau were filled with people, many of them unknown to me, celebrating my victory." For de Marigny, his acquittal represented not only the victory of a good defence team but also a triumph of human rights. He was convinced that he had public opinion on his side. "The champagne flowed, not for me alone, but for the underdog in each of us. Hundreds gathered on the lawn outside my home, singing, dancing, cheering."

THE DE MARIGNYS may have thought that the ordeal was over—but it was not. Back in the courtroom, the chief justice watched the celebration with an amused eye, then turned back to James Sands, who had not finished speaking. Three significant statements had almost been lost in the hubbub.

Sir Harry and Lady Oakes strolling through London's Green Park in 1938.

The pretty colonial architecture of Parliament Square in Nassau.

Nassau's affluent Bay Street in the 1930s. THE BAHAMAS NATIONAL ARCHIVES (BNA)

Nassau docks and the sponge fleet, with Christ Church Cathedral, where Oakes's memorial service was held, in the background. BNA

Harold Christie (far left) showing the island of San Salvador to Sir Harry Oakes (left) and two friends. Oakes subsequently bought the island. GETTY IMAGES 515332568

Eunice Oakes and her husband enjoying his golf course. AGEFOTOSTOCK

Children raised in Nassau's Grant's Town had little hope of an education. BNA

The Duke of Windsor was a frequent guest at Oakes's polo matches. The Duchess and Lady Oakes are in the stands behind their husbands. GETTY IMAGES 515118134

"Count" Marie Alfred Fouquereaux de Marigny and Nancy Oakes, both good-looking and reckless.
GETTY IMAGES 107808125

The blood-spattered, partly burned bed on which Oakes was bludgeoned to death.
GETTY IMAGES 53007672

The blood-stained Chinese screen, which played a crucial role in the trial.
GETTY IMAGES 53007677

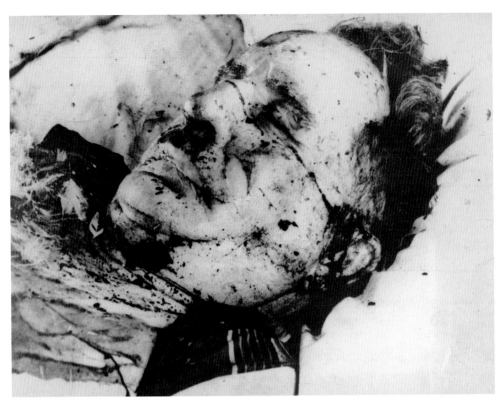

Police photo of Sir Harry Oakes's battered head. GETTY IMAGES 53007674

The Supreme Court building in Nassau, with war memorial in front. BNA

The biggest story the island
newspapers ever covered.
BNA

Freddie de Marigny arriving at the preliminary hearings.
PRIVATE COLLECTION

Left to right: Attorney General Eric Hallinan,
Justice Daly, and defence lawyers Godfrey
Higgs and Ernest Callender study a plan of de
Marigny's house. GETTY IMAGES 50623020

The killer of multimillionaire Sir Harry Oakes
has never been identified. . . . Perhaps it suited
his associates to leave the murder unsolved. BNA

The first two statements suggested that doubts had rippled through the jury's deliberations. First, Sands said that the verdict was not unanimous, despite Sir Oscar's hopes—the vote to acquit was 9–3. Second, the jury regretted that Colonel Erskine-Lindop, who as Nassau's police commissioner had been one of the first at the crime scene the previous July, had been allowed to leave the colony without giving evidence in the case. In mid-September, two weeks after de Marigny had been committed to trial, Erskine-Lindop had been abruptly promoted to deputy commissioner of the larger Trinidad Police Force. The departure of the most senior member of the Nassau constabulary, and the man who had informed the Duke of Windsor about the murder, had left the field entirely open to the two Florida detectives to fortify the Crown's case. Because Erskine-Lindop missed the trial altogether, he was never questioned under oath about the appearance of the crime scene before it had been thoroughly contaminated. Perhaps the twelve sturdy Nassauvians on the jury resented the way that this chain of events had allowed Melchen and Barker to shoulder aside the local force and make a mess of the case.

Sands's third statement to the judge was the most significant. The jury had added a rider to its verdict. It recommended that, despite his acquittal, de Marigny should be immediately deported from the colony.

The chief justice observed that the court had no authority to order the deportation of de Marigny: this was a decision for the political authorities. However, he said, he was sure that their recommendation would carry weight with the governor.

He was absolutely correct. Both Attorney General Eric Hallinan and Harold Christie had sent daily reports on the trial to the Duke of Windsor while he and the duchess were travelling in the eastern United States. The duke could not have been more eager to get rid of a man he loathed. De Marigny's continued presence in Nassau would inevitably provoke comment on the governor's foolish decision to call in the two Miami detectives and their subsequent eagerness to convict the Mauritian, perhaps with fabricated evidence. So, within hours of the verdict, presumably following instructions from the absent governor, the acting governor of the Bahamas was cabling the Colonial Office in London. "Am strongly of opinion that deportation order should be made," read the telegram from Leslie Heape, an old-school colonial bureaucrat with little sympathy for French-speaking outsiders.

The telegram also contained a request for a military aircraft or vessel to execute the order. I can imagine how outrageous the Westminster mandarins, preoccupied by bloody military campaigns in Europe, found this demand. It would have confirmed their opinion of the former king's lack of judgment. The request was summarily refused.

The duke was not the only Nassau official who wanted to see the back of de Marigny. The executive council of the Bahamas, which included amongst its members Harold Christie, defence lawyer Godfrey Higgs, and Attorney General Hallinan, called a special session to discuss whether the acquitted man should be deported. Christie, Higgs, and Hallinan were all present when the council voted to expel immediately not only de Marigny but also Georges de Visdelou-Guimbeau. Higgs was one of the few who refused to jump on the deportation bandwagon, yet even he was unenthusiastic about his former client. Council minutes recorded his view that, "while it was desirable that Mr. de Marigny leave the colony, he should be permitted to leave of his own accord and that no deportation order should be made."

Telegrams continued to fly between Nassau and Westminster. Colonial Secretary Heape, who was acting governor in the Duke's absence, reported that de Marigny was widely believed to be guilty and had been acquitted only because the Miami detectives had done such a poor job. The newspapers in Nassau, Heape added, were out for blood: "Retention of these men will create discord in the community." Heape, presumably prompted by the governor, insisted that everything might calm down "if we can get de Marigny and Guimbeau out of the Colony."

The Colonial Office would not budge on its refusal to divert an RAF Transport Command aircraft to Nassau to do the duke's imperious bidding and ship de Marigny off to Mauritius. London officials pointed out that there were no legal grounds to deport somebody for being "undesirable." This drove the Duke of Windsor to new levels of frustration. By now he was back in Nassau, where he received a letter from de Visdelou-Guimbeau asking for a six-week grace period to put his affairs in order— not an unreasonable request from a man who had barely been involved in the Oakes murder trial. Nevertheless, de Visdelou's request was refused, and the governor fired off another testy cable about de Marigny to Westminster: "His matrimonial history shows him to be an unscrupulous adventurer. Twice divorced and three times married since 1937. Despoiled second wife of £25,000 and then married daughter of a millionaire. Has evil reputation for immoral conduct with young girls. Is gambler and spendthrift. Suspected drug addict. . . . Evaded Finance Control Regulations by obtaining divorce from second wife."

The cable continued in this vein for two more paragraphs, trotting out unsubstantiated accusations that de Marigny and de Visdelou were sexual predators, harassing young women and perhaps even slipping drugs into their drinks, then raping them. Perhaps there was some truth in these allegations. The two reckless Mauritian playboys were so offensive to both the Bay Street Boys and the starchier members of the British expatriate community that many people were happy to assume the worst on the flimsiest of evidence.

IN THE SHORT term, Alfred and Nancy de Marigny were too elated to pay any attention to the deportation order and the cables that would soon be shuttling between Government House and Westminster. At Godfrey Higgs's house, they had been joined by many of their supporters, paid and unpaid, including the private detective Raymond Schindler and Professor Leonarde Keeler, the inventor of a lie-detector apparatus, whom Schindler had brought into the case. Justice Daly had not allowed Professor Keeler to demonstrate his polygraph kit in court, but Keeler had it with him now and was keen to show it off. "In my euphoria, I volunteered to take the test," de Marigny recalled. "Higgs objected, as any lawyer would. I had nothing to fear." The jury had declared him not guilty; would this new machine do the same?

The cuff was fastened to de Marigny's wrist and connected to the detector by electrical cables that would measure vital signs such as his pulse and temperature, then activate pens recording the activity on graph paper. Erratic movement of the pens would reveal any uncertainty. Keeler began his interrogation, interspersing irrelevant questions with questions related to Sir Harry's murder:

Q: Is your name de Marigny?
A: Yes.
Q: When you took your guests home on July seventh, did you come straight home yourself?
A: Yes.
Q: Do you live in Nassau?
A: Yes.
Q: Did you enter Westbourne?
A: No.
Q: Did you kill Sir Harry Oakes?
A: No.
Q: Do you know who killed Harry Oakes?

A: No.

Q: Did you put your hand on the Chinese screen between the time of the murder and the discovery of the body?

A: No.

Raymond Schindler would attest in a magazine article the following year: "The graphs showed that de Marigny was telling the truth. He was jittery and high strung, but his reactions to the important questions were no more marked than those to such queries as, 'Do you live in Nassau?'"

De Marigny would triumphantly write: "That night, and for the rest of his years, Keeler, a pioneer in scientific crime detection, swore that there was no doubt of my innocence." Perhaps. But the accuracy of polygraph testing (unlike fingerprint evidence) has always been controversial, and Professor Keeler's apparatus was an early model that had received little scientific validation. Today, there are very few jurisdictions where polygraph test results are admissible in court.

But in November 1943, Alfred de Marigny believed that Keeler's apparatus had vindicated him. He was also triumphant that the verdict had confirmed public opinion in Nassau, particularly amongst the black population, that he was innocent. In his 1990 memoir, he enjoys relating an episode that reinforced this confidence, although the incident appears in no other account of the night after his acquittal. After he and Nancy left Higgs's party, de Marigny claimed, he dropped his wife at their Victoria Street house and then continued to drive around the little colonial capital, enjoying his liberty after four months in the cramped, dirty jail cell. Then he heard a distant singer, and he recalled the music that had wafted into his cell. He drove in the direction of the music and found himself in front of a nightclub. "Some of the blacks at the entrance to the club recognized me. . . . I walked inside, and a cheer greeted me. When I could finally regain my voice, I ordered drinks for everyone. 'Sorry, boss man,' said the owner. 'You buy no drinks for anyone. We buy *you* a drink.'"

The following day, when de Marigny first heard about the jury's recommendation that he be deported, his first reaction was to resist. Dressed in grey slacks and a loud checked jacket, he graciously welcomed reporters into his Victoria Street sitting room for a press conference. With his wife at his side, he told his audience that he had no plans to leave the Bahamas. He had never worried about the verdict: "I am a good Catholic. See, here are my prayer beads. . . . That's what kept my faith while I was in prison. . . . I had never thought I'd be found guilty."

The de Marignys put on a great performance for the press, starring Freddie as the handsome hero and Nancy as the glamorous minx. Nancy smiled at her husband and commented, "I'm a complete jinx." The "dapper adventurer" (as *Newsweek* labelled him) turned to her and said, "She is like most women. She has bad taste." His wife enquired, "In what respect?" He replied, "In marrying me."

It was the same old carefree attitude that both de Marignys had always enjoyed projecting. Freddie even announced that he and Nancy were going to remarry: he had the bishop's permission to validate their union in St. Francis Xavier Church, despite his two previous civil ceremonies. The following afternoon, Father Bonaventure waited for an hour at the appointed time, but the bridal couple never showed up. The priest shrugged, "It takes two to make a wedding."

A new wrinkle cast a shadow on Freddie's legal status. Gasoline was strictly rationed on the island, but he and Georges de Visdelou had illegally acquired four drums of gasoline that bore RAF stencils. A few days after the Oakes murder trial finished, the two Mauritians were convicted and fined £100 for possession of the gasoline drums. The presiding magistrate announced that, if they were not on the point of being deported, he would jail the pair of them.

De Marigny decided to go quietly. Even if ordinary Bahamians were happy at the verdict, he knew that the island's elite remained convinced of his guilt, couldn't wait for his departure, and would likely boycott his businesses. His reputation was ruined; a casual enquiry about entry into the United States brought the sharp response that he would have to "breathe elsewhere." He set about selling his possessions; Godfrey Higgs acquired *Concubine*, his racing yacht, and Eric Callender got his car—probably as partial payment of their considerable legal fees as his defence team. After attending a dinner in his honour at the Nassau Yacht Club, Freddie and Nancy de Marigny sailed for Cuba on December 6, 1943. They had already said goodbye to Georges de Visdelou, who was moving to Haiti.

One of de Marigny's final initiatives in Nassau was to call in at James Sands's grocery store—motivated, he claims in his 1990 memoir, by an impulse to thank him for the manner in which he had led the jury. Sands led him into a back room and explained why the jury had added the deportation rider to the verdict. According to de Marigny, Sands told him that four members of the jury were Plymouth Brethren—fervent Christian fundamentalists who were shocked by de Marigny's lifestyle and were prepared to believe anything about him. Sands explained, "To them you were more than a criminal, you were a person who broke the law of God. Not only did you sail on Sundays, but you enticed their sons and daughters to sail with you. Those four stuck together like glue. Without that rider, we would have had a hung jury and you would have spent many more months in jail."

So Sands struck a deal with the four men: in exchange for the deportation request, one of the jurors shifted his vote.

BY NEW YEAR'S DAY 1944, the Bahamas were sinking back into international oblivion, and military campaigns in Italy and the Far East occupied the front pages of most newspapers. Crime reporters had already moved on to a new society murder in New York, where a young Canadian playboy named Wayne Lonergan had been accused of strangling his wife, heiress to a New York beer fortune, and crushing her skull with a silver candelabra. The outcome of this trial was more predictable, and fit easily into newspaper headlines. In the short term, the "not guilty" verdict in distant Nassau was too inconclusive for the likes of Erle Stanley Gardner.

The main actors in the courtroom drama had either returned to their regular, sleepy routines or left the island. Sir Oscar Daly was back on the golf course that Harry Oakes had built. James Sands could be seen each evening, walking his dog along the seashore. Lady Oakes had flown out of Nassau a few days before the verdict and retreated to the Bar Harbor estate. She and her children would continue to spend time in the Bahamas, where they had friends and several properties, although her visits were never lengthy.

But there had been no convenient closure to this story. Freddie de Marigny had been acquitted, but did this mean he was innocent? And if he was, who and where was Sir Harry Oakes's killer? Was he sipping a whisky and soda at the bar of the Prince George Hotel, racing a sailboat before the Royal Nassau Sailing Club, or talking business in a Bay Street office? Or had he been acting under orders, and was either far away or had been quietly eliminated, perhaps in the deep waters off Hog Island? According to

Time magazine's correspondent, Attorney General Eric Hallinan grimly declared the search for the murderer closed. But as Nassau society ramped up for its winter season, one prominent hostess confided, "I'll always have to wonder whether I'm dancing with the murderer of Sir Harry Oakes."

The de Marignys were trying to settle in Cuba, where they were guests of Freddie's friend Ernest Hemingway at his *finca*, an hour's drive outside Havana. Their marriage was already beginning to come apart. Part of the problem was that, even after the sale of his Bahamian assets, de Marigny was essentially broke, and his wife had no access to her assets, which were in sterling and were locked into the Bahamas by Britain's wartime currency controls. More fundamentally, once the trial was over, their fundamental incompatibility surfaced. De Marigny was a jaundiced thirty-three-year-old roué who was happiest when hunting and drinking with his friend Ernest. Nancy was a nineteen-year-old heiress who had enjoyed being in the spotlight during the trial but now found herself left alone with Hemingway's smart and scornful third wife, the brilliant war correspondent Martha Gellhorn. Nancy de Marigny soon left, to return to her mother's house (she could not afford her own) and her lively social life in Nassau. The de Marigny marriage would be annulled in 1949; the couple went in different directions, neither of them finding stability or serenity in the years ahead. In subsequent years, Nancy embarked on a series of affairs (including a fling with Jack Hemingway, Ernest's eldest son) and started to obsess over what had happened to her father's fortune.

The Oakes story was not over for them, or for the colony. As Étienne Dupuch wrote in the *Tribune* the day after the verdict, "Today Bahamians are looking around for someone to scalp for the unsolved murder of Sir Harry Oakes. In this 'Tragedy of Errors,' the question for the public to decide is who made the first and biggest error that led to the greatest fiasco in a criminal trial in this country."

Poor Harry Oakes. His image as the Bahamas's great benefactor was already overshadowed by the sensational murder trial, the evidence of his intemperate rows with his son-in-law, and the fevered speculation as to his murderer's identity. In the decades ahead, whenever his name arose anywhere in the world, it prompted only one question: "Who killed him?"

CHAPTER 15

"An Unconvicted Murderer, of a Particularly Savage Type"

It was common knowledge that men from the Klondike to the Congo had felt the weight of Sir Harry's fist. Many others had tasted the equally crushing weight of his influence.

RAYMOND C. SCHINDLER, INSIDE DETECTIVE

I n October 1944, *Inside Detective*, the largest-selling detective magazine in the world, had a riveting cover. Under an illustration of a glamorous blonde in elbow-length purple gloves and gold hoop earrings, it featured the cover line: "'I Could Crack the Oakes Case Wide Open!' by Raymond C. Schindler, celebrated private detective."

Schindler, hired by Nancy de Marigny the previous year as part of her husband's defence team, had already made thousands of dollars out of the Oakes murder case. (His fees were $200 to $300 a day, plus expenses, although it is unlikely that the de Marignys ever paid all his bills.) But after the verdict, he had no intention of allowing the case (or his own name) to disappear from the headlines. I suspect that he was also genuinely frustrated at the lack of a resolution in what he described as "the Twentieth Century's most mystifying crime." So he plunged into the pages of the garish true-crime tabloid to publicize his views.

Schindler was first out of the gate in the post-trial rush to speculate about Sir Harry's murderer, but other "experts" would soon follow. There would be three waves of Oakes obsession in the years ahead. Each illustrates how the past is always seen through a contemporary lens, so that it resonates with current fixations. No new evidence was ever produced, but that didn't stop authors from claiming "breakthroughs." Besides, in addition to the missing perpetrator, there were so many tantalizing loose ends to fuel speculation about the case. The murder weapon had never been found. The bloody "handprints" (perhaps just smears) on the walls of Oakes's bedroom had been ignored, and then scrubbed off. The mystery of the failed attempt to burn the body remained unsolved. Had the body been moved? Had more than one person battered the sleeping baronet to death? Had the murderer or murderers been acting under orders from someone else?

In the immediate aftermath of the trial, those who tried to identify the murderer largely stuck to descriptions of the crime scene as they pursued their own agendas. As the trial faded from memory, the second wave began with promoters spinning increasingly fanciful explanations rooted in contemporary interests rather than new evidence. The third wave gathered momentum as those directly involved in the trial died, the twentieth century drew to a close, and speculation and fiction became interwoven.

Each successive wave further obscured the character and achievements of Sir Harry Oakes. The dead millionaire—a complicated, flawed, and not particularly attractive man—did not hold the interest of any of the writers, and he became a blurred shadow of his real self as writers stumbled onto new insights and pursued their agendas. His extraordinary and ultimately triumphant search for gold, and his philanthropy in Kirkland Lake, Niagara Falls, and New Providence, were forgotten. His truculence and towering rages were endlessly replayed.

Schindler's angle in his self-promoting article was that forensic science could "tear aside the veil of doubt and confusion which has shrouded the case for more than a year." He announced that he had written to the Duke of Windsor the previous June, offering to take over the official Oakes investigation without charge, because "it is my considered opinion that the murderer of Sir Harry [Oakes] can be found, identified, convicted and brought to justice." Now, he catalogued the various scientific approaches that should be employed to explore exactly what had happened in Sir Harry's bedroom on the night of July 7 of the previous year. "The murder room, I am informed, has not been touched," he wrote. FBI laboratory experts should test the burned carpet and bedding to identify what inflammable liquid had been used.

Next, Schindler insisted that witnesses should be questioned again, but this time they should be wired up to Leonarde Keeler's lie-detector apparatus. He also urged that Oakes's body be disinterred, so that medical experts might perform a more thorough autopsy that would include tests to determine whether the dead man had been drugged and what weapon had caused the four head wounds. "Island authorities should remove the handcuffs from scientific crime detection," the portly private dick thundered.

Schindler strayed from science when he trundled off in a new direction—one that says a lot more about Schindler's imagination than it does about the Oakes murder. Photographs of the corpse, the American detective argued, showed that a concentrated flame had been applied to Sir Harry's eyes and genitals after his death. (These macabre details had not been mentioned in medical reports, or at the trial.) Schindler asked why, before advancing his deliciously gruesome explanations. Perhaps the murderer was spurred to mutilate the body by jealousy over a woman, or perhaps this was part of "some mysterious pagan ceremony." In a previous article, the detective had floated the idea that "there are aspects of voodooism in the modus operandi. Burning the eyeballs is one." He went on to write, "The theory of abnormal revenge can't be ruled out. It was an abnormal crime."

After raising this ghoulish scenario (catnip to his readers), Schindler reverted to his support for men in white lab coats. Scientific crime detection, he insisted, "stands ready to prove itself in the Oakes case. . . . I am sure the microscopes and retorts of the laboratory are capable of solving Sir Harry's murder if the green light is given." Today, given the role that DNA testing can play in detection, Schindler's appeal to science would make sense. But in 1943? Perhaps, although the only forensic evidence that offered much certainty was fingerprint evidence.

Nevertheless, in the rush to arrest de Marigny, the police had indeed ignored other possible suspects, and a more rigorous examination of Sir Harry's bedroom might have yielded more clues.

Schindler's article did not prompt any response from Bahamian authorities. But the article achieved its other objectives. *Inside Detective* was the most successful of the nearly two hundred true-crime periodicals that were wildly popular in the days before *People* magazine and twenty-four-hour cable news. These breathlessly written publications thrived in the 1930s and 1940s, and at their peak some six million copies were sold every month in North America. Their covers featured femmes fatales and attention-grabbing headlines, and between the covers were grainy black-and-white images of crime scenes, heroic lawmen, and menacing suspects. They fed a vast public appetite for gory tales of crime and scandal.

Schindler's article included a photo of "Count Alfred de Marigny" and his rich wife, both as groomed and stylish as stars of Hollywood noir, as well as a photo of Oakes's scorched corpse and a diagram of the second floor of the Oakes mansion, with the helpful labels "Bloody Hand Prints on Walls" and "Body Found Here." Accompanying the article about the Oakes case was a glowing blurb about "Detective Schindler," the "shrewd, imaginative pioneer in new investigative methods" who had cracked high-profile murder cases and smashed an Atlantic City graft ring. The profile claimed, "It is generally conceded that he played a large part in securing the acquittal of de Marigny." Readers of *Inside Detective* would never know that Alfred de Marigny and his lawyers fiercely disputed this claim, since Schindler had contributed so little to the defence.

Raymond Schindler achieved his objective; he could not have paid for better publicity for the Schindler Bureau of Investigation. The article had the dual effect of making him look as if he had the inside scoop and making everyone else look clueless. Such tactics are the hallmark of private investigators to this day.

As THE WAR dragged on, the Duke and Duchess of Windsor continued to grumble about their exile in Nassau and their treatment by the British government. The duchess told their friend Rosita Forbes, "They only murdered Sir Harry Oakes once. They will *never* stop murdering the Duke of Windsor." Nevertheless, the duke's secretary sent a polite but curt note to Schindler, refusing his offer to find the murderer.

However, government officials in Nassau knew that the murder and botched investigation cast a long shadow over the colony. When the Windsors finally returned to Europe in the spring of 1945 to live out a life of grudges and indolence in France, the duke's successor as governor, Sir William Murphy, took action. He asked the colonial secretary for a further examination of

Oakes's business affairs and of the evidence against de Marigny. In London, Sir William's boss did not give much priority to this request, and it was quietly shuffled off to Scotland Yard. There, in February 1947, a Detective Inspector Deighton produced a 130-page report based solely on the transcript of the 1943 trial.

Deighton had rigorously scrutinized the evidence produced four years earlier, in a courthouse more than 4,000 miles away. But he had not travelled to Nassau to talk to the local police there, to pick up further information (and gossip), or to re-interview any of the witnesses. His limited approach meant that he stayed within the parameters of the Crown's case; from the start of his report, he had de Marigny in his gun sights. After describing de Marigny's threats against his father-in-law (with little mention of Sir Harry's churlish behaviour towards his son-in-law), Deighton wrote in his introduction: "If any person was a suspect that person was de Marigny, and his motive was revenge and gain." The British detective listed the circumstantial evidence against de Marigny, which he considered damning, then commented: "With the assistance of the accused's many friends, the defending solicitors built up a clever defence and took advantage of the mistakes by the investigating officers, to bring about so much doubt regarding the vital clues, that the Jury (supported in my opinion by His Lordship's summing up) returned a verdict of 'Not Guilty' and the accused was acquitted."

As far as Deighton was concerned, de Marigny remained the only real suspect. He lambasted the way that the police had done their job: "In my opinion de Marigny was given too much consideration and latitude, and if more time had been devoted to his interrogation and an *early* search been personally conducted by the officers at his house, garage, farm etc., it is highly probable that other valuable circumstantial evidence would have been obtained. I am reluctant to leave the matter at this stage as I feel so much could have been accomplished if more 'punch' had been put into the practical side of this investigation." The British detective shared the same tunnel-visioned approach as the Nassau police, Barker, and Melchen. He brushed aside de Marigny's alibi, the awkward questions about Harold Christie's movements, and the lack of a murder weapon, and he chose to accept Barker's dodgy fingerprint evidence. But he was also a traditionalist who deplored the confused lines of authority ("too many senior officers") and sloppy police work. Reading his report, I have no doubt that if he had been in charge, the investigation would have proceeded lickety-split and de Marigny would have swung from a rope in no time. "I am of the opinion that the accused committed the crime," he wrote, adding that Georges de Visdelou was probably de Marigny's accomplice and should have been interrogated properly.

Deighton's official conclusion, submitted to the Colonial Office, was that reopening the investigation would not "serve any good purpose," despite the fact that Bahamians must be "disgusted with the manner in which this investigation was conducted and the subsequent result." De Marigny could not be retried for the murder after he had already been acquitted, and there was no enthusiasm for pursuing the case against Georges de Visdelou when so much time had elapsed.

The Bahamas had been useful to the wartime British government as a holding pen for the Nazi-sympathizing Windsors, but now that the war was over and the Windsors were discredited, this obscure little colony slipped out of view. By the 1960s, Britain was keen to shed its colonies, and the Bahamas took their first steps towards self-government in 1964. Meanwhile, in time-honoured British tradition, the Oakes report was quietly buried in the Colonial Office Archives, with a note that it should remain classified until 2022. (It was released in 2001.)

The government had fulfilled its duty to answer the governor's request. Now it could let sleeping dogs lie.

A copy of the report was, however, sent to Sir William Murphy in Nassau, who presumably shared it with his executive council—a government body that included Attorney General Hallinan, Harold Christie, and others who had been intimately involved in the de Marigny trial. They would have welcomed Deighton's conclusion: any serious attempt at further investigation would have involved another round of finger pointing and mutual suspicions within Nassau's tight little society, and might have revived gossip about the Oakes–Christie–Windsor financial dealings. Instead, everyone could simply deplore the fact that de Marigny had allegedly got away with murder, while congratulating themselves for shipping him off the island and out of sight.

YET A STEADY flow of articles about the unsolved murder continued to titillate writers and readers in the English-speaking world. Every questionable event in New Providence immediately became part of the Oakes murder mystery. The day after Sir Harry was killed, Rawlins and Cordner, two black Bahamians who had been employed as night watchmen for Westbourne and the country club next door, failed to show up for work. They may have simply decided to stay out of the way of the police, fearful of somehow being implicated. But suspicion quickly blossomed that they had been bribed to leave New Providence immediately because they could identify who had entered Sir Harry's bedroom that night.

This theory was endlessly whispered in Nassau, and then reported in various gossipy articles about Oakes's death. Alfred de Marigny would later claim that he had run into Rawlins in Freeport, Grand Bahama, in the 1980s. According to de Marigny's 1990 account, Rawlins told him that he and Cordner had seen Frank Christie, Harold's brother, drive two unknown men to Westbourne's entrance. Frank remained in the car while the two men climbed the outdoor staircase to Sir Harry's room. After a few minutes, de Marigny wrote, the watchmen had seen the orange glow of fire in the room, then watched the intruders descend the staircase, to be driven by Frank Christie in the direction of Lyford Cay.

But in the official 1943 investigation, despite the possibility of a connection between the vanished watchmen and the murderer, no effort had been made to locate them. And by 1990, after de Marigny had spent nearly half a century brooding on the murder, officials in Nassau had no interest in pursuing a theory based on a conversation for which the long-departed de Marigny had no witnesses, of which he had made no record, and that conveniently removed any suspicion from him but incriminated someone else.

Crime lovers also had a colourful selection of cranks to listen to, some of whom claimed to know the identity of the murderer, and a couple of whom claimed to *be* the murderer. There was no proof for any of these claims. Lady Oakes received several letters from correspondents claiming that they would tell her the name of her husband's killer if she would forward to them a bank order—usually for £5,000. One particularly aggressive letter writer, a taxi driver named Nicholas Musgrave, was sent to prison for threatening behaviour.

In 1950, the half-naked body of a thirty-seven-year-old Washington-based lawyer named Betty (occasionally spelled Bettie) Renner was found stuffed down a well outside Nassau. Her family and her legal colleagues insisted that she was in the Bahamas as a tourist, but this didn't scotch the rumour that she had been investigating the Oakes murder. The *Toronto Daily Star* then trotted out a widely reprinted story from an English-born Toronto resident who was described as a "personal friend" of Betty Renner, and who claimed that Renner had told her the murder had been organized by the "King of the Island"—a powerful local businessman. The son of a white man and a "Negro" woman, this island oligarch had allegedly hired a man to commit the crime. The friend suggested that "everybody in Nassau knows he did it and that he did it because he thought Lady Oakes would marry him, but he is so powerful that nobody from the governor down dares touch him." But one woman's assertion, with no corroborating testimony, went nowhere—except, of course, to stoke lingering suspicions of Harold Christie, although this was the first suggestion that he had hopes of marrying Lady Oakes.

Apart from a lack of evidence, there was another reason why the *Toronto Daily Star* story died. Nassau's ruling clique had a much more pressing priority: building up the Bahamas as a dazzling vacation destination. Any lingering suspicion that a ruthless killer remained in Nassau would have been bad for business. The tourist industry benefited from the vast improvement in air transportation to the islands, helped by the wartime bequest of two modern airports. It also got a sharp boost in 1959, when Fidel Castro seized power in Havana. Barred from swarming into Cuba's casinos and clubs, American gamblers and sun seekers switched their attentions to the Bahamas. Income from tourism alone exploded from then until the end of the century. At the same time, the Bahamas' image as a tax haven blossomed. Chief beneficiaries of this new economy were white realtors and lawyers, whose Bay Street offices featured lengthy lists of locally registered companies. Before the war, there had been only one bank and one trust company in Nassau; by the 1950s, there were dozens.

No one did better out of the boom than Harold Christie,

who, thanks to his association with Sir Harry Oakes, had been able to amass a huge amount of seafront property, including the 448-acre estate that he and Oakes had been developing on the west end of New Providence: Lyford Cay. This lavish sanctuary was a magnet to big shots looking both for a tax shelter and a secure second home.

Christie continued to be a superb salesman, soft-voiced and persuasive. Each winter, he exchanged his casual Caribbean shirts and sandals for pinstriped suits and leather brogues, and spent a few weeks in New York City, Toronto, and London, entertaining potential buyers with photos of glowing sunsets and pearly white sands. (In London he stayed at Claridge's, one of the most elegant hotels in the world; in Toronto he preferred the baronial Royal York.) Jovial in manner and generous with drinks, he shrugged off any suggestion that ordinary tourists, let alone millionaires, might be at risk. He was so persuasive that, in the mid-1950s, he sold the Lyford Cay Club estate to the Canadian millionaire and horse owner E. P. Taylor. Lyford Cay's future residents would include Greek shipping tycoons, Wall Street hedge fund owners, heirs to fortunes made from automobiles, rum, supermarkets, toy stores, and construction, plus the actor Sean Connery, the author Arthur Hailey, and a smattering of minor royals.

But the fascination with the great unsolved crime lingered, particularly amongst those who had been part of the courtroom drama. In April 1956, another accomplished self-publicist wrote a long feature in the *American Weekly* under the title "My Most Baffling Murder." Erle Stanley Gardner, who had covered the trial for the Hearst newspaper chain and was now billed as the "creator of Perry Mason and author of 'The Case of the Terrified Tailor,'" described the murder and the death scene in vivid detail. Then he eagerly trotted out clues that he had noticed but the police had ostensibly missed.

Why had nobody paid any attention to the feathers that stuck to the body? Who had moved the body before the police were called? Why were the contents of Sir Harry's stomach never analyzed to eliminate the possibility that he had been poisoned? (They had been, and were not found to include any toxic substance.) "I had first-hand opportunity to observe significant photographic evidence (such as the clue of the blood that ran uphill) which points toward reappraisal of some facts which seemingly have hitherto escaped the authorities." (Harold Christie may have inadvertently created the "blood running uphill" impression when he clumsily wiped the murdered man's face.) When Gardner himself had visited the scene of the crime, he "got down on my back and looked under the bed." The other reporters laughed, but it gave him a significant clue: the underside of the mattress had been destroyed by fire, but Sir Harry's pyjamas had not. Gardner therefore insisted that "the body must have been placed on the bed *after the burning*."

It is hard to know what to make of these mysterious details and surmises. They were not featured in the police reports at the time—but as Deighton had noted, the police work had been shoddy. However, like Schindler, Gardner went on to build a more gruesome scenario, although his version didn't include voodoo. Gardner suggested that there must have been more than one killer, since it would have taken at least two individuals to move the body. He proposed that enraged killers had set two fires, although he did not explain why two were necessary or why they were enraged. He suggested that Sir Harry might have hidden gold bars under his bedroom floor, and when he heard intruders, got out of bed to check on them. (There was no evidence that he had been roused by the killer, nor that he had a cache under his floorboards, nor that his body had been moved.) Gardner raised the possibility that one of the murderers had entered Christie's bedroom—thus accounting for the blood-stains found on his bedroom door—to look for him, "perhaps to eliminate him as a witness," but repeated the rumour that Christie was not in the house at the time. (Christie himself could have smeared blood on his door when he rushed back to his room after trying to revive Sir Harry. The police had not flagged these bloodstains as significant.)

After sowing confusion about what had happened, Gardner did not manage to weave together a convincing answer to the question "Who killed Harry Oakes?" Perhaps he felt inhibited by the constraints of nonfiction. Still, his decision to write the piece was prompted by the same impulse as Schindler's decision to publish in *Inside Detective*. The *American Weekly* was a great platform for a popular writer; a Sunday supplement carried in all the Hearst newspapers across America, it claimed a circulation of over 50 million readers.

Meanwhile, various themes emerged from Gardner's article that played well in Nassau. The piece confirmed Sir Harry Oakes as an unsympathetic character whom many people had good cause to dislike. It suggested that the solution to this "most baf-fling murder mystery of all time" likely lay in Oakes's gold-mining days, long before he arrived in his tax-sheltered paradise. "He was a man of direct action, of strong likes and dislikes. He had many enemies. . . . Is it possible that Sir Harry Oakes was fire-tortured as a result of some weird facet of his past?"

Almost as an afterthought, Gardner raised the possibility of random, ruthless thieves. Wherever Harry Oakes had lived—in Niagara Falls, in Sussex, and in New Providence—there had been rumours that the distrustful millionaire had buried caches of gold bars and coins on his property. Now Gardner heard that, on Great Exuma Island, southeast of New Providence, Bahamians had been finding gold coins. The oldest were dated 1853, the newest 1907, so they were not from the piracy era. The Bahamian police had already investigated this cache and found no link between the Exuma gold and the Oakes murder, but that didn't stop Gardner speculating. He wrote, "There is a persistent rumor that, after Sir Harry's death, gold coins could be purchased on one of the outlying islands at 50 percent of their face value. Was Sir Harry tortured to make him divulge information connected with this?"

Most important, Gardner did not even consider the possibility that Harold Christie, who had been so helpful to him in 1943 while Gardner was covering the trial, played a role in the killing of Sir Harry. The official story in the Bahamas for the next few years was that the murder had likely been committed either by de Marigny, as the Deighton report argued, or by someone else—perhaps from Sir Harry's gold-mining past—who had long since fled the islands. I can well imagine Christie's relief that he had escaped mention in this article, as he continued to cast wide his international net for millionaires who might flutter into his tax-sheltering paradise.

HAROLD CHRISTIE'S GROWING influence was evident in the first full-length book about the "Murder of the Century," as it was frequently tagged, which was published sixteen years after Oakes's death. *The Life and Death of Sir Harry Oakes,* from which I have already drawn colourful details about Oakes's early life, was the work of Geoffrey Bocca, a suave thirty-nine-year-old British writer who had been a war correspondent for London's mass-circulation *Daily Express* during the Second World War. He subsequently moved to New York, cultivated a taste for silk ties and gold cufflinks, and established a very successful career as a freelance correspondent for such bestselling magazines as *Saturday Evening Post, McCall's,* and *Reader's Digest.* But he always kept in close touch with his former employer Lord Beaverbrook, the Canadian-born press baron who owned the *Daily Express*, *Evening Standard*, and *Sunday Express*. Wealthy, gregarious, and impatient, Beaverbrook gave Bocca entrée into the social circles to which the author aspired.

The Oakes biography was Bocca's fourth nonfiction book; the first three were fawning accounts of various royal figures, including *The Woman Who Would Be Queen*, a sycophantic portrayal of the Duchess of Windsor. Bocca's nonfiction books conformed to magazine style: racy and compelling, but with no indexes or endnotes, and only the briefest bibliographies. (Liberated from picky magazine fact checkers, he also included lively dollops of invented dialogue.) After exploring the Harry Oakes story, he would go on to publish several more nonfiction titles, as well as a series of sado-masochistic erotic novels featuring Commander Amanda Nightingale, a shapely English spy.

Bocca had first stumbled onto the Oakes story when he visited New Providence to conduct research for his 1954 book about the former Wallis Simpson. He did not warm to the colony. "Nassau is a village community with a compelling capacity for inspiring dislike," he wrote, going on to describe its "smallness, meanness and tourist-chiselling." During that visit, Bocca had got to know Harold Christie, and quickly came to rely on him for insider information about Nassau society and the duchess's hairdresser and wardrobe. At this point, the author did not spend much time on the Oakes murder, other than to record (or invent) the duchess's first "breathless" reaction to news of Sir Harry's death: "Well, never a dull moment in the Bahamas!"

The author's only comment on the murder in his 1954 book was provocative. He didn't buy the official story that the killer had long since departed from New Providence. Instead, he dropped in the throwaway line that "an unconvicted murderer, of a particularly savage type, lives and works today in the tiny community of Nassau. Yet three succeeding Governors have made no attempt to reopen the case, although the stain of evil it has left behind remains a pervading and ominous force in the island . . . causing a deep degeneration in its communal character."

As a freelance writer, Bocca was always on the lookout for a good subject, so it is no surprise that he returned to such a popular story as the Oakes murder. Moreover, he felt he had an excellent source for his book: Lord Beaverbrook. Beaverbrook, who had been a confidant of the former Edward VIII during the abdication crisis, had already supplied Bocca with the names of people with whom the author might discuss the Duchess of Windsor. The press baron, who made frequent fishing trips to the Caribbean, knew New Providence and its government elite well. He had a residence, known as Pancake House, in Nassau, and he had made it his business to get to know Étienne Dupuch, owner of the *Nassau Tribune*, because he liked his crusading anti-racism editorials. In February 1953, Bocca had written to Dupuch, "Lord Beaverbrook tells me you are prepared to help me in my biography of the Duchess." He quizzed the *Tribune*'s editor about the relationship between the Windsors and the Oakes family, and the duke's role in the investigation of the Oakes murder.

Initially, when Beaverbrook heard that the New York publisher Doubleday had commissioned a book on the Oakes murder from Bocca, he received the news warmly, promising to publish extracts in the *Sunday Express*. By March 1958, Bocca was already well launched on his Oakes project, and he told the British press lord, "The Oakes story will be first rate. I have drafted an opening chapter so hair-raising it even scares me." He wrote Beaverbrook that he had made arrangements to call on Raymond Schindler, still active in New York City, and to visit Maine, to see Harry Oakes's childhood home and work in the files of his alma mater, Bowdoin College. "I am to finish the book by October."

Bocca planned to travel to Nassau in July, and, hoping that his association with the British baron would enhance his own credibility, he made a bold request. "I hope you will find this liberty of mine pardonable," he began his next letter to Beaverbrook, before going on to ask if he might stay in Pancake House while doing research in Nassau. He explained that he didn't want to "write about death, murder and creeping evil from a room in the British Colonial Hotel." On the other hand, if he was alone in Pancake House, "the story writes itself from there."

Beaverbrook snapped back the following day, in a completely different tone. "I am opposed to the book about Oakes. I disassociate myself from it altogether because of the implications in relation to other people. . . . Now you are asking me to house you in Nassau. This I will not do. And I will repudiate any association with you in this venture."

The final line in this curt note is enigmatic: "You are a good boy when you are a good boy."

What caused Lord Beaverbrook's volte-face? I could find no clues in the Beaverbrook correspondence. But I speculate that amongst the "other people" whom he apparently wished to protect were not only the Duke of Windsor, to whom he felt a residual loyalty, but also members of the Nassau elite whom he knew socially. He was definitely acquainted with Axel Wenner-Gren, and may have had a small tax-shelter corporation in Nassau himself. Bocca's line in his biography of the duchess about Nassau's "unconvicted murderer" would have rung alarm bells.

Geoffrey Bocca apologized profusely to Beaverbrook in his next letter: "I certainly didn't mean to offend you." But he was committed to the Oakes book, and he still hoped to sell it to the *Express* newspapers. Within months, the complete manuscript was at Doubleday's New York office. Upon publication the following year, it would be promoted as "the sensational story, never before told, of the Maine Yankee who found a gold mine, bought a British Knighthood, and was murdered in Nassau in the classic crime of the century."

Despite this overheated blurb, Bocca offered the blandest possible explanation for Sir Harry's death. Two aspects of his story suggest that he had decided to be, in Beaverbrook's enigmatic phrase, "a good boy," and to present a black-and-white narrative to which no Nassau tycoon could object.

First, his description of the murder victim was the harshest characterization yet of Oakes, and far more negative than any other portrayal of Sir Harry in Canada or the Bahamas. In Northern Ontario, Bocca wrote, Oakes had made "hundreds of enemies whom he would not forgive and who would not forgive him. . . . His drive and determination almost from the start had been sparked and spontaneously combusted in hate and bitterness." According to Bocca, success had unleashed "everything that was worst in [Oakes's] nature. . . . He had done what every gold prospector across the face of the earth sought to do—he had found his Holy Grail—but the gold had turned to the gold of Midas, corrupting, destroying."

Once in the Bahamas, Bocca claimed, "His temper became even more violent. . . . He enjoyed outraging [Nassau residents], grating their cultured nerves, swaggering into the British Colonial Hotel, sweating freely in his heavy lumber shirt and sand-caked top boots. His language and manners were filthier than ever." Bocca quoted an anonymous source's remark to the millionaire: "A skunk you were born, Harry Oakes, and a skunk you will die." In the year before his death, according to Bocca, Sir Harry had begun to drink. "As he drank, his moods and his temper grew progressively blacker." In his final pages, Bocca concluded,

"He found his gold and it destroyed him"—implying that his brutal death was almost self-inflicted.

This was a brutal murder, but for Oakes's unreliable biographer Geoffrey Bocca, there was a soothing symmetry to the event. "Sir Harry Oakes was dead, a long, bitter and violent life violently terminated."

By contrast, Harold Christie emerges from Bocca's account as "a remarkable man," a cross between a saintly parish priest and a visionary entrepreneur. "Had he chosen to engage his personality in a wider sphere, say in the affairs of his mother country, Britain, he would have achieved international stature and received many honors and decorations." Christie's growing fortune meant nothing to him, wrote Bocca; his only concern was the welfare of his beloved Bahamas. "People followed him everywhere" with their problems, and "somehow everything was settled, everyone satisfied." Bocca dismisses any notion that Christie was involved in the murder. In his view, "Only those for whom the Oakes case is the wildest hearsay have misinterpreted Harold Christie's unhappy position."

Having flattened these two characters into caricatures, Bocca then wove an elaborate tale about a professional hitman being hired in Miami by a "syndicate of financial adventurers involved in an intricate plot to get their hands on Oakes's fortune." His theory of whodunit added up to nothing; he offered no proof and only two limp suggestions as to how the case should be reopened: that Sir Harry's body be exhumed so it could be examined for more clues, and that Raymond Schindler take another crack at the case. His tone is sanctimonious to the end. "Whoever it was who cut Harry Oakes down on July 8, 1943, one can say this, that Harry asked to be killed." The author had abandoned his own conclusion in his earlier book that the killer was still in the Bahamas.

The Life and Death of Sir Harry Oakes, which was eventually published by Weidenfeld, sold well, and its glib theorizing had a lasting impact on the Oakes story. It confirmed Harold Christie, now sixty-three, as the Bahamas' greatest salesman— the "Man Who Put the Bahamas on the Map" according to one admirer—as well as a benevolent godfather to residents, tourists and property buyers alike. Whatever suspicions might be muttered about him, Christie had risen above them—and, moreover, taken everybody by surprise by finally getting married. His wife was a charming American designer, Virginia Campbell. Five years later, Christie was knighted for services to the Bahamas. As the Christies entertained at their elegant Nassau mansion, Sir Harold radiated the glossy confidence of the islands' most important patriarch. He remained on friendly terms with the Oakes family, and he had the largest real estate business in the Bahamas. His position and reputation seemed unassailable.

Meanwhile, Bocca's portrait of Sir Harry Oakes as a bitter brute who deserved to die would fuel the next wave of Oakes exposés.

Other residents of New Providence Island remembered Sir Harry not as a selfish monster but as a man who had done much to make his employees' lives easier. According to Dame Doris Sands Johnson, a teacher and formidable black activist who in 1961 became the first woman to run for political office in the Bahamas, Oakes was a marked man because he had challenged the colony's entrenched racial segregation. In her memoir *The Quiet Revolution in the Bahamas*, Johnson quoted "Over-the-Hill gossip" (that is, talk amongst black Bahamians) that "Sir Harry was killed because he was so generous and fair to Bahamian laborers and had vowed to bring about the downfall of one of the 'Bay Street Boys.'" At the edge of Oakes Field, an imposing memorial was erected; the inscription on its base read, "In memory of Sir Harry Oakes, Bt., 1874–1943. A great friend and benefactor of the Bahamas." The monument's white Vermont marble was paid for by Lake Shore Mines in Kirkland Lake, Ontario.

But the white marble gradually lost its gleam in the Bahamian humidity. And there was no redemption for Sir Harry in the next wave of curiosity about his unsolved murder.

CHAPTER 16

Darker Questions

Saturday, 10 July, [1943]. . . . Still a bit stunned by all that has taken place. I can't quite piece it together yet. . . . At the very least you have to accept that the Duke colluded in the implication of de Marigny. At the very least, the Duke of Windsor, the Governor of the Bahamas, the ex-King of the United Kingdom and the British Empire, was guilty of conspiracy to pervert the course of justice. At the very least. This, as I say, is the kindest interpretation one can make. Many other, darker questions arise.

LOGAN MOUNTSTUART IN *ANY HUMAN HEART*,

A NOVEL BY WILLIAM BOYD

I n the early 1970s, two deaths pushed the Oakes saga into a new phase.

The first death was that of the Duke of Windsor in May 1972. The former British monarch and governor of the Bahamas died of throat cancer at his home in Paris, just before his seventy-eighth birthday. He and his wife had remained in virtual exile from Britain ever since his abdication thirty-five years earlier. In the obituaries, there was no mention of his pro-Nazi activities before the war; the abdication was explained exclusively in terms of the unsuitability of Wallis Simpson, a divorced American commoner, for the role of royal spouse.

Sixteen months later, on September 28, 1973, a headline in the *New York Times* read, "Sir Harold Christie Dies at 77; Spurred Growth of Bahamas." Sir Harold, "one of the largest landowners in the Bahamas," had collapsed during a business trip to Frankfurt, West Germany. The obituary went on to describe how "his company, H. G. Christie Real Estate, was one of the first to realize the potential of the Bahamas as a vacation land and played a major role in the development of Nassau and the outer islands in the West Indies Archipelago."

Dead men cannot sue. Now that two of the principal actors in the Oakes murder drama were gone, the second wave of interest in "the greatest unsolved crime of the century" gathered momentum.

Writers of the next rash of books were for the most part hit-and-run maestros of popular culture who had sharpened their writing skills on the scandal-loving tabloids of London's Fleet Street. They were drawn to the crime not because of any personal connection but because they could reshape it to fit the bestselling genres of their times. Most of these books offered no citations, skimpy bibliographies, and inadequate indexes. The authors' interest in the murdered man was negligible; like the victim in the murder mystery board game *Clue*, Sir Harry was simply a corpse to jumpstart some fun. His fate was now to be marginalized with a few choice words selected from Geoffrey Bocca's caricature. One author dismissed Oakes as a "rough, ruthless, uncouth" man who "made more enemies than friends." Another shrugged him off as "a broad-backed, brash prospector with no social graces." A third described him as "a man so coarse, so rude and so awkward to handle that he was often likened to a warthog."

The lack of new evidence meant that authors and filmmakers broke no fresh ground, but that didn't hinder speculation that roamed further afield than previous treatments of the murder. A new villain was then introduced into the story: American organized-crime kingpin Meyer Lansky. Lansky wanted Oakes dead, went the theory, because Oakes was resisting his plans to develop casinos on the Bahamas.

This idea first appeared in a 1972 book originally titled *King's X: Common Law and the Death of Sir Harry Oakes*, which was reissued in 1976 under the title *Who Killed Sir Harry Oakes?* The author was Marshall Houts, a former FBI agent, lawyer, and author of forty-four books, whose area of expertise was courtroom procedure and whose work inspired the television series *Quincy, M.E.*, about a crime-solving Los Angeles medical examiner. Houts spent most of the book discussing arcane legal arguments, but then he raised the possibility that Oakes's death was a "mutilation gangland killing." He suggested that Lansky had secured the Duke of Windsor's approval to open casinos, and was working with Harold Christie to build them. Oakes allegedly disapproved of the plans, so some of Lansky's henchmen were sent to Nassau to "persuade" him. Houts constructed an elaborate narrative about Oakes meeting Lansky's men on a powerboat in Nassau Harbour, on which Sir Harry unexpectedly died. Houts speculated that Christie then took the corpse back to Westbourne and arranged a fake murder scene. (Had this actually happened, Christie would have had to remove his friend's false teeth, since they were found the next morning in a glass at the bedside.)

Houts's melodramatic account was followed in 1983 by another imaginative tale along the same lines: James Leasor's *Who Killed Sir Harry Oakes?* (reissued in 2001 and 2011). The British-born Leasor was an even more prolific author than Houts; according to his *Times* obituary, he published more than seventy books. He wrote both fiction and nonfiction in a flamboyant style he'd honed while working on the *Daily Express*, and most readers couldn't tell the difference between the two, since he invented dialogue and facts for both. The first half of his book on Oakes followed the standard account of the murder and trial, but the tone was transformed in the second half, which described a plot generated by the Mob (called here "the Outfit") to build casinos in the Bahamas. Cathleen LeGrand, public services librarian at the College of the Bahamas, Nassau, has described these chapters as reading "like a sub-standard gangland thriller, complete with Leasor's own original mobster characters spouting stereotypical tough-guy dialogue." Leasor's book became the basis of a terrible 1989 made-for-TV movie, *Passion in Paradise*, starring Rod Steiger as Oakes.

Mafia villains popped up amidst the palm trees again in 1988 thanks to John Parker, another British journalist who spent several years in the Bahamas on the *Nassau Daily Tribune* before returning to London to work on the tabloid *Daily Mirror*. By the standards of Houts and Leasor, Parker's literary output was modest—only thirty-five books—but his prose rivalled theirs for breathless pacing and racy conspiracies. His book, *King of Fools*, was a biography of the Duke of Windsor. Parker adopted the Houts theory that Oakes's murder was ordered by Meyer Lansky because Oakes was resisting the introduction of casinos to the Bahamas. Parker added the intriguing suggestion that the duke already had business connections with Lansky. Parker also repeated the gossip that Barker and Melchen, the two Miami detectives, were on the Mob's payroll. (There was some truth in this. By now it was known that Barker had connections with organized crime; the FBI had identified him as the source of leaks about bureau activities to Miami gangsters.)

This upsurge in theories linking organized crime to the murder of Sir Harry Oakes is at first puzzling because the supposed motive—the idea that Sir Harry had thwarted Meyer Lansky—doesn't make sense. Although gambling was not a big tourist draw in the Bahamas, it was already legal there; a tourist-only casino, the Bahamas Country Club, had been operating in Nassau since 1920. Pressure to build more casinos would not come until more than sixteen years after Oakes's death, when Fidel Castro banished American businesses from Cuba. Until then, Meyer Lansky and his pal Charles "Lucky" Luciano did not need the Bahamas. Apart from their lucrative interests in the United States, they were busy making a fortune from their control of Cuba's racetracks and casinos, secured through kickbacks to Cuban dictator Fulgencio Batista.

Why the impulse to link Oakes's murder to the Mob? Because in the 1970s and 1980s there was a huge market for Mafia-related books. The phenomenon was no different from the proliferation of vampire novels a few years ago. Interest had surged after the American author Mario Puzo published *The Godfather* in 1969, a book that became, according to the *New York Times*, "one of the most phenomenal successes in literary and cinematic history." The first of several Mafia novels, *The Godfather* topped bestseller lists for months, sold more than 21 million copies, and spawned three popular movies. Publishers rushed to commission books with Mafia-linked plots, while NBC aired an ambitious thirteen-part miniseries called *The Gangster Chronicles*, based on the lives of Mob bosses. This was the bandwagon onto which Houts, Leasor, and Parker—all relentlessly commercial authors—leapt with enthusiasm.

THE MAFIA WAS not the public's only fixation in the 1970s and '80s. The death of the Duke of Windsor unleashed several volumes about the former king. Most of these focused on the

Windsors' Nazi links, and their exile in the Bahamas was given only cursory treatment. But a handful gleefully explored the duke's relations with Sir Harry Oakes and Harold Christie, and took the murder story in a different direction—but one just as popular at the time as Mafia activities.

British author Michael Pye plunged into the business links between the Duke of Windsor, Harold Christie, and Harry Oakes in *The King over the Water,* published in 1981. Pye's preoccupation was illicit currency trading—a hot topic at the time, thanks to highly publicized accounting frauds, pyramid schemes, and securities manipulations by such wheeler dealers as Bernie Cornfeld and Robert Vesco. Pye was a newspaperman who ricocheted between London and New York in the 1970s and '80s, writing for publications as varied as the London *Sunday Times* and the *Daily Telegraph,* and the American magazines *Esquire, Geo,* and *Atlantic Monthly.* Before he wrote his book about the Windsors, he had already published two juicy books on American show business (*The Movie Brats,* coauthored with Linda Myles, and *Moguls*).

The thesis of Pye's book about the Windsors is that their Bahamian sojourn was a period of relentless decline for the royal has-beens, exacerbated by the moral corruption and white-supremacist attitudes of the colony's ruling class. In *The King over the Water,* the author asserts that the Duke of Windsor and Sir Harry Oakes were allies in the search for ways to protect their money from the financial chaos in Europe and to invest it where there was a good chance of making money. The duke was perennially anxious about money (his wife had *very* expensive tastes) and was therefore happy to sell his influence in return for being bankrolled. For Oakes, the problem was that his sizable Lake Shore dividends were trapped inside his Nassau holding companies. He was barred by Britain's wartime exchange controls from sending funds outside the sterling area (which included Canada), and he was afraid that the British government might seize his assets to cover its military costs.

Pye writes that Oakes and the duke were persuaded by Axel Wenner-Gren, the svelte and sinister Swedish entrepreneur, to consider Mexico as a safe and lucrative destination for British currency. Far removed from wartime hostilities, Mexico offered possibilities for investment in highways and railways, particularly if the investor had political influence. Given Oakes's view of government tax grabs, the prospect of putting some of his millions out of reach of Westminster would have been attractive. The challenge was to get the funds there.

Wenner-Gren, according to Pye, was prepared to stake the Duke of Windsor as an investor. This was why the duke had received Maximino Ávila Camacho, brother of the president of Mexico, at Government House in 1941, against all the advice of professional British diplomats. "Royal hospitality was an excellently seductive start" to Wenner-Gren and Oakes's investment schemes, suggests Pye. The author's speculation about how Wenner-Gren shifted Oakes's fortune into Mexico is more elaborate. "It is possible," he writes, that the Swedish financier "was responsible for physically shipping bullion for Oakes from the Bahamas and Canada to Mexico."

The idea that Wenner-Gren's sleek yacht, the *Southern Cross*, cruised around the Caribbean with gold bars from Kirkland Lake stashed in its hold is compelling, although Pye offers no proof. However, by 1941 Oakes had emerged as a sizable stockholder in a newly established bank in Mexico City, the Banco Continental. And he may have been considering abandoning his investments in the Bahamas and relocating to Mexico. This was Pye's supposition, and the basis for his explanation of Oakes's murder and the incompetence of the investigation.

Pye had no doubts about the murderer's identity. In his view, Harold Christie panicked when he realized that Sir Harry was on the verge of moving himself and his fortune to Mexico. If Oakes left Nassau, Christie would lose his best client. But if Oakes were to die, control of his estates "would pass to his trustees—Lady Oakes (to whom Christie was close), Kelly, the business manager (a friend of Christie), and Walter Foskett, the Palm Beach lawyer. Christie would still have some say in the running of Sir Harry's fortune, would still take his commissions and give his advice."

After establishing a motive for Christie, Pye goes on to explain the Duke of Windsor's role. For the duke, the Oakes murder was shocking not for its brutality but because it "meant questions about Oakes's money—where it had gone, how it had gone, who else had been involved in the economic network Wenner-Gren had instigated. The Windsors would at the very least appear greedy and amoral—sending money illegally from a struggling Empire to invest alongside blacklisted neutrals." So the governor summoned Edward Melchen, a Miami policeman he trusted more than Scotland Yard officers, because "he wanted a quick solution." Melchen and his colleague Barker "understood." Pye, keen to chart the decline of the Windsors, implies that Melchen framed de Marigny to suit the duke's needs. The murder of Sir Harry Oakes was allegedly collateral damage in the more shocking story of the Duke of Windsor's moral and financial corruption.

"This explanation is, of course, speculation," writes the author towards the end of *The King over the Water*. This belated admission did not handicap sales of the book, despite one reviewer's comment that its thesis about illicit currency trading was "a morass of innuendo and conjecture." Financial shenanigans attract as many readers as Mafia plots.

=

IF THERE'S A subject that is bound to outsell both Mafia and money crimes, it is royal scandal. This was particularly apparent a few years later, with the appearance of a 1988 biography of the Duchess of Windsor. *Mrs. Simpson: Secret Lives of the Duchess of Windsor*, which was republished in an updated edition promising "fascinating new revelations" in 2004 and would sell over 1.4 million copies.

This sensational bestseller was written by yet another prolific and scandal-loving British author, Charles Higham, who had moved to Los Angeles to become the Hollywood correspondent for the *New York Times*. By the time he turned his attention to the former Mrs. Simpson, he had published gossipy books on Katharine Hepburn, Errol Flynn, Bette Davis, and Audrey Hepburn, amongst others. In the words of his *Telegraph* obituary, much of what Higham wrote about celebrities "was regarded by many critics as the product of an overactive and self-serving imagination."

His lip-smacking "revelations" about the duchess included allegations that she was the mistress of Count Galeazzo Ciano, who was later Mussolini's foreign secretary, as well as Ribbentrop, the German ambassador in prewar London, and that her attractions included exotic sexual techniques that she had acquired in the brothels of Beijing. One reviewer observed that, if the duchess had been guilty of even half the peccadilloes attributed to her, "early on she would have succumbed to exhaustion."

Charles Higham's imagination certainly did not fail him when he wrote a chapter entitled "Murder in Nassau." Once again, the murder of the multimillionaire was a sideshow in the author's larger thesis—that the Duchess of Windsor was not only far more able and resourceful than her husband but also a committed Nazi. Once again, the portrait of Sir Harry Oakes was taken almost verbatim from Bocca's descriptions. "His coarse, loud-mouthed, vulgar personality had not changed from the days when he had explored the wilderness armed with a pick and shovel," Higham wrote.

The murderer, Higham deduces in his book, must have been Harold Christie. He repeats Pye's allegations about the schemes between Wenner-Gren, Oakes, and the Duke of Windsor to invest money in the Banco Continental in Mexico City. He adds an extra layer of intrigue by suggesting a deal gone wrong between Oakes and Christie. Oakes, he argues, had been negotiating to buy land for an air base from Christie, but then discovered that Christie had gone behind his back and sold it to an American syndicate. But it is Higham's account of Oakes's death that takes the mining mogul's story to a new plane.

In Higham's version, on the night of the murder, Harold Christie had laced Sir Harry's nightcap with a powerful sedative, then left the sleeping millionaire to be bludgeoned to death by a hired hitman from Florida—a "very short but powerfully built spear fisherman" who belonged to "the diabolical cult of Palo Mayombe." While Christie stayed at his girlfriend's house, the killer slipped into Westbourne, thrust his spear four times into Sir Harry's head, sprayed his victim's chest with insecticide that he then set alight, and finally stabbed a pillow and scattered the feathers over the burning body "in the time-worn practice of the exponents of the Palo Mayombe black arts."

Higham described several more steps in the ritual killing, then surmised that the murderer left the island before dawn. Meanwhile, Christie had returned to Westbourne and sounded the alarm. When the news reached Government House, the duke deduced immediately that "this was a black crime with sinister overtones," and that he and his wife were in danger. When the duke then summoned detectives from Miami to investigate the crime, Melchen and Barker "clearly knew that a cover-up would be involved, since they deliberately left behind the fingerprint identification camera."

This overheated account (further elaborated upon in the second edition of *Mrs. Simpson*) is jigsawed together from the original autopsy report, the photographs of the crime scene, FBI files—and Higham's own imagination. Vague talk about voodoo rituals that had floated around Nassau at the time of the murder had never been specific and had gained little traction at the time. The author did not substantiate any of these sensational details from either written or oral sources.

Critics focused on the depiction of the Duchess of Windsor in Higham's biography, and their opinions ranged from "distasteful" to "political melodrama of the highest consequence." By and large, they ignored the gruesome picture of Sir Harry Oakes's death, although, as with the other sensationalized accounts of the murder in the second wave, the various conspiracy theories likely boosted sales.

This particular surge of interest in the Oakes case continued to play itself out as the twenty-first century opened. One of the last, and certainly the most thoughtful, nonfiction treatments of the whole story was *A Serpent in Eden* by an English lawyer-turned-journalist named James Owen. Owen had a particular connection to the case: his grandmother had spent eighteen months in Nassau during the war and knew many of those involved in the subsequent investigation. Owen was able to interview a handful of elderly survivors, including Nancy Oakes.

Moreover, Owen had done extensive research into the recently released FBI records on Sir Harry Oakes, Alfred de Marigny, Axel Wenner-Gren, the Duke of Windsor, and Harold Christie. These files yielded a few tidbits of new information on secondary characters in the story, especially Wenner-Gren, but no smoking gun that revealed the identity of Sir Harry's murderer.

However, Owen introduced a new suspect into the mix: Walter Foskett, Sir Harry's sleek American attorney and adviser, who had helped encourage his client's distrust of de Marigny, and who was a trustee of the Oakes estate. After Oakes's death, Foskett had moved quickly to take charge of the estate and was soon a powerful influence over his widow.

Foskett's hold on Lady Oakes infuriated Nancy Oakes, who was convinced that the smooth-talking lawyer had swindled the family out of valuable land that Harry Oakes had bought north of Palm Beach. With dimming eyes and a thirst for rum, Nancy returned to her long-time obsession: the whereabouts of the Oakes fortune. A few months before her death, Owen asked her if she thought that Foskett had been behind her father's murder. "As I made the suggestion, I can remember her turning to me as she was stretching for the tumbler, and glaring at me with her almost sightless eyes. 'Well,' she said indignantly, emotion for once colouring her drawl, 'wouldn't *you* think so?'"

After a careful review of testimony from the trial and of official records, Owen came up with no firm answer to the crucial question of whodunit. He couldn't find any evidence to link Foskett to the crime (although he turned up interesting information about the devious lawyer's double-dealing). Owen's reluctant and predictable conclusion was that there were two obvious suspects—de Marigny and Harold Christie—and not enough on either of them to hang them.

ONE PARTICULAR THREAD runs through all the colourful speculation about the Mafia, illicit currency deals, property swindles, and black arts: Harold Christie was fingered, with increasing frequency, as the leading suspect. His protestations of innocence had never entirely convinced many observers at the time of the trial. If he had spent the entire night of the murder at Westbourne, why had he not heard the sounds of a struggle? If he had in fact been with a mysterious lady friend (likely Mrs. Dulcibel "Effie" Henneage), why had she not come forward to provide an alibi for him? Why had Captain Edward Sears of the Bahamas Police Force insisted that he saw Christie driving through Nassau shortly after midnight? And why, when he was giving evidence during the trial, was Christie so visibly nervous?

Christie had faced the rumours himself. At one point, he was a guest of Lord Beaverbrook at La Capponcina, the press baron's villa on the French Riviera. It had been a raffish gathering of aging politicians, second-rate writers, and alcoholic aristocrats. One of the chief guests was the former Diana Mitford, who had an unexpected link with the Harry Oakes story—her father was the same Lord Redesdale who had briefly moiled for gold near Kirkland Lake. Now she was Diana Mosley, wife of the disgraced British fascist Oswald Mosley and future biographer of her close friend the Duchess of Windsor. Mosley relished a particular exchange at the Beaverbrook table. Their host had turned to Christie as they were sitting down for dinner, and, with a mischievous grin, asked, "Come on, Harold. Tell us how you murdered Harry Oakes." According to Mosley, the joke "evoked a tired smile from Christie."

Such a question was rarely asked in Nassau, where the Bay Street Boys closed ranks around their powerful colleague. Christie could claim so much credit for transforming the Bahamas from a shabby little British colony into a Mecca for the super-rich that he had made himself unassailable. British novelist William Boyd discovered this fact during the 1980s, more than a decade after Christie's death. Boyd was in the Bahamas, researching his novel *Any Human Heart*, in which his main character finds himself spying on the Duke and Duchess of Windsor during the war.

One evening, at a crowded drinks party in an opulent Lyford Cay mansion, Boyd started asking about the murder of Sir Harry Oakes. "It's a case that fascinates me," he later explained in an article in the British newspaper *The Guardian*.

At first, Boyd's linen-suited fellow guests were happy to talk about Harry Oakes and who might have killed him: "I am asking leading questions and am receiving a number of very animated and interesting answers." Suddenly a burly man in a loud silk shirt appeared at his side, followed by two Bahamian servants. "The man smiles at me. Dead eyes. 'Are you the person asking questions about Harry Oakes?'" Boyd said he was, then asked the man's identity. His interrogator snapped, "This is my party. And if you ask one more question, I'll have these guys throw you out." Boyd promised not to ask any more questions about the case. But he resolved to put the murder in his novel. *Any Human Heart*, published in 2002, includes a full account of the Oakes murder, identifies Christie as the murderer, and indicts the Duke of Windsor for his attempt to pervert the course of justice and incriminate an innocent man in order to save himself from embarrassment.

Unconstrained by a nonfiction writer's obligation to cite sources, the novelist could allow his imagination free rein. But he says that his imagination did not have to work too hard for this section of the novel. "At the party in Lyford Cay where my questioning so offended my host, everybody knew that Christie was the guilty man. . . . I was told it repeatedly—though the motives often strayed into the realm of fantasy."

Boyd's novel formed part of the third wave of books to feature the death of Sir Harry Oakes. By now, the unsolved murder had become a meme for fiction writers—an intriguing mystery that provoked literary speculation. The story of the gold digger who became the richest man in the British Empire, and who was then brutally murdered, never lost its fascination. It was not simply the whiff of Mafia involvement or the perennial attraction of royal scandal. It was also the mythological undertone. In Greek legend, King Midas asked the gods to turn everything he touched to gold. When the gods granted his wish, he discovered that the divine gift meant even food and drink were transformed into the precious metal. Helpless, he starved to death.

One of the first novelists to exploit the "death was inevitable" theme was Canadian author Timothy Findley. In his bestselling novel *Famous Last Words*, published in 1981, Findley delved deeply into the Duke and Duchess of Windsor's Nazi connections, and put Sir Harry Oakes in the centre of the action. In his novel, the Canadian millionaire is outraged when he discovers that the Windsors are about to make their way onto a German submarine in the dead of night. Findley's portrait of Oakes is unusually positive; he depicts him as a patriot who gets in the way of the Windsors—particularly the duchess. Oakes's wealth had propelled him into a deadly predicament, and there was no escape; he had to die. The author told the Canadian journalist Roy MacGregor that he believed his intriguing scenario was not only plausible but "very, very real."

Alice Munro, the Nobel laureate for literature, also invoked the name of Sir Harry Oakes in a story called "Spaceships Have Landed," published in the 1994 collection *Open Secrets*. The story opens in a bootlegger's house in rural Canada, where a bunch of men are drinking and playing cards. One man starts talking about a prospector who had stumbled on asbestos, which was lying all around him while he answered the call of nature in the bush. "And from that mine came a fortune!" he declaims. Another man offers the opinion that the fellow who found the asbestos would not be the one who got rich: "It never is." Immediately the name of Harry Oakes is invoked. "Some have found gold and got the good of it," a third says. "Billionaires. Sir Harry Oakes, for instance. He found it. He got to be a millionaire!"

But the punch line comes from the drinker who said that the one who finds the wealth never gets the benefit. "Got himself killed," he points out triumphantly. "So that's how he got the good of it!"

Nemesis stalked poor old Harry Oakes.

Why has the murder of Harry Oakes lingered on in popular culture, and attracted so much speculation? A couple of years ago, I met William Boyd in London to talk about the Oakes murder and his experiences in the Bahamas. Later, I asked him why the story refuses to die. He said it was because of its unique ingredients. "The murder of a multimillionaire on a tropical island in the middle of World War II would be pretty exotic in any event—but throw in the abdicated, Nazi-loving ex-monarch of the UK and his charming wife, and the brew becomes even more alluringly toxic."

Boyd argues that it is the involvement of the Duke of Windsor that is the most compelling ingredient. "The playboy son-in-law was acquitted (having been fitted up by corrupt US detectives) and the case was closed. It is a scandal—and even more so if you accept that the Duke of Windsor conspired to manipulate the evidence, pervert the course of justice, and was never called to any kind of account." But the royal element only goes so far. The murder of the richest man in the British Empire, the cover-up, and the lack of resolution continue to titillate—with or without the involvement of a second-rate royal.

CHAPTER 17

Unhappy Legacies

My father, being the youngest child, was only 10 when his father, Sir Harry, was killed, and any information I have is very general in nature. The Sir Harry story was not something that we discussed often when we grew up [because] it was a painful experience for my father when he was very young. I could ask my father if he would be interested in having a discussion with you; however, he has not been very receptive over the years due to some of the previous books written. My father is 85 and lives in the Bahamas.

EMAIL FROM HARRY OAKES, FEBRUARY 2018

The lack of an answer to the question of who killed Harry Oakes is emotionally unsatisfying. There is no villain to boo. Over time, Alfred de Marigny's innocence has been accepted, mostly on the strength of his alibi and because of his and his wife's insistence that murder was not in his character. At the same time, the assumption that Harold Christie likely benefited most from the murder, and may therefore have organized it, is persuasive. However, I cannot claim to have found any more incriminating evidence than have previous writers. Too many questions remain, including this one: If Christie organized the killing, why did he choose to spend the night in Sir Harry's house rather than providing himself with a rock-solid alibi elsewhere?

Nevertheless, once the trial of Alfred de Marigny ended in acquittal, I'm convinced that it suited both the snobbish, indolent white Nassau elite and the wartime British government to abandon any attempt to pursue the murderer. And I also recognize how the historical imprint of Harry Oakes has been shaped not by the extraordinary achievements of his early life but by the ambitions of writers eager to manipulate the tale of his brutal death.

Author Geoffrey Bocca, who came to the story sixteen years after the murder, suppressed his own assumption that the murderer was a resident of Nassau. Under pressure, I suspect, from Lord Beaverbrook, he presented Sir Harry Oakes as such a monstrously unpleasant man that he deserved to die. The Bocca portrait then congealed into accepted wisdom. His 1959 book was the starting point for all the subsequent treatments of the story that dismissed Oakes as an unmannered bully and used the brutal manner of his killing as rich material for sensational theories.

Perhaps there was some truth in the speculation about the involvement of organized crime, currency smuggling, or royal treachery. Or perhaps there was a much simpler explanation— that Harold Christie might have arranged Sir Harry's murder in order to keep the Oakes fortune in the Bahamas. Christie was a major source for all the journalists and authors who arrived in Nassau intent on solving the mystery. It is his soft whisper that echoes through the breathless prose that describes both his own close friendship with the murdered man and the motives others had to get Oakes out of the way.

But the murder had real consequences for those most affected. It blighted Sir Harry's family, whose members drew apart from one another. Lady Oakes remained convinced that her husband had been murdered by Alfred de Marigny, the son-in-law she abhorred because of the way he treated her daughter. Christie, who continued to advise her on family interests in the Bahamas, would have been happy to encourage this belief out of self-interest—as would Walter Foskett, the lawyer who was the executor of the Oakes estate. Both men, aware of the suspicions against them, remained close—very close—to Sir Harry's widow; there was gossip that each of them hoped to marry her.

Lady Oakes never remarried, although as a wealthy and attractive forty-four-year-old widow she must have had many suitors. Instead, she continued to spend her winters at Prospect Ridge, another Oakes residence in Nassau, and her summers in Maine. Her eldest son, Sydney, who at the age of sixteen had inherited the baronetcy after his father's death, lived in Oak Hall in Niagara Falls for several years, and Lady Oakes stayed with him from time to time. She was always warmly received in Niagara Falls.

Lady Oakes also retained some affection for Kirkland Lake, where she had spent the early years of her marriage. Residents of the little northern town who were strolling down the town's potholed Government Road in May 1969 were intrigued to see a chauffeur-driven white limousine drive slowly by. Then word spread: it was Lady Oakes, revisiting the town on the fiftieth anniversary of its incorporation. The limousine drove on to her former home, the Chateau, which was now the Museum of Northern History. There, she shook hands and smiled, savouring the expressions of gratitude from weather-beaten old-timers who shared with her their admiration for her husband's prospecting successes. An observer later recalled her regal manner and "most beautiful blue eyes."

Ten years later, when she was eighty-one, Sir Harry's widow drove north again for the town's diamond jubilee, and was guest of honour at the anniversary dinner. She died at Prospect Ridge, in Nassau, in 1981, and her ashes were interred in the Oakes family plot in Maine. The local paper in Niagara Falls marked her death with an obituary reminding readers that, thanks to Oakes generosity, "Niagara Falls became a much more pleasant city to live in. Citizens of all ages will always owe thanks to the Oakes family."

All five of Sir Harry's children continued to spend time at the various Oakes properties in and around Nassau after their father's death. Nancy's life ricocheted between glamour and pathos. She had enjoyed membership in Nassau's fast set in her late teens, and she had revelled in the press attention she received as the devoted young wife at the 1943 trial. Her taste for clubs, cocktails, and paparazzi persisted. Some time after her marriage to de Marigny fell apart, she moved to Hollywood, where her reckless nature, good looks, and string of actor boyfriends provided fodder for gossip columnists. "Heiress Nancy Oakes and Philip Reed [a leading man in dozens of films in this period] are Movietown's Big Talk," columnist Walter Winchell wrote in a typical item. She had an affair with the British actor Richard Greene, star of the television series *Robin Hood*, and they had a daughter, Patricia. In 1952 she married a member of the German nobility, Baron Ernst-Lyssardt von Hoyningen-Huene; photographs of Baroness von Hoyningen-Huene, sporting glittering jewellery and a haughty expression, appeared frequently in glossy publications. During this short-lived marriage, she had a son, Alexander.

Next, there were rumours of a liaison with Lieutenant-Commander Michael Parker, an Australian playboy who had served as the Duke of Edinburgh's private secretary until he was forced to resign after his divorce. But her third wedding, conducted in a quiet ceremony at the British ambassador's residence in Mexico City, was to a colourful Irishman named Patrick Tritton, who, like Nancy, was a heavy drinker. (Tritton established a reputation as incorrigible while still a student at Cambridge, when he took his horse to lectures.) This marriage also fell apart, and Nancy never remarried again; instead, she reverted to her second husband's title. She spent her days brooding over her father's murder and the fate of his fortune; over the years, her conviction grew that her parents' professional advisers had siphoned off a chunk of the Oakes millions. The Baroness, as she liked to be known, died in 2005 in London, England, and was buried in Nassau.

Accompanying many of the obituaries of Nancy Oakes was a photograph of her in her wild prime—bare-legged in a beach chair, with strong-boned features and the tough expression of a woman who is damned if she's going to be a victim. But damned she was. "If ever proof were wanted that money cannot guarantee happiness, it could be found in abundance in the life of Nancy Oakes von Hoyningen-Huene," ran the opening line of her obituary in *The Times*. Nancy had never found her footing. Married at eighteen, she had been scarred first by the vicious tension between the most important men in her life, then by the death of her father and the arrest of her husband for his murder, and finally by the collapse of her relationship with her mother and siblings. Alcohol may have been the only constant in her life.

If Nancy's life verged on pathos, the lives of three of her siblings were scarred by calamity. Two of her three brothers predeceased their mother. William Pitt Oakes, Lady Oakes's fourth child, was only twenty-seven when he had a heart attack in New York City in 1958. His health was already compromised by heroin addiction and a liver ailment, and he died in a Bronx hospital nursing home. Eight years later, his older brother Sir Sydney, who had left Niagara Falls and moved back to the Bahamas, was killed when the green Sunbeam Alpine sports car he was driving at high speed crashed into a utility pole in Nassau. He was thirty-nine. The headline in the Nassau newspaper now known simply as *The Tribune* read, "Latest in Chain of Family Tragedies." His son Christopher, then seventeen, inherited the baronetcy.

The Oakes's second daughter, Shirley, appeared set on a happier course. After studying in Paris, she attended Vassar (where she was a classmate of the future Jacqueline Kennedy) and qualified as a lawyer. But in 1981, when she was fifty-two, her marriage to an American named Allan Churchill Butler broke up and she was involved in a car crash. Driving back from a party at Lyford Cay to Nassau, she had noticed the driver behind her flashing his lights. He was trying to signal that she had left her purse on the roof of her car; she interpreted the high beams as an invitation to speed up. She lost control of her car as she accelerated down West Bay Street, hit a tree, and was left in a coma. She never recovered, and she died in 1986.

Only the youngest of the Oakes children, Harry Phillip, appears to have remained unscathed. Ten years old when his father died, Harry always shunned publicity. While attending university (he spent time at both McGill University and the University of Toronto), he worked one summer at the Lake Shore mine under an assumed name, so that none of his workmates knew his identity. With his German-born wife, Christiane Botsch, he spent much of his adult life in Canada. At first, he chose to work in a "regular job" in a friend's accounting firm in Niagara Falls, until the demands of his family's financial interests required all his attention. Because of disagreements about the administration of the family assets, he was barely on speaking terms with his sister Nancy.

Alfred de Marigny displayed fortitude and resilience in the years after the murder, even as his life dwindled into a series of arrests and pleas for asylum. He remained with his friend Hemingway in Cuba for only a few months (Nancy left even sooner) and began an unhappy odyssey of deportations. Branded as the man "accused of the murder of Harry Oakes," he was thrown out of the Canadian merchant navy, in which he had enlisted towards the end of the war, and was refused permission to become a Canadian resident. He was also forced to leave Haiti, and then Jamaica. He attributed all these reversals to the malign influence of the Duke of Windsor. He also had to face his third wife's spite; Nancy was determined to secure not simply a divorce but an annulment of their union on the grounds that their marriage was improperly conducted. As he wrote in his memoir *A Conspiracy of Crowns*, Nancy wanted to "squish me into the gutter."

De Marigny finally gained entry to the United States. For a while, he was so broke that he had to rely on handouts, menial jobs such as dog walking, and selling his blood. Eventually, thanks to funds that his lawyer had mislaid but then recovered, as well as a successful fourth marriage, he managed to lose some of his notoriety and settle quietly in Houston, Texas. However, he could never put the past behind him; at this point he embarked on his second memoir. Untroubled by modesty, he carefully curated his self-image in *A Conspiracy of Crowns*, describing himself as "tall, elegant, well born, but irreverent about class and wealth." He went on to argue strenuously that Harold Christie "should have been tried and hanged for the murder of Sir Harry Oakes. While hired hands acted for him, it was Christie who ordered the fatal act."

In a book riddled with invention and self-congratulation, the only part of de Marigny's account that is convincing is his contention that the Crown's case against him was both dishonest and badly constructed.

Most of the other people involved in the trial of Alfred de Marigny slipped into the shadows. Axel Wenner-Gren emerged unscathed from accusations of Nazi links, and after the war he invested in early computer technology, monorail systems, and speculative railway projects in western Canada. Still a very wealthy man, he died in Stockholm in 1961. Walter Foskett continued his law practice in Palm Beach, where he mingled with some of America's wealthiest businessmen. By the time he died in 1973, he had quietly amassed a considerable fortune as a director of the Alleghany Corporation, the holding company for several major railways. A more modest fate awaited de Marigny's great friend Georges de Visdelou-Guimbeau, who went to live in Britain, published a book about Mauritius, and died in 1989 in the starchy seaside town of St Leonards-on-Sea in East Sussex.

The two discredited Florida detectives both came to unhappy ends. Captain Edward Melchen succumbed to a heart attack only five years after the trial. Captain James Barker had a more dramatic death. A proven snitch to the Mafia, he had an "altercation" with the head of a Florida vice squad who had been investigating corruption charges, and Barker broke his nose. Barker was first suspended, then took early retirement. Addicted to prescription drugs and heroin, he became a menace to himself and others—particularly to his son Duane, also a Miami policeman. Father and son had a violent fight on Christmas Day, 1952. James Barker pulled his gun, the two men wrestled for it, and it went off. The bullet killed the older man instantly.

But the story of the millionaire owner of a gold mine whose murder has never been solved wouldn't die. In the absence of compelling evidence—no deathbed confessions, no new revelations—the spell cast by Bocca held powerful sway.

THE MURDERER'S IDENTITY is only part of the Oakes mystery. The second issue is what happened to the Oakes millions. This matter, too, is riddled with conjectures.

One of the few available sources on the Oakes estate is a lengthy feature article written six months after the murder by the award-winning investigative journalist Ruth Reynolds for the New York *Sunday News*. According to Reynolds, by 1939 Oakes had well over US$32 million in Bahamian corporation stock and real estate. The costs and operating expenses of his various projects there—waterworks, houses, the airfield, tropical gardens—may have amounted to nearly US$2 million. That left over US$30 million—and this was the money that the tax exile worried, once war had broken out, might be "borrowed" by the British government. That never happened, and money continued to roll in besides. By Reynolds's reckoning, the Nassau holding companies would probably have been worth upwards of US$34,713,500 at the time of Sir Harry Oakes's death. She asked around to confirm her estimate. Walter Foskett told her the estate was "in the neighbourhood" of US$25 million, and Canadian tax experts offered the figure of US$30 million. (Comparisons over time are always difficult, but an estate of US$25 million in 1943 would be worth between US$354 million and US$2 billion today.)

Given the published reports from the late 1930s that Oakes's estate was worth over $200 million, and that he was perhaps the richest man in the British Empire, these estimates seem extraordinarily low. But it was Lake Shore Mines that was worth $200 million at its mid-1930s peak, and Oakes owned only half its shares. Moreover, once the Lake Shore gold seams ran dry, its major shareholder's annual income and net worth must have shrunk rapidly. It is possible that Sir Harry was never as wealthy as his reputation suggested. Compelling rags-to-riches stories always breed exaggeration.

After Sir Harry's death came the taxmen. The will that had been published a few days before the trial dealt only with his personal property, amounting to US$14.7 million, rather than his holdings in Bahamian corporations. The tax bill for the Bahamas was easy to settle: 2 percent on the personal property, or US$293,720. Under Bahamian law, there were no death duties, and only personal property was taxable, not real estate. Moreover, there was no gift tax in the islands, so Sir Harry might already have handed over substantial sums to his wife and children. Reynolds reported: "Lady Oakes is reputed to have US$4,000,000 in her own right."

The attempt at a much bigger tax bite came from Ottawa. The Department of National Revenue was hell bent on collecting about 90 percent of the total estate, on the grounds that although Sir Harry was resident in the Bahamas, he was domiciled in Canada. Ottawa was prepared to take the case to the Supreme Court; the claim, wrote Reynolds, was "based upon the fact that his wealth and income sprang from Lake Shore Mines, in Canada." The relentless reporter also reported that the Oakes trustees "hooted" at such a claim. Meanwhile, the US Internal Revenue Service was sniffing around at the capital and real estate that Oakes had accumulated in Palm Beach in the interval between his departure from Canada and his arrival in Nassau.

"It appears that the Oakes estate will be tied up for years," wrote Reynolds. However, there is no evidence that the US recaptured lost taxes or that Canada ever managed to claw back anything from its wealthiest tax exile. Then, as now, the super-rich can shield fortunes from revenue departments, and keep lawsuits going for years.

The only Oakes properties liable to Canadian taxes were the real estate holdings in Niagara Falls. But as far as I can see, most of them stayed in the family. Today, Welland Securities Ltd., a company formed by the family in 1964, is one of the largest owners of real estate in the Niagara Falls area. Another family company, HOCO Ltd., owns 30 acres of prime real estate on Clifton Hill, next to the falls, and includes most of the loudest, kitschiest, most popular (and, presumably, most lucrative) tourist entertainments there, including the Ripley's Believe It or Not! museum. The president of HOCO is Harry Oakes, son of Harry Phillip, the murder victim's youngest child. I asked him if he would speak to me about his family history. He graciously but firmly brushed me off.

And the Lake Shore mine, once known as the "Jewel Box of the North"? The mine that made Sir Harry such a rich man? Already in decline before his death, its share value collapsed and its dividends dried up; soon, some family members might have found themselves living off capital. The Oakes connection was completely severed when Lake Shore was bought out by the mining company Little Long Lac in the late 1950s. The mine was closed down in 1965. Within a few years, the office complex and headframe were gone, and a shopping mall had been built on the site of the old mill. Between 1918 and 1965, it had produced almost 8.5 million ounces of gold—a fabulous amount, worth over US$10 billion in today's terms—and represented over a third of all the gold produced in Kirkland Lake.

Nancy Oakes was always convinced that at least one of the family's professional advisers had siphoned off a large chunk of her father's fortune. She was likely referring to the sale of large tracts of North Palm Beach and parts of Palm Beach Gardens that Harry Oakes had bought in the 1930s. Walter Foskett arranged the sale of these prime oceanfront holdings to billionaire John D. MacArthur in the 1950s, and today it is some of the most valuable real estate in the United States. There is also the question of what happened to any money that found its way to Mexico. If Harry Oakes had already transferred a large amount of capital there with the help of Wenner-Gren, that money might have disappeared with his death, since the transactions were illegal and his family was likely unaware of them. However, his shrewd lawyer, Foskett, would have known about them, and would likely have had signing authority over them. But as with so much of this story, this is all speculation: the Lake Shore earnings were never invested in publicly traded companies, so information is scarce.

THE BAHAMAS HAVE a well-deserved reputation as a holiday destination. Islands like Eleuthera, Andros, and Inagua are extraordinarily beautiful, with their warm breezes, quaint settlements, and brilliantly clear ocean. You can walk for miles along the soft pink sand of deserted beaches, snorkel over coral reefs, or enjoy exotic bird life. But the years have not been kind to the capital city of Nassau.

My first reaction when I arrived there to research this book in 2017 was disappointment. The island of New Providence is now completely dependent on tourism and tax exiles. Mass tourism dominates the shops, bars, and restaurants in the few central blocks of Nassau, at the eastern end of the island, which are geared to the midday trade from visiting cruise ships. Once the pastel-shirted passengers have returned to their floating hotels in the midafternoon, the gift stores and most of the restaurants put up their blinds. The pink government buildings in the centre of the capital have retained their charm, and Government House remains an impressive stone building encircled by well-weeded flowerbeds and iron railings. But on the other side of the hill on which Government House perches, untouched by the ocean breezes, are the kind of jerry-built shacks and dirt streets that Harry Oakes saw when he first arrived in the island.

Nassau police are still clad in immaculate white uniforms and solar topees, and evidence of the former colony's British links is everywhere—the statue of Queen Victoria, the shortbread and woollen garments on sale in the stores. Most of Cable Beach's pearly sands are invisible behind a wall of luxury tourist hotels. Westbourne, where Sir Harry spent his final night, has long since been demolished, as has his other mansion, The Caves. Axel Wenner-Gren's private island, now renamed Paradise Island, is packed solid with hotels, bars, clubs, a golf course, an aquarium, and a casino.

Twenty-four kilometres west, at the other end of New Providence, is the tax-exile enclave that no cruise ship passenger is likely to see. Trespassers are stopped at the gatehouse. Lyford Cay, the development originally masterminded by Harold Christie, now boasts more than three hundred villas, an eighteen-hole golf course, twelve tennis courts, a private international school, 2 kilometres of private beach, and its own post office. Royal palms, casuarina trees, and brightly coloured hibiscus surround lavish, multi-bedroomed mansions painted in pastel shades.

This is the billionaire bunker that Christie first envisioned in the 1930s, and that Harry Oakes helped him to build—either directly or thanks to the fees that Christie received as Oakes's adviser. Harry Oakes set an example of wealth management and tax avoidance that has been followed by hundreds of other tax exiles, since the government of the Bahamas still does not charge its expatriate residents income tax, corporate tax, capital gains tax, or wealth tax. In the twenty-first century, wealth is more footloose than ever, and Nassau boasts legions of tax advisers, and firms that manage investments.

In between these island extremes are acres of flat, rocky soil, covered in low scrub. Much of this land is still owned by the Oakes family.

The Oakes presence persists. In the lobby of the Hilton Hotel in Nassau, where I stayed, there is a bust of a thin-lipped, heavy-jawed man. The plaque underneath reads, "Presented to the British Colonial Hilton by the Oakes Family, in memory of Sir Harry Oakes, Former Proprietor." I realized I was on the site of the former British Colonial Hotel, which, according to fable, Harry Oakes had bought because he was so enraged by the maître-d's high-handed behaviour.

On the southern outskirts of Nassau lies Oakes Field, now a sports ground. There I found the memorial obelisk paid for by the people of Kirkland Lake. I never discovered the grave of Sir Harold Christie, or any monument to his benefactions to the community. However, H. G. Christie Ltd., "founded in 1922 by the legendary Sir Harold George Christie," continues to thrive in Nassau as "the trusted authority in Bahamas real estate."

The Oakes legend persists too. Every now and then during my stay, I would diffidently mention to someone that I was exploring the life and death of Sir Harry. My admission sparked some surprising reactions. When I told the porter at the Hilton Hotel, he offered his own guess at those responsible. "It was the Mafia. Those guys were thrown out of Cuba by Castro, so they wanted to come here and Harry wouldn't let them." The Mob is now so entrenched in Oakes folklore that I didn't bother to point out that Oakes was murdered sixteen years before Castro seized power in neighbouring Cuba.

In the Graycliff Restaurant, one of the few dining establishments that remains open in the evenings (and, judging by its prices, caters to the Lyford Cay crowd), I discussed the case with the Italian owner. He launched into memories of Nancy Oakes, who had frequently spent long, boozy evenings on the Graycliff's elegant porch. I asked who had murdered her father. He looked at me sombrely and gave me the best and most bizarre theory that I had yet heard. "It was the Canadian Mounties. He owed them his gold."

Gold has always bred its own myths and convictions, from the legend of King Midas to speculation about Nazi gold holdings still in Switzerland. The layers of false facts and half-truths surrounding Sir Harry Oakes's death have ballooned over the years. But the tale of the complex and dynamic man who staked, developed, and owned one of the most lucrative gold mines in the world, and helped build a mining industry that still defines Canada, has almost disappeared. Instead, conspiracy theories— provoked by the glitter of celebrity, scandal, and gold—have swamped a more human story.

SOURCES

I list here the major sources for each chapter, so that readers may see where I found my material. More precise endnotes, including references to newspaper articles, are available on my website (www.charlottegray.ca).

In addition to the books and archives mentioned, I relied on two online reference works for information about key figures and background events. Both the *Dictionary of Canadian Biography* or *DCB* (www.biographi.ca/en) and *The Canadian Encyclopedia* (www.thecanadianencyclopedia.ca/en) are consistently accurate and lively resources that are a pleasure to read. We are lucky to have them, as they cover the broad span of the Canadian historical landscape for both academic and general audiences.

INTRODUCTION
Details about the murder scene are drawn from newspaper reports, and from the evidence presented at the preliminary investigation into the death of Sir Harry Oakes by Dr. L. W. Fitzmaurice, acting chief medical officer, and Dr. H. A. Quackenbush, medical practitioner.

The Canadian author Timothy Findley wrote about the Oakes murder in his 1982 bestseller *Famous Last Words*, and the British author William Boyd included it in his 2002 bestseller *Any Human Heart*.

The quotation from Jean-Paul Sartre can be found in *The Family Idiot: Gustave Flaubert*, vol. 1 (Chicago: University of Chicago Press), x.

CHAPTERS 1-5

I relied on several books for background on the history of mining in Northern Ontario in the early twentieth century. Particularly valuable were *Free Gold: The Story of Canadian Mining*, by Arnold Hoffman (New York: Associated Book Service, 1958); Philip Smith's *Harvest from the Rock: A History of Mining in Ontario* (Toronto: Macmillan of Canada, 1986); *Steam into Wilderness: Ontario Northland Railway, 1902–1962*, by Albert Tucker (Don Mills, ON: Fitzhenry & Whiteside, 1978); *The Opening of the Canadian North, 1870–1914*, by Morris Zaslow (Toronto: McClelland & Stewart, 1971); *Mine-Finders: The History and Romance of Canadian Mineral Discoveries*, by B. F. Townsley (Toronto: Saturday Night Press, 1935); D. M. LeBourdais's *Metals and Men: The Story of Canadian Mining* (Toronto: McClelland & Stewart, 1957); H. V. Nelles's *The Politics of Development: Forests, Mines and Hydro-electric Power in Ontario, 1849–1941* (Toronto: Macmillan of Canada, 1974).

Nobody has done more to record the history of Kirkland Lake (KL) and other communities than Michael Barnes, former principal of Queen Elizabeth School and subsequently Central School, in the community. He is the author of more than thirty-five books, most notably *Gold in Kirkland Lake* (Renfrew, ON: General Store Publishing House, 2011). I also found useful information in an unpublished master's thesis by Ralph Deline, available in the KL Teck Library.

An excellent source on KL history is S. A. Pain's *Three Miles of Gold: The Story of Kirkland Lake* (Toronto: Ryerson Press, 1960).

Glimpses of Harry Oakes during his prospecting years are drawn from Hoffman's *Free Gold* and from two lively memoirs: James A. McRae's *Call Me Tomorrow* (Toronto: Ryerson Press, 1960) and Brian Martin's *Ernie's Gold: A Prospector's Tale* (Renfrew, ON: General Store Publishing House, 2011).

I took information about Oakes's early years from the first book that covered the murder story—Geoffrey Bocca's *The Life and Death of Sir Harry Oakes* (New York: Doubleday, 1959). However, I tried to confirm all details from other sources, for reasons that become obvious later in this book.

Another source on Oakes's life is Bob Cowan's *Sir Harry Oakes, 1874–1943: An Accumulation of Notes* (Cobalt, ON: Highway Book Shop, 2000).

The impact of the mineral rush on the local Ojibwa people, in particular Chief Ignace Tonené of the Temagami band, is noted in an undated document by Bruce W. Hodgins and James Morrison in the archives of the Museum of Northern History, Kirkland Lake. I found in the same museum some invaluable reminiscences from old-timers, recorded by local historian Carolyn O'Neil in the 1970s, who generously shared her knowledge with me in several phone calls.

For the business side of the mining industry, I drew on several sources. Two were particularly useful: Christopher Armstrong's *Blue Skies and Boiler Rooms: Buying and Selling Securities in Canada, 1870–1940* (Toronto: University of Toronto Press, 1997), and mining reporter Stan Sudol's articles in various publications, including the *Sudbury Star* and the *Huffington Post*.

CHAPTER 6

Much of the information about Niagara Falls comes from local historian Sherman Zavitz, author of *It Happened at Niagara: Stories from Niagara's Fascinating Past* (Niagara Falls, ON: Lundy's Lane Historical Society, 2017). I also relied on *Images of a Century: The City of Niagara Falls, Canada, 1904–2004* (Niagara Falls, ON: City of Niagara Falls Centennial Book Committee, 2004). In the Niagara Falls Public Library, I located a useful unpublished 1980 thesis by McMaster University student Sam DiMartino, "A Report on the Past and Present Land Uses of Properties Acquired by Sir Harry Oakes and Welland Securities Ltd. in the City of Niagara Falls, Canada."

My sources on tax policy included Robert Bryce's *Maturing in Hard Times: Canada's Department of Finance through the Great Depression* (Montreal and Kingston: McGill-Queen's University Press, 1986); J. Harvey Perry's *Taxes, Tariffs, and Subsidies* (Toronto: University of Toronto Press, 1955); and the article "Ontario Millionaire Finds Haven in Tax-less Bahamas," by Gregory Clark, in the *Toronto Daily Star*, February 11, 1938.

Information about William Wright's finances comes from Maggie Siggins's *Bassett: John Bassett's Forty Years in Politics, Publishing, Business, and Sports* (Toronto: Lorimer, 1979).

CHAPTER 7

For background on the Bahamas, I drew heavily on two excellent histories: Michael Craton's *A History of the Bahamas*, 3rd ed. (Waterloo, ON: San Salvador Press, 1986); and Gail Saunders's *Race and Class in the Colonial Bahamas, 1880–1960* (Gainesville: University Press of Florida, 2016). I also read all the copies of *The Bahamas Handbook*, an annual review of the islands, available in the Archives of the Bahamas. Several contained personal reminiscences of island history and of Oakes.

Oakes's activities in New Providence are covered in several books about his murder and in a lengthy article by Ruth Reynolds, "Sir Harry Oakes, The Incorporated Baron," published in the New York *Sunday News*, January 23, 1944. Rosita Forbes's comments about him appeared in *A Unicorn in the Bahamas* (London: Herbert Jenkins, 1939). Most information about Walter Foskett's legal manoeuvres also comes from Reynolds.

Axel Wenner-Gren is covered in "The Lord of Paradise—His Rise and Fall: The Axel Wenner-Gren Paradox" in *The Bahamas Handbook* (Nassau: Dupuch Publications, 2002) and in a laudatory profile published in 2012 by the Wenner-Gren Foundation: "Reality and Myth: A Symposium on Axel Wenner-Gren" (www. wennergren.org).

CHAPTER 8

Gregory Clark described his visit with Oakes in his *Toronto Daily Star* article "Ontario Millionaire Finds Haven in Taxless Bahamas," cited above. Sir Orville Turnquest, who would serve as governor general of an independent Bahamas between 1995 and 2001, described Oakes's activities in New Providence, including his election, in *What Manner of Man Is This? The Duke of Windsor's Years in the Bahamas* (Nassau: Grant's Town Press, 2016).

Prime Minister Mackenzie King's comments on Oakes and the Bahamas are accessible online in his diaries, which constitute one of Canada's most intriguing political documents and are available at Library and Archives Canada (www.bac-lac.gc.ca).

Information about Oakes's properties in England comes from Barbara Denny and Carolyn Starren's *Kensington Past* (London: Historical Publications, 1998) and from Mrs. Judith Jawad, the current owner of Oak Hall in Sussex. The papers of Sir Joseph Ball are in Oxford University's Bodleian Special Collections, Weston

Library; the material on Harry Oakes can be found in "Papers Relating to Honours for Sale c. 1933–1939" (MS Eng. C.6658).

CHAPTER 9

There is no shortage of books and articles about the Duke and Duchess of Windsor, and most include an account of their unhappy stay in the Bahamas. A few are admiring, such as Philip Ziegler's *King Edward VIII: The Official Biography* (New York: Knopf, 1991) and Diana Mosley's *The Duchess of Windsor* (London: Gibson Square Books, 2012). Many wallow in speculation about the duke's financial intrigues and his role in the Oakes murder enquiry, most recently Andrew Morton's *17 Carnations: The Royals, the Nazis and the Biggest Cover-up in History* (New York: Grand Central, 2015). A few, such as Charles Higham's *Mrs. Simpson: Secret Lives of the Duchess of Windsor* (London: Sidgwick & Jackson, 2004) and Michael Bloch's *The Duchess of Windsor* (London: St. Martin's Press, 1997), are unreliable. In addition to reading most of them, for this chapter I also drew for atmosphere on the ghosted and self-justifying memoirs of both the duke and the duchess. Their correspondence gives a more candid picture.

Several more books focus exclusively on the Windsors' Nassau years, including John Marquis's *Blood and Fire: The Duke of Windsor and the Strange Murder of Sir Harry Oakes* (Kingston, Jamaica: LMH Publishing, 2006). They are also covered in Alfred de Marigny's 1990 memoir, *A Conspiracy of Crowns* (London: Bantam, 1990). However, all these books are rife with unsubstantiated claims.

The duke's comments on executive council members and on the racial divide are quoted in Turnquest. Information on the Burma Road Riot and its aftermath is mainly drawn from Turnquest, Saunders, and Sir Randol Fawkes's *The Faith That Moved the Mountain* (Nassau: Author, 1979).

CHAPTER 10

For some insight into the complicated relationship between the Duke of Windsor, Axel Wenner-Gren, Oakes, and General Maximino Camacho, see Ziegler, Cowan, and James Owen's *A Serpent in Eden* (London: Little, Brown, 2005).

The most elaborate but least reliable sources on Alfred de Marigny are his two autobiographies: *More Devil Than Saint* (New York: Beechhurst Press, 1946) and *A Conspiracy of Crowns*. Additional information about his relations with Nancy Oakes and her family, and details of the two dinner parties on the evening of July 6, 1943, are drawn from contemporary newspaper accounts that were collected and published in 1959 as *The Murder of Sir Harry Oakes, Bt.* by the *Nassau Daily Tribune*.

CHAPTERS 11-14

Details about the murder of Sir Harry Oakes and the trial of Alfred de Marigny are almost all drawn from the *Nassau Daily Tribune*'s collected reportage (which includes clippings from other papers) and de Marigny's two memoirs. Social notes about Nassau, and details of the Duke of Windsor's correspondence with the Colonial Office, come from Owen.

The uncatalogued correspondence between Higgs and Dr. W. P. St. Charles is in the Museum of Northern History archives.

CHAPTERS 15-16

Schindler's cover story on the Oakes investigation appeared on pages 18–23 of the October 1944 edition of *Inside Detective*. The Deighton report on the Oakes murder enquiry, "Unsolved Murder of Sir Harry Oakes at Nassau, Bahamas, on 8 July 1943" (MEPO 2/9532), is available at the National Archives, Kew, England. Erle Stanley Gardner's article "My Most Baffling Murder" was published in the *American Weekly* on April 8, 1956.

The several books about the murder and trial that I mention can be found in the selected bibliography that follows. Geoffrey Bocca's correspondence with Lord Beaverbrook is in the Beaverbrook Papers, UK Parliamentary Archives, BBK/C/46.

Cathleen LeGrand's article "Another Look at a Bahamian Mystery: The Murder of Sir Harry Oakes" was published in the *International Journal of Bahamian Studies* 16 (2010), pages 92–101.

William Boyd's account of the party at Lyford Cay was published as "The Real-Life Murder Case behind Any Human Heart" in *The Guardian*, November 10, 2010.

CHAPTER 17

There are several uncatalogued documents and clippings about the lives of Sir Harry's widow and children in the archives at the Museum of Northern History. I have also drawn on Cowan and Owen for further information. De Marigny gave one version of his own story in his 1990 memoir; other sources include obituaries from the *New York Times* and the *Globe and Mail*.

Details about the Oakes estate come from the 1944, New York *Sunday News* feature by Ruth Reynolds, cited above, and from Eliot Kleinberg's *Palm Beach Daily News* article "Cold Case Murder: Who Killed Rich Palm Beacher 75 Years Ago?" (July 10, 2018.)

The indefatigable Michael Barnes made the calculations about the total output of the Lake Shore Mines in his invaluable 2011 publication, *Gold in Kirkland Lake*.

ACKNOWLEDGEMENTS

As I mention in the text, there are very few Oakes papers available to researchers; Harry Oakes does not appear to have been a man either given to much reflection or interested in committing himself to paper. I did not speak to anybody who had known him personally, but I did talk with several people who knew his story well and were vividly aware of both his achievements and the impression he made on others at different stages in his colourful life . . . and death.

KIRKLAND LAKE
Reconstructing Harry Oakes's mining career in Northern Ontario, and understanding the evolution of Kirkland Lake, would have been impossible without the help of several residents, past and present, of the area. I am particularly grateful to Carolyn O'Neil, Tom Wright, Janet Christie-Seeley, Roger Dufresne, and Marion Botsford Fraser. Kaitlyn McKay, manager of the Museum of Northern History, and the staff at KL's Teck Library went out of their way to provide me with resources. Ralph Deline generously

ACKNOWLEDGEMENTS

shared with me his thesis on the growth of Kirkland Lake. I am also grateful to Dr. Christopher Armstrong, Stan Sudol, Joseph Martin, and Jonathan McQuarrie for their information on the development of Ontario's mining industry and issues concerning the threat of taxes that drove Harry Oakes out of the country. Thanks to Jamie Benidickson for information about Chief Tonené and the Beaver House Lake Band.

NIAGARA FALLS

Sherman Zavitz, the official historian of Niagara Falls, gave me an excellent tour of the city; Suzanne Moase, curator at the City of Niagara Falls Museum, showed me its Oakes material and put me in touch with a former Oakes employee; Cathy Roy at the Niagara Falls Public Library brought to my attention material about the Oakes family and Niagara Falls in the 1930s. I am particularly grateful to Jim Hill and David Adames at the Niagara Parks Commission, who showed me around Oak Hall, which now houses the commission, and discussed the continuing importance of Oakes's business ventures in the city.

BAHAMAS

Many thanks to Patrice M. Williams and the staff at the Department of the Archives, Nassau, Bahamas, for assistance with clippings, books, court records, and photographs. I would also like to thank Dr. Gail Saunders at the University of the Bahamas.

There are several others who enriched my research. In the US, Lawson Hunter and Bill Fox introduced me to Palm Beach opulence. In England, Judith Jawad, current owner of Oak Hall in Sussex, was as intrigued as I was to find out who had visited the Oakes family there. (Sadly, we did not locate a visitors book.) In London, Patricia Potts walked up and down Kensington Palace Gardens with me, identifying which gracious mansion had belonged to Oakes. I am particularly grateful to William Boyd, who discussed the Oakes case at length with me over coffee at the legendary Groucho Club, sharing his own experiences and conclusions.

THERE ARE MANY others to whom I owe thanks: Jane Lagesse and Margot Gualtieri, for copies of Alfred de Marigny's contradictory memoirs; Ralph Deline, for sending me a copy of his research paper; Mark Bourrie, for providing information about William Wright; staff at the Bodleian Library for assistance with Sir Joseph Ball's papers; staff at the House of Lords Archives for assistance with Lord Beaverbrook's papers; the ever-helpful librarians and archivists at Library and Archives Canada; friends who asked penetrating questions about the Harry Oakes case, including Wendy Bryans, Maureen Boyd, Judith Moses, Cathy Beehan, Julie Jacobson, and Jane Clark. As usual, Dr. Sandy Campbell and Dr. Duncan McDowall were the most careful and helpful readers that any nonfiction writer could ask for.

Frances Middleton, Anna Kuntz, and my three sons, Alexander, Nicholas, and Oliver, gave me endless encouragement (a special thanks to Anna for technical support!). My greatest debt of thanks goes to my husband, George Anderson, who accompanied me on research trips to Kirkland Lake, Nassau, Miami, Sussex, London, and Oxford, helped me sort out financial details, and was generous with time and good advice.

As usual, my agent, Hilary McMahon at WCA, has been helpful, available, and supportive at every stage of the process. At HarperCollins Canada, I enjoyed working with a remarkable team led by my editor, Jennifer Lambert, and including Stephanie Conklin, Victoria Ryk, Lloyd Davis, Camilla Blakeley, Mary Rostad, and Mike Millar.

ACKNOWLEDGEMENTS

Finally, I am grateful to the Office of Cultural Affairs in the City of Ottawa and to the Canada Council for financial assistance and for their steadfast support of creators in my hometown and in my country. Their commitment to writers and readers is invaluable, and underlines their larger commitment to a crucial priority: Canadian storytelling within a global literary community.

SELECTED BIBLIOGRAPHY

Armstrong, Christopher. *Blue Skies and Boiler Rooms: Buying and Selling Securities in Canada, 1870–1940*. Toronto: University of Toronto Press, 1997.

Barnes, Michael. *Gold in Kirkland Lake*. Renfrew, ON: General Store Publishing House, 2011.

———.*Gold in Ontario*. Erin, ON: Boston Mills Press, Ontario, 1995.

———.*Kirkland Lake*. Erin, ON: Boston Mills Press, 1994.

———.*Roza Brown of Kirkland Lake*. Cobalt, ON: Highway Book Shop, 1973.

———.*The Town That Stands on Gold*. Cobalt, ON: Highway Book Shop, 1978.

Berton, Pierre. *Niagara: A History of the Falls*. Toronto: McClelland & Stewart, 1992.

Bocca, Geoffrey. *The Life and Death of Sir Harry Oakes*. London: Weidenfeld & Nicolson, 1959.

———.*The Woman Who Would Be Queen*. New York: Rinehart, 1954.

Boyd, William. *Any Human Heart*. London: Penguin Books, 2009.

Chicanot, E. L., ed. *Rhymes of the Miner: An Anthology of Canadian Mining Verse*. Gardenvale, QC: Federal Publications, 1937.

Cowan, Bob. *Sir Harry Oakes, 1874–1943: An Accumulation of Notes*. Cobalt, ON: Highway Book Shop, 2000.

Craton, Michael. *A History of the Bahamas*, 3rd ed. Waterloo, ON: San Salvador Press, 1986.

De Marigny, Alfred. *More Devil Than Saint*. New York: Beechhurst Press, 1946.

De Marigny, Alfred, with Mickey Herskowitz. *A Conspiracy of Crowns*. London: Bantam, 1990.

Denny, Barbara, and Carolyn Starren. *Kensington Past*. London: Historical Publications, 1998.

Dupuch, Sir Étienne. *A Salute to Friend and Foe*. Nassau: The Tribune, 1982.

Forbes, Rosita. *Islands in the Sun*. London: Evans Bros., 1949.

———.*A Unicorn in the Bahamas*. London: Herbert Jenkins, 1939.

Higham, Charles. *Mrs. Simpson: Secret Lives of the Duchess of Windsor*, rev. ed. London: Sidgwick & Jackson, 2004.

Hoffman, Arnold. *Free Gold: The Story of Canadian Mining*. New York: Associated Book Service, 1958.

Houts, Marshall. *King's X: Common Law and the Death of Sir Harry Oakes*. London: Robert Hale, 1972. Republished as *Who Killed Sir Harry Oakes?* London: Robert Hale, 1976.

Inglis, Alex. *Northern Vagabond: The Life and Career of J. B. Tyrrell*. Toronto: McClelland & Stewart, 1978.

Johnson, Doris Sands. *The Quiet Revolution in the Bahamas*. Nassau: Family Islands Press, 1972.

Leasor, James. *Who Killed Sir Harry Oakes?* Boston: Houghton Mifflin, 1983.

LeBourdais, D. M. *Metals and Men: The Story of Canadian Mining*. Toronto: McClelland & Stewart, 1957.

Lonn, George. *The Mine Finders*. Toronto: Toronto Pitt Publishing, c. 1966.

MacDonald, Cheryl. *Murder! The Mysterious Death of Canadian Mining Magnate Sir Harry Oakes*. Toronto: Lorimer, 2009.

Marquis, John. *Blood and Fire: The Duke of Windsor and the Strange Murder of Sir Harry Oakes*. Kingston, Jamaica: LMH Publishing, 2006.

Martin, Brian. *Ernie's Gold: A Prospector's Tale*. Renfrew, ON: General Store Publishing House, 2011.

McRae, James A. *Call Me Tomorrow*. Toronto: Ryerson Press, 1960.

Mosley, Diana. *The Duchess of Windsor*. London: Gibson Square Books, 2012.

Nassau Daily Tribune. *The Murder of Sir Harry Oakes*. Nassau: The Tribune, 1959.

Nelles, H. V. *The Politics of Development: Forests, Mines and Hydro-electric Power in Ontario, 1849–1941*. Toronto: Macmillan of Canada, 1974.

Newell, Dianne. *Technology on the Frontier: Mining in Old Ontario*. Vancouver: University of British Columbia Press, 1986.

Newman, Peter C. *Flame of Power: Intimate Profiles of Canada's Greatest Businessmen*. Toronto: Longmans, Green, 1959.

Owen, James. *A Serpent in Eden*. London: Little, Brown, 2005.

Pain, S. A. *Three Miles of Gold: The Story of Kirkland Lake*. Toronto: Ryerson Press, 1966.

Palu, Louie, and Charlie Angus. *Industrial Cathedrals of the North*. Toronto: Between the Lines, 1999.

Parker, John. *King of Fools*. London: St. Martin's Press, 1988.

Pye, Michael. *The King over the Water*. New York: Holt, Rinehart & Winston, 1981.

Rouleau, Leonard. *The Rugged Life of Sir Harry Oakes*. Laval, QC: Author, 1971.

Saunders, Gail. *Race and Class in the Colonial Bahamas, 1880–1960*. Gainesville: University Press of Florida, 2016.

Smith, Philip. *Harvest from the Rock: A History of Mining in Ontario*. Toronto: Macmillan of Canada, 1986.

Stafford, Ellen, ed. *Flamboyant Canadians*. Toronto: Baxter, 1964.

Stortroen, Magne. *An Immigrant's Journal*. Cobalt, ON: Highway Book Shop, 1982.

Taylor, A. J. P. *Beaverbrook*. New York: Simon & Schuster, 1972.

Townsley, Benjamin Franklin. *The Mine-Finders: The History and Romance of Canadian Mineral Discoveries*. Toronto: Saturday Night Press, 1935.

Tucker, Albert. *Steam into Wilderness: Ontario Northland Railway, 1902–1962*. Don Mills, ON: Fitzhenry & Whiteside, 1978.

Turnquest, Sir Orville. *What Manner of Man Is This? The Duke of Windsor's Years in the Bahamas*. Nassau: Grant's Town Press, 2016.

Williamson, O. T. G. *The Northland Ontario*. Toronto: Ryerson Press, 1946.

Zaslow, Morris. *The Opening of the Canadian North, 1870–1914*. Toronto: McClelland & Stewart, 1971.

Zavitz, Sherman, *It Happened at Niagara: Stories from Niagara's Fascinating Past*. Niagara Falls, ON: Lundy's Lane Historical Society, 2017.

INDEX